DALIT FREEDOM FIGHTERS

DALIT FREEDOM FIGHTERS

MOHAN DASS NAMISHRAY

GYAN

NEW DELHI-110002

Dalit Freedom Fighters

Rs. 750

ISBN: 978-81-212-1020-1

Published in 2009 in India by
Gyan Publishing House
Gyan Kunj 23, Main Ansari Road, Darya Ganj,
New Delhi-110002
Phones : 23282060, 23261060
Fax : 011-23285914
E-mail: books@gyanbooks.com
Website: www.gyanbooks.com

Lasser Type Setting by: Rudra Computer Graphics, Delhi
Printed at : G. Print Process, Delhi-35

To

The Martyrs of the Freedom Struggle whose Sacrifices Paved the Way for the Country's Independence and Social justice

Contents

Preface

The history of freedom fighters of India is unique for new generation. The real life stories of valour and heroism of these freedom fighters has served as a great source of inspiration to the present generation. A great deal has been written about India's struggle for independence. Most of this literature has been written either by the Britishers from their colonial point of view or by the Indian elite class consisting of caste Hindus and has, accordingly, been inclined to emphasise the history of caste Hindus, and the role of the masses and their leaders mainly consisting of the Backward Communities including Dalits and Tribes has been left from the scenario. Udham Singh (a Dalit fighter for freedom) and his movement were evaluated too late. The fight for independence has largely been conceptualized as a dual game. The history of the Freedom Struggle Movement written by the Indian elite class and the Congress sponsored historians is lopsided leaving aside the significant roles of the masses and their leaders. This path breaking study is a dissection and revelation of the heroic and uncompromising roles played by these Dalit leaders in the struggle for Indian independence.

Though it is the rich experience in the early period (from Maharana Pratap to Shivaji Maharaj) that the militancy was preserved among Dalits and Tribes. But the concept of Martial race has groves within groves and circles within circles. The Punjabis, irrespective of their religion, caste and creed, are considered a brave people. Then within the State the Sikhs are claimed to be braver. Among the Sikhs, too the Jat Sikhs are considered the bravest. India has an unbroken record of military defeats, may be to great extent because of the "Divide and Rule" introduced in Hindu Society became basis of mundane functioning of the society, by passage of time. Only about one-fourth of Hindus Kshatriyas were considered capable of fighting and governing and consequently brought humiliations for centuries of come and ruins to the country. As and when invasions took place, it became the duty of the Kshatriyas or Rajputs only to fight and defend and the rest of the peace became silent spectators to death and destruction wrought in the country. Nationalism explains national power predominantly in terms of national character and according to Hans J. Morgenthau, ultimately degenerates metaphysic of racism.

In his classic work "A matter of Honour," Philips Mason of the Indian Civil Service; traces the history of the British Indian Army and its travail and is candid in recording that the division of the people into "martial and non-martial classes was not an invention of the British. It was recognition of something already implicit in the Indian social system." The British Army, which has the widest possible experience in fighting colonial and continential wars and with considerable success, bases its own fighting units on zonal basis, something akin to our "one class" and "fixed class" units.

Ambedkar advocated introduction of compulsory military training for all adult young persons. He stressed that the recruitment to all standing army must be open to all communities. He repeatedly said, "War cannot be abolished by merely refusing to fight when attacked; to abolish war, you must win war and establish just peace. He urged the Mehar youths to preserve high martial traditions and suspend their studies and qualify themselves for miliraty commissions. Dr. Ambedkar was appointed on the Defence Advisory Committee during July, 1941. He asked the government to raise Mehar battalions and not to make distinctions as martial and non-martial races.

Dr. Ambedkar attacked the British Government on the senseless distinction of Martial and non-Martial races and appealed to the British Government to keep faith and confidence in Mehars and not to abolish them from the army after .the World War II was over.

Amongst the untouchable communities in the fold of Hindu Society, the Mehars are a robust, adaptable, intelligent, fighting, brave community. Mehars were the original inhabitants of Maharashtra. Mehars were the first to come into contact with the Europeans in India. They also formed part of the army. But the recruitment of Mehars in the army was discontinued after 1882. Ramji, father of Ambedkar, protested against this unjust order and approached M.G. Ranade and sought interview with the Governor of Bombay. The order banning the untouchables in the army was withdrawn on February 6, 1917 and a Mehar Battalion was raised in the First World War, 1914-1918.

History is a witness that when during the struggle for Indian independende, the union Jack was being protected by the so called martial races, while Dalits, tribes and backwards other backwards and so-called criminal tribes, challenged and ultimately succeeded against the right of the British Empire.

In developing his argument about the future defence of India and the composition of the armed forced Ambedkar drew extensively on the information compiled by a writer in Ramanand Chatterjee's Modern Review. The pre-Mutiny Bengal Army which had conquered North and North Western India and also areas outside India was essentially a Brahmin-Kshatriya army of the Ganga basin. It was during the Mutiny that this army disintegrated and its remaining units were disbanded. It was the deliberate post-Mutiny policy of the British Government which changed the character of the British-Indian Army. Ambedkar thought that the whole British rationalization of their policy in regard to the martial races was bogus. "The division between martial and non-mrtial classes is, of course, a purely arbitrary and artificial distinction. It is as foolish as the Hindu theory of Caste, making birth, instead of worth, the basis for recognition."

Of course, past is something unique and every nation is proud of its past. But if we entirely depend on the past it would be a folly and if we dream of the past and do nothing for present and the future, we will be presumed to be living fools paradise.

In my view the meaning of Freedom is different as other political thinkers define the freedom in the context of India. We should have the idea of development of awareness in any society. The age-long problem-whether man is an end or a means or both, is basically related to the concept of freedom. And the concept of freedom is related to human nature. It varies from thinkers to thinkers, because they consider human nature from different angles. It further gives rise to the conflicting notions – such as, induviual good or common good (social good).

Lohia agrees with Laski's view on human nature – that, "... it is, of course, vital to the structure of political philosophy that man should not be merely a creature of impulse, but also the possessor of reason."

Ambedkar in his writings has expressed his views on many political issues. They comprisesed the theoretical as well as practical sides. From the function of the state to the intricacies of every small detail of the Consitution, he has ennumerated his political thought. This is an attempt to outline his thoughts on various topics in political science.

He did not agree with Hobbes, Hegel and Bosanquet, the supporters of the absolute theory of the state. He accepted the idea of state as a human organisaation, but not the final one, as its supporters believed, because there were many other sources of thought and action. To him, stability of the state rested on difference and sympathy. Ht was therefore against the doctrine of civil disobedience. He remarked, "To believe in civil disobedience is to believe in anarchy. He conceived the state as an organization the aim of which was "(1) to maintain the right of every subject to life, liberty and pursuit of happiness and to free speech and free exercise of religion; (2) to remove social, political and economic inequality by porividing better opportunities to the submerged classes, and (3) to make it possible for every subject to enjoy freedom from want and freedom from fear". The state has to serve the interests of man and society as a servant and not as a master. So he stood for people's freedom and rights in post independence India. He attached more importance to the eternal struggle of man for freedom. To him, the true freedom of man was not merely political. It was also social, economic, intellectual and spiritual.

The writings on Indian National Movement have been brought out by many historians and scholars in different historiographic perspectives. The Cambridge School of historians perceive the Indian Struggle against the British Rule as a 'Mock Battle'. They deny that India was in the process of becoming a nation and believe that what is called India in fact consisted of religions, castes, communities and vested interests of some particular groups.

These historians further assert that the Indian National Movement was not a people's movement but a product of the needs of the interests of the 'elite groups' who used it to serve their vested interests by mobilizing the masses. In this game, the chief political brokers were Gandhi, Nehru and Patel, who, in turn, promoted the second level leaders who were called by these historians as 'sub-contractors'.

The Marxist School, on the other hand, led by R.P. Dutt and A.R. Desai, takes into account the inner contradictions of the Indian society and the process of nation-in-making. They relate the anti-imperialist struggle with the class and social struggle. They see the Indian National Struggle as the bourgeois movement. They say that the bourgeoisie played a dominant role in the movement. Furthermore, they equate the Congress national leadership with the bourgeoisie or capitalist class.

A group of historians, known as 'subaltern', dismisses all historical writings, including that of Marxist School and claims to write the history on Indian National Movement in the perspective of subaltern or common people's approach. These historians say that the Indian people were never untied in a common anti-imperialist struggle and there was no such entity as Indian National Movement. They further state that there were two distinct movements, viz., the real anti-imperialist stream led by the common masses due to their socio-economic exploitations and the bogus national movement of the elites led by the self-centered groups. These elite groups, led by the leaders of the Indian National Congress, were more interested in throwing the authority of the British and distribute the power amongst themselves consisting of educated elites and bourgeoisie. These groups were least bothered about ameliorating the socio-economic condition of the masses consisting of peasants, workers, backward communities, dalits, muslims and tribes.

Another approach of historiography is that of 'Nationalist Historians'. They completely ignore inner contradictions of the Indian society both in terms of class and castes and, rather focused on the exploitative character of colonialism and recognized the process of India becoming a nation without any justification.

If we make a comparative analysis of all the four known schools vis a vis the socio-economic and anti-imperialist struggle of the pre-independent India and socio-economic and political condition of the post independence period, we come at the conclusion that the history of the India's Freedom Struggle Movement should have been written in the perspective of subaltern or common people's approach who give a true picture of the socio-economic and anti-imperialist movement going on at the grass root level in the country side as well as in the urban and semi-urban areas.

More than a hundred books have been published on the Indian Freedom Struggle Movement. All these books have been written in political perspective illustrating the major developments in the transformation of power from the 'British Raj' to 'Ram Raj', the goal which had been perceived by Gandhiji throughout his entire political career as the objective of his life. I would give a brief description on the pseudo facet of the Gandhiji's 'Ram Raj' in the next chapter. The hidden conspiracy of the Indian National Congress, under the tutelage of Gandhiji, was indefatigably challenged by Dr. B.R. Ambedkar, the leader of the Dalit masses, who declared in unambiguous terms that 'the Non-Cooperation Movement inaugurated by Gandhi in late 1920's was a movement to get Swaraj but the Civil Disobedience Movement was aimed at the establishment of 'Ram Raj' in India.' It may be recalled that in 1920's, the initial years of Gandhiji in the Indian politics, the Indian National Congress got engaged in the peasants' movements and other socio-economic movements in order to expand its scope amongst the masses.

It's my effort to define the India's Struggle for Freedom in new way based on 'subaltern' approach. Reminiscences of the local people in the country side provide an insight into different types of socio-political orientation of a section of the community for assertion of its separate identity. Throughout the Freedom Struggle Movement, there had been a challenge before Dalits of this motherland since they were seriously involved in dual struggle, i.e., 'political' as well as 'socio-economic'. Politically their fight was with the English empire. Simultaneously, they wanted to get free from the socio-religious cage of four *varna system* propounded and perpetuated for last more than two thousand years by the caste-Hindus. Throughout this national movement, the Dalits remained followers of Dr. Ambedkar as well as the companions of Gandhiji. Their goal was more important to that of a caste nationalist. They wanted freedom not only from the British but also from autocratic and deplorable socio-economic system set-up by the caste Hindus.

Rebellions of Dalits against the authority of any established administration are mostly the conflicts between rulers and ruled.

Whatever course these clash may take, it is always a hopeless struggle of the weak against the strong. Under the British Empire, the capitalists, mill-owners, landlords and zamindars were making very large profits. Zamindars and agents of the Britishers were sucking the blood of the masses. There was nationwide unrest amongst the poor. This is our proud legacy and historic obligation.

In my view, the freedom was not the achievement of the struggle of any particular caste or political party. But, it was the consequences of combined efforts and sacrifices of each and every Indian who was committed to the nation and his own liberation from the shackles of poverty and social bondages. We should not forget the thousands Railway workers and other factory labrourers all over India acquired anti-Imperialist consciousness with far greater force than any sections of the working class and so-called reformists.

I am indebted to many of my friends and colleagues for writing this book, which has been taking shape in my mind for a very long time. My first and foremost debt is to my nephew Shri Sanjay Singh working in Rajya Sabha Secretariat, Parliament of India. He has keen interest in the history of political change as well as social awakening amongst the Dalits. Without which, I would not have been able to write this book. I am also indebted to Indian Institute of Advanced Study Library, Rashtrapati Nivas, Shimla, and Central Secretariat Library, Shastri Bhavan, New Delhi, where I consulted many valuable books and met the senior persons, who guided me on the concerned subject. For this book I would like to thanks my friends, those who have written a book, article etc in Hindi as well as in English on the same subject. Most are mentioned in the book, but notably Shri Mata Prasad, Ex. Governor of Arunchal Pradesh, Shri D.C. Dinker, and Badri Narayan, Sh. K.L. Chnchrik social activist and the writer.

I am also indebted to Shri Ranajit Guha, Shri David Arnold and Shri David Hardiman for their subaltern studies. I acknowledge with thanks the cooperation and assistance provided by Gyan Publishing House towards completing the research.

While writing this book, I have adopted a neutral understanding of the national movement and its relationship with different social groups and classes. The end of the British rule in 1947 was undoubtedly a milestone in the path of modern Indian history. But the history of nationalism during the independent Indian politics is not land mark. The most telling evidence in the era are the emergence of Dalit, in various form of struggles. What we witness now-a-days the atrocities on Dalits. The English have not taken India, we have given from the darkest chapter of the history, we must learn something. The purpose of history is the same as Polybins says ...

"These events are rich in lessons useful in the redress of human errors... Men have, infact, two ways of correcting themselves. Either they learn from their own mistakes or they benefit from those of others. If one method is more effective, the other is les costly."

Lastly if caste Hindus had followed the path suggested by Ambedkar, we would not have found the major portion of Dalits and Tribes in the social & financial dismay in which we find them today, even after 50 years of independence find them today. For bringing equality and fraternity caste Hindus have to wakeup and decide for the healthy society and build the strong nation. I hope that my contribution encourages the readers to join this great cause. If this socio-economic imbalance is not corrected very soon by the caste Hindus and capitalist class, then time is no far away when there will be social disturbances, class struggle, riots and small mutinies. The growing influence of *naxalism* is an example of this class struggle. In his book ***'India- A Million Mutinies Now'***, V.S. Naipaul has written...

The Dalits for instance. If they still have been only the mahatma's Harijans, children of God, people for whom good things might be done, objects of sentiment

and passing piety.... but a certain amount of money had come to the people once known as Harijans, a certain amount of education, and with that then had also come the group sense and the political consciousness. They had ceased to be abstractions. They had begun to do things for themselves. They had become people stressing their own particularity, as better off groups in India stressed their particularities.

According to Naipaul, during the British rule, India had the Mutiny of 1857, but in the post-independence era, these mutinies are multiplied everywhere in India. In his justification, he has stated that **the freedom has awakened the people everywhere in India about who they are and what they owe themselves. The liberation of spirit that has come to India could not come as release alone. In India, with its layer below layer of distress and cruelty, it had to come as a disturbance. It had come as rage and revolt. India was now a country of a million little mutinies.**

14 April, 2008

Mohandass Namishray

1

Dalits and Memories of 1857

The literature on freedom struggle movement has been written either by the Britishers from their colonial point of view or by the Indian elite class consisting of caste Hindus and has, accordingly, been inclined to emphasise the history of caste Hindus, and the role of the masses and their leaders mainly consisting of the Backward Communities including Dalits and Tribes has been left from the scenario. The literature written by the Indian elite class and the Congress sponsored historians is lopsided leaving aside the significant roles of the masses and their leaders. The heroic and uncompromising roles played by these Dalit leaders in the struggle for Indian independence by these historians who have been termed by the entire Dalit and backward communities as traitors. The Dalit litrary class has unearthed a number of prominewnt leaders and figures who have played dominating role in India's struggle for independence. The Dalits thus feel that there are sufficient grounds to explore their contribution to the freedom struggle and gain compensation for it in the present.

The Dalits have an emotional link with the 1857 War of Independence because they believe it was initiated by them. They claim that it was the revolt against the British that commenced in Jhansi in 1857, which snowballed into the War of Independence. It was a War of Independence since the Dalits were fighting for their motherland rather than to gain power. The war was led by *Bhau Bakshi* and *Puran Kori* and with them was *Jhalkaribai*. The dalit narrative of the first freedom struggle is filled with stories about brave women martyr belonging to the oppressed communities, including *Jhalkaribai, Avantibai, Pannadhai, Udadevi* and *Mahaviridevi*. In the dalit narrative, *Matadin Bhangi* emerges as the source of inspiration for the first spark of the revolt. The story is as follow:

There was a factory in Barrackpore where cartridges were manufactured. Many of the workers of the factory belonged to the untouchable communities. One day, one of the workers felt thirsty. He asked a soldier for a mug of water. That soldier was Mangal Pandey. Mangal Pandey, a Brahmin by caste, refused to take water from him because the worker was an untouchable. This was very humiliating for the worker. On this, that worker retorted....

"Bara awa hai brahaman ka beta. Jin kartuson ka tum upayog karat ho, unpar gaaye or suar ki charbi lagawal jaat hai, jinhe tum apan daatun se torkar banduk me bharat ho. O samay tomka jati aur dharma kahan jawat. Dhikkar tumkhare is brahmanatwa ka. [You claim to be a highly respectable Brahmin, but the cartridges which you bite with your teeth and insert into your guns, are all greased with the fat of cows and pigs. What happens to your caste and religion them? Curse on your brahminism].

Hearing this, the soldier was taken by surprise. That untouchable was none other than *Matadin Bhangi*, who opened the eyes of the Indian soldiers and ignited the first spark of India's independence in the cantonment. The words of Matadin Bhangi spread like wildfire through the cantonment. Very soon the torch of independence was lit. On the morning of 1 March, 1857, Mangal Pandey broke the line during the parade. Accusing the British of hurting their religious sentiments, he started firing indiscriminately at them. This was the moment when the first battlelines against the British were drawn. Mangal Pandey was arrested in an injured condition. He was court-martialled and hung from the gallows in front of all the soldiers. Mangal Pandey's sacrifice became an inspiration for the soldiers. On 10 May,1857, the floodgates of the independence movement burst open in Barracpore and many brave sons of India became martyrs. In the charge-sheet that was made, the first name was that of Matadin Bhangi, who was later arrested. All the arrested revolutionaries were court-martialled. Matadin was charged for treason against the British.

S.R. Sajeevan Nath, in his book *1857 ki Kranti ka Janak: Nagvanshi Bhangi Matadin Hela,* also narrates a similar story in which Matadin Bhangi has been claimed to be the father (janak) of the 1857 rebellion. In these narratives, Matadin Bhangi is presented as the moving force behind the revolt. They also show how the upper-caste soldiers refused to hand a glass of water to the untouchables although they bit cartridges rubbed with cow's fat. Thus, these narratives also question and strongly criticise the hierarchical structure of Indian society, in which the untouchables are not allowed to go near the upper-caste persons because of their 'low birth' and ritual 'dirtiness'. To prove the historicity of this event, a book written by one Shri Acharya Bhagwan Deb, titled *the Immortal Revolutionaries of India,* has been quoted by Dinkar.

Dalit celebrate the memory of Matadin Bhangi and his contribution to the nationalist movement in a number of ways. Many songs have been composed in his honour that are sung in rallies and functions, both cultural and political. Plays are staged at commemorative functions held in his honour in both towns and villages. Special issues of magazines are brought out with articles by eminent writers highlighting his contributions. A fortnightly newspaper *Dalit Kesri* published a special issue on the 1857 Revolt in which the lead article was on Matadin Bhangi. *Anarya Bharat*, another dalit newspaper that is published from Mainpuri in UP, brought out a special feature on the contribution of dalits to the revolt of 1857. All these publications project Matadin Bhangi as a pioneer of the First War of Independence. *Himayati*, a dalit literary magazine, in its May 1996 issue celebrating the memory of 1857, published a special feature and lead article of the contribution of Matadin Bhangi. Dr. Sohanpal Sumankshar wrote very strongly in the same issue that the first person who sowed the seed of the revolt of 1857 was Matadin Bhangi, but unfortunately historians have forgotten his contribution.

In this manner, the elite nationalist history has subverted the prominent roles played by the dalits in their favour. Kunwar Singh, Tantia Tope and Nana Saheb do not figure in the dalit narrative of the 1857 freedom struggle. The people who figure are *Chetram Jatav, Balluram Mehtar, Banke Chamar* and *Vira Pasi* who were martyrs born in the lower stratas of society. Although the elite nationalist heroes are not negated, they are ignored in the Dalit narratives. The narratives emphasise the sacrifice of the Dalit martyrs for the nation in spite of their 'low birth' and poor socio-economic status. The story of Balluram Mehtan and Chetram Jatav has been described in the following manner:-

Although the dalits were born in the lowest caste of the Indian caste hierarchy and suffered great hardship because of their poor socio-economic status, they never sold the interests of their country for their own benefit. No one can accuse a single Dalit of doing so. Whenever the need arose, they sacrificed their lives for their motherland. Among the brave sons of the country, the names of Balluram Mehtrar and Chetram Jatav are written in shining letters.

As soon as the news of the Barrackpore revolution reached the people, a mob of revolutionaries took to the streets. Mr.

Phillips, who was an officer of the Etah District, tried to control the mob. On 26 May 1857, in the Soro region of Etah district, Chetram Jatav and Balluram Mehtar joined the Barrackpore revolution without caring for their lives. In this revolution, Sadashiv Mehre, Chaturbhuj Vaish and others were also present. Chetram Jatav and Balluram, who were the moving forces behind the revolution, were tied to trees and shot. The rest were hung from trees in the Kasganj area.

The bravery of martyr Banke Chamar is also described. He lived in village Kuarpur of Macchli Shahar in Janpad Jaunpur. When the movement failed, the British declared Banke Chamar and 18 of his associates as baghi (rebels). After being arrested, Banke Chamar was ordered to be hung. Thus this brave revolutionary laid down his life for the country.

The Dalits, through their narratives of the 1857 Revolt, have also tried to dethrone the existing upper-caste heroes from the mainstream narratives. For instance, in the story of Jhalkaribai, by not recognizing Rani Lakshmi Bai as a martyr, they want to prove that she was hungry for power. Rani Lakshmi Bai did not want to rebel against the British, but did so only under the influence of Jhalkaribai. At the end of the 1857 struggle, Rani Lakshmi Bai did not become a martyr but hide herself in the estate of Partapgarh.

The myth is a part of the popular memory of the people of Bundelkhand region and is narrated in several versions. It has still survived in people's memory and is often resurfaced in folklores, folk stories and discussions at the village squares (*chaupal*).

In the words of Raj Kumar Koree, a singer in the *Jababi Kirtan Mandali*, "U to *durga rahin*" (She was Goddess Durga). *Jababi Kirtan* is a popular cultural performance in this region and the story of Jhalkaribai and her brave deeds is a common subject of most *Kirtan mandalis* (devotional song groups)

Jhalkarbai was a real historical character and not a myth; but the memories about her vary between different communities. They are in a continuous process of reconstruction and modification, especially among the lower castes. This is so because it helps these communities to revise their identity and juxtapose it against that of the other communities. Contesting images of Jhalkaribai are still being circulated in the Bundelkhand region, and it has also become a theme of political and social contention. This can be illustrated from the fact that in Kachnara village in the Hamirpur district of Bundelkhand, the old and illiterate Ram Narayan Shukul, a Brahmin, subverts Raj Kumar Koree's version by saying that 'Jhalkaribai koi khas nahi thi' (Jhalkaribai was not very important). She was just a Korin and a maid servant of Rani Laxmibai. The two resembled each other physically. When the Rani came out of the fort with her army to face the British, Jhalkaribai dressed herself as the Rani and confused the British about her true identity.

In the written historiacl record of that period, one can, however, find a mention of her in the book, *Majha Pravas*, written by Vishnu Rao Godse, who refers to her as "*Jhalkari Korin*". *Majha Pravas* is a travelogue based on the author's travels in the central part of India during the 1857 Rebellion. In the book she is mentioned to be a maid of Rani Laxmibai (Godse 1907).

Another reference to her myth can be found in "*Jhansi ki Rani*", written by the eminent litterateur, B.L. Varma (1951:255). He created a sub-story in his novel based on Jhalkaribai for which he interviewed Jhalkaribai's grandson. A detailed version of Jhalkari is presented here. Varma himself belonged to the Bundelkhand region. While depicting her character, he too addresses her as a Korin who resembled Laxmibai. He narrates the story as follows:

There was a Jhalkari Korin. Her features, the contours of her nose, the colour of her eyes, her complexion and physical stature all resembled those of the Rani. The Rani liked her very much. Her husbands name was Puran Koree. She was not Laxmibai's servant but someone who was very close to her. She learnt archery, wrestling and shooting from the Rani and, later, became a member of the female army created by the Rani. Jhalkari inspired her husband to fight and die for Rani and the country. Subsequently, he became a topchee (cannon operator) posted at the main gate of the fort. When Laxmibai proceeded to fight the British, the British began to chase her. Jhalkari dressed as the Rani, approached the British commander, General Rose, who mistook her for the Rani and arrested her. Laxmibai was thus saved from being captured. The confusion continued for a week and it was only after it was revealed that Jhalkaribai was not the Rani that she was released (Varma 1951).

In 1951, Ram Chandra Heran, a progressive writer in the Bundeli language, wrote a noval called *Maati*. This novel was not centered on Jhalkaribai but it gave a small narrative about her in which she was depicted as a chivalrous and a valiant martyr (Heran 1951).

The first biography of Jhalkaribai was written in 1964 by Bhawani Shankar Visharad, a Dalit intellectual. He picked up the story of Jhalkaribai from Varma's novel and, with the help of the oral narratives of the lowercaste people living in Nayapueva in the vicinity of Jhansi fort, he reconstructed it.

Since 1990 several booklets, dramas and songs have been composed by Dalit activists, politicians and writers, narrating the story of Jhalkaribai. Efforts have been made to rewrite and reread the story of Jhalkaribai with the avowed objective of placing her on an equal footing with Laxmibai.

Many other Dalit writers and composers have narrated the myth of Jhalkaribai, glorifying her brave deeds. Bihari Lal Harit composed a folk balled in 1995, called *Virangana Jhalkari*. Earlier in 1990, Mata Prasad, (then the governor of Arunachal Pradesh) composed a drama on her called *Jhalkaribai Natak*. It can, therefore, be seen that these writings further corroborate the argument that it is the reconstruction of history that is the driving objective of the depressed castes.

In this narrative, Jhalkaribai was placed on the same pedastal as Rani Laxmibai. Both of them excelled in martial arts, the only difference being that Laxmibai was a queen and Jhalkaribai a Korin. According to this version, Jhalkaribai was treated by the Rani as her *Bahin* (sister) and the Rani's military strategies were planned by her. *It was on account of Jhalkaribai's friendship with Laxmibai that the conspiracies of the upper castes could not concretize. She was eventually arrested because of the treachery of Thakur Dulhaju. In this version, she is projected as a patriot greater than any person belonging to a higher castes* (ibid).

The upper stratum of society finds such an interpretation unacceptable because, on the one hand, Jhalkaribai is depicted as an equally significant strategist as Laxmibai while, on the other hand, a Thakur is characterized as a traitor. Here a depressed caste is, by the logic of facts, represented as being more patriotic. Not a single low-caste member, in this version, is shown to be a traitor.

D.C. Dinkar (1990:24-25) presents a very interesting story about Jhalkaribai. According to him, 'Rani Laxmibai had a lust for the crown. She was not interested in revolting against the British. Jhalkaribai stopped her from compromising with them. In fact, she was the person who inspired the Rani to fight and struggle for freedom.

Dalit writers also construct the martyr-ology of Dalit freedom fighters in the 1857 Rebellion. In this martyr-ology, Jhalkaribai and Udadevi are glorified as significant contributors to Dalit heritage or dedication and patriotism. Through these narratives, the Dalits attempt to highlight their role in the freedom movement. Another purpose of the construction of a martyr-ology is to stiffen the endurance of survivors and induce courage and confidence in them. Martyrdom has been considered to be a supreme dedication for the nation. It symbolizes patriotism, which forms the basis of emotional nationalism.

Table as given below has a chronological list of the books that have been written featuring the history of Jhalkaribai.

	Author	Title of the Book	Date
(i)	Vishnu Rao Godse	*Majha Pravas*	1907
(ii)	Brindaven Lal Varma	*Jhansi ki Rani*	1951
(iii)	Ram Chandra Heran	*Maati*	1951
(iv)	Bhawani Shankar Visharad	*Veerangana Jhalkaribai*	1964
(v)	Piyush	*Jhansi ki Rani natak*	1972
(vi)	D.C. Dinkar	*Swatantra Sangram Mein Achhuton ka Yogdan*	1990
(vii)	Chokhe Lal Verma	*Jhalkaribai Natak*	1990
(viii)	Mata Prasad	*Veerangana Jhalkaribai Kavya*	1993
(ix)	Bihari Lal Harit	*Veerangana Jhalkari*	1995
(x)	Mohandass Namishray	Jhalkaribai	2002

The Dalits of Bundelkhand also invented celebrations and commemoration around the legend of Jhalkaribai. They organized a function every year at Jhansi in the Fort of Rani Laxmibai to commemorate the memory of Jhalkaribai. A tower near Unnao Gate and Anjani Toria is named after Jhalkaribai. The Dalits of Jhansi have instituted a Polytenchinc Institute in her memory. They have also credted a *Veerangana Memorial Trust* to ensure the transmission of the story of Jhalkaribai.

The Role of Harbolas in First War of Independence

The tradition of Harbolas is also very deeply rooted and related to the Dalits and down-trodden communities, while crossing the forests, vallies and mountains they sang the songs, full of patriotism. These Harbolas, who were a variour class, however, are placed out of the Varna System of the Brahminism.

In the year of 1857, the people of this region got awakened who had important role in the first war India's Independence. Really, they were the true and committed messengers who used to sing *ballads* from place to place. Thieer messages for the war were echoed in nick and corner of the Bundelkhand region. They were called *Madari, Bewriya, Soot, Bazigar, Nat*, etc. With the help of Harbolas, the queen of Jhansi, Rani Laxmibai, established her detective department.

The contribution Rani Laxmibai in the First Independenec War was brought to the world by none other than Harbolas. A famous aphorism sang by the Harbolas is... *'Khoob Lari Mardani, Weh to Jhansi Wali Rani Thi. Harbollon ke Mukh Se Sunhi Yeh Kanahani Thi.'*. It has been elaborately described by a famous a Hindi Poet, Subhadra Kumari Chauhan. Once Subhadraji met her brother in the Imprisonment, who was an Inspector, she listened this aphorism from the mouth of an imprison.

Due to the commitment in the 1857 Freedom Struggle, they had been victimized by the British Empire. The message of Revolution and mutiny was spread from door to door by these Harbollas.

Unfurtunately, the Harbollas of today are living their lives in obscurity since they have not been accepted and recognized in the society.

Vira Pasi is another Dalit who is remembered as a brave warrior in the dalit narrative. He was a security guard of Raja Beni Madhav Singh of Murar Mau, in Rae Bareli (Uttar Pradesh). The raja was arrested for taking part in the Revolt. One night, Vira Pasi entered the prison and helped the king to escape. This was a big insult to the British administration. They decided to capture Vira Pasi dead or alive, and placed a reward of Rs. 50,000 on his head. However, they were unable to capture him.

Another narrative tells the story of village Magarwara, about ten kilometers from Unnao on the Lucknow highway. On 20 July, 1857, a small battalion of the British army under the leadership of General Henry Havelock was passing through Magarwara to help another battalion that had got stuck in the Residency. Nearly 2,000 Pasis came out of their hamlets and pelted the battalion with stones, forcing it to return to the Kanpur cantonment. On 4 August, 1857, the same battalion came to the village, this time with a lot of preparations. When the Pasis tried to stop the battalion from moving forward, a battle ensued and nearly 2,000 Pasis were killed.

Yet another story narrated by the Pasis is about village Bani on the banks of river Sai, close to Magarwara. This region consisted of many small Pasi hamlets. When the British army passed by this highway, it faced stiff resistance from the Pasis. Angered by this, the British officers asked the Pasis to vacate the area within five minutes. When the Pasis refused, the British announced that they would blow up the hamlets with cannons. This caused great alarm for the people and their families. Many Pasis were killed in the cannon firing. The British found this region very salubrious and decided to build a fort where their soldiers, who had faced stiff resistance from the Pasis after leaving the Kanpur cantonment, could rest and recuperate. This story is part of the collective memory and oral tradition of the Pasis of this region is often presented in plays and songs. One of the songs is as follows:

Bani bani kati bani, ban ke bigri bani
Angrezon ke tope se urhi, phir bani rahi bani.
(The village Bani was made, then destroyed,
Again made and again destroyed;
The cannon balls of the British blew it apart;
Then Bani was once again made and remained Bani.)

As the story goes, General Havelock once again moved forward the next day with his troops to free the soldiers trapped in the Residency. Once again he had to face the wrath of the Indian freedom fighters, this time at the Alambagh Bhavya Bhawan. Many soldiers, both Indian and British, lost their lives in this battle. When the General reached Dilkushbagh, he had to fight again. These incidents took a toll of the British soldiers and drained the energy of General Havelock. He fell ill and finally succumbed to his illness on 24 November 1857. He was buried at the British cemetery in Alambagh. This story was recorded in a documentation of the Pasis to the freedom struggle, from where it was once again transmitted to the oral memory of the dalits.

Another story that is narrated in glowing terms is about the husband of Udadevi, *Makka Pasi,* who, like his wife, laid down his life for the sake of the country. The incident took place on 10 June 1857, when a small battalion of British soldiers under the leadership of Henry Lawrence was passing through Barabanki on its way to Chinhat from Awadh. At village Chinhat, Makka Pasi gathered an army of 200 Pasis and was able to kill many British soldiers before Captain Lawrence shot him dead. It is said that **Udadevi and Makka Pasi are the only couple in world history where both the partners have become martyrs**. **This couple has brought glory to not just the Pasi community but the entire country. Every Indian should be proud of such a couple**.

The Pasi community believes in its golden age past. It emphasizes that the pasi community had, at one time, ruled over a large area of Avadh. Centuries of Pasi history lies buried beneath mounds, ancients settlements and deserted places that were once densely scene of being neglected in the writing of the history of the nation. R.K. Choudhury, an eminent Pasi leader and minister in the Mayawati-led government, writes:

Historians have not written books on the Pasi empire. Scholars have never ibentified the history of this chivalrous community for their research. Neither did the government departments, established for the purpose of protecting cultural heritage, ever attempt to collect information about the Pasi empire. Not a single book is available in libraries in which details about the Pasi empire are even mentioned. (Choudhury 1997:3)

Some educated Pasis outlined that the British authors have mentioned Pasi rulers in different gazetteers and other books, but Indian writers almost completely eliminated those chapters from history.

This sence of deprivation from history led the Pasis to invent their own histories. As the assertion for a new identity acquired momentum with the rise of Bahujan (Dalit) politics in U.P.

Mayawati wrote: *Among the Pasi rulers, the names off Maharaja Bijlee Pasi, Maharaja Satan Pasi, maharaja Lakhan Pasi, Maharaja Suhaldeo, Maharaja Chheta Pasi and Maharaja Daldeo deserve to be mentioned in golden letters. But unfortunately, the history of these chivalrous and majestic kings has received only negligible treatment in a few books.*

The role of Udadevi in the Revolt of 1857 has been elaborately narrated as follows:

There was a peepal tree, heavy and thick at the centre of Sikanderbagh in Lucknow. Under it were kept earthen vessels, many filled with cold water. When the bloodshed in the battle stopped, many soldiers went there to rest, quench their thirst and enjoy the cool shades of the tree. Under this tree, many British soldiers, belonging to the 53rd and 59th regiment of the British army, were found lying dead. But Dawson (Captain of the British army troop) noted that from the wounds of the soldiers, it was evident that the bullets that hit and killed them had been fired from above. Captain Dawson soon came out of the shade of the tree and called Wallace so as to confirm whether there was someone on the tree. He said that the death of the British soldiers in the battlefield did not occur on account of attacks by bullets from the opposite direction, but by bullets fired from above the tree. Wallace had with him loaded gun. Cautiously moving backwards, he started searching for the person on the tree. Immediately, he called out to caption dawson, saying that he had seen a person and lifting his gun, he said that he would fulfill his promise before God. Thereafter, he fired at the target and the body of a person fell on the ground. This person was wearing a red coloured jacket and a tight trouser. It was discovered that the person was not male but female. She had two pistols of an old model. Of these, one pistol was full of cartridges and other was exhausted. She had in her pocket live cartridges, which had been manufactured very cautiously. When Wallace saw that the dead body was not of male but female, he started weeping, saying 'Had I known that she was a woman I would have died thousand times but never harmed her. This lady was none other than Udadevi.

This story is being narrated by the Pasis who believe that this incident took place on 16th November, 1857.

The Pasis of the region believe that Begum Hazrat mahal, in the struggle for freedom, organized an army of women soldiers after her husband's arrest. According to popular belief, the Commander of this army was Udadevi. She belonged to Ujrion village near Lucknow. Her husband Makka pasi was also a soldier in the army of Hazrat Mahal. He laid down his life while fighting the British at Chinhat. In this battle, Begum Hazrat Mahal herself participated, accompanied by Udadevi. It is said that the Begum herself looked after the wounded soldiers and covered shrouds on the bodies of the martyrs. Udadevi suddenly shuddered on seeing dead body of her husband, Makka Pasi, and wept bitterly. It was then that Udadevi vowed to avenge the killing of her husband, and this resulted in the killing of 36 British soldiers from the top of a tree and her subsequent martyrdom (Dinkar 1990:35). The East India Company had made General Cambell the commander and sent him to Avadh. On 10th November 1857, Campbell reached Dilkusha from the fort of Bijlee Pasi. As per the plan, he was to meet General Outram and Henry Havelock at Moti Mahal in Lucknow. But due to their fear of facing brave Indians, he changed his route. It was on this new route that his forces encountered Udadevi and her troop of women soldiers.

The 1971 Census records mention that, according to the Pasi respondents, a Pasi *paltan* (a platoon) rescued Begum Hazrat Mahal from being arrested by the British doing the 1857 Revolt (Census of India 1971:2). From 1980 onwards, the story of Udadevi began to emerge out of the story of Begum Hazrat

Mahal. After 1990, with the formation of the *Virangana Udadevi Smarak Sansthan*, this story found organizational support for its transmission and celebration. It is narrated in the Lucknow region of central UP, which is still, demographically, Pasi dominant. From these narratives has also emerged the iconographically, Pasi dominant. From these narratives has also emerged the iconographically of Udadevi. Since she was linked with a Muslim woman-Begum Hazrat mahal-she is described as wearing a long skirt and a head cloth and holding a pistol in her hands. Motivated by the same tale, the statue shows her wearing a short-sleeved blouse (as opposed to the attire of an upper-caste Hindu woman) and is projected as an average Pasi woman.

16th November is observed as *Udadevi Martyrdom Day* for which a conference is organized by people belonging to the Pasi caste, a souvenir is published and *Pasi Ekta* (unity) rallies are organized as a token of remembrance of virangana Udadevi.

Maharviridevi is another popular Dalit woman leader who was a resident of the Muzaffarnagar region of western UP. Plays based on her life are regularly performed and many folk poets have composed poems on her life. Popular folk singer Arjun Gayak of Agra sings:

Mahaviri Bhangin ke ganwa bhaiya gave ke part
San sattavan ke gadar main di usne kurbani
Angrezon ke samne usne haar kabhi na manni

The English version of the above-mentioned poem is as followes:

(Brother, you will have to sing the song of Mahaviri Bhangin
She sacrificed her life in the 1857 Rebellion
She never accepted defeat before the British.)

Deval kavi, a poet born in Muzaffarnagar but settled in Agra, recites the following poem:

Chamak uthi san sattavan ki vah talwar purani
Mahaviri Bhangin thi bari mardani

The English version of the above-mentioned poem is as followes:

(The old sword of the 1857 Rebellion shone brightly
Mahaviri Bhangin was very masculine.)

Through such poems and songs, a popular image of Mahaviridevi Bhangin has been created in the minds of the people.

The historicity of these narratives is questionable, but the politics behind the creation and narration of these stories is aimed at dethroning the established heroes of the mainstream narratives. A three dimensional discursive strategy was adopted to achieve this aim. The first dimension makes allegations about the way mainstream writings distort the events of the 1857 struggle. The second seeks to establish their own heroes as freedom fighters who fought for their motherland. The third tries to prove that *zamindars*, feudal lords, and the wealthy classes of society who were on the side of the British rulers. The educated Indian intelligentsia is also claimed to have been hand-in-glove with the British. In the preface to his 1997 booklet, *Sepoy Mutiny 1857-58: An Indian Perfidy*, A.K. Biswas, a dalit from West Bengal who later became an IAS officer, wrote:

The Indian history has been subjected to calculated distortion at the hands of educated Indians. Instances are galore in many walks of life. The Sepoy Mutiny (1857-58), though not even two centuries old and though there is vast mass of contemporary literatures, has suffered the same mindless perversion,where truth has been swept under the carpet. In other words, it has not been allowed to come to the light. The Sepoy Mutiny is hailed today universally as the first war of Indian Independence when the mutineers unfurled the banner of revolt against a mighty Empire. The contemporary literature, however, gives a very different, rather baffling picture. The sepoys have been held therein as seditious, perfidious, evil and wrong doers, etc. They were condemned in strongest terms by Indian journalists who are held as pioneers and doyens. The feudal class, on the other hand, lent

strong moral and material support to the imperial forces which crushed the uprising. The glaring contradiction does not find any mention in the textbooks of history of our times for our times for the reasons not far to seek, nor is it known to the generation of the day.

Through these narratives of the past, the dalits want to acquire power in the ongoing social struggle. It is also an attempt to reshape the fractures and competing pasts from the standpoint of the present and acquire a position of authority for themselves. This process of remaking the past is based on their current experience of socio-political and cultural discrimination, which they face in their everyday lives. They link their experiences of recent times with those from their remote past and authenticate the latter by establishing their historicity. Invention of history for the dalits is thus a process of acquiring legitimacy for their identity by establishing that their community's tradition of sacrifice for the nation and society has a long history.

Why is important for the dalits to link themselves with the 1857 War of Independence and why are the icons related to this incident more important than those associated with other incidents? Why is 1857 so important for them? The reason, perhaps, is that the events from this period are not well documented, allowing the dalits plenty of space to invent their history and posit their leaders in it. the popular imagination of the 1857 revolt is a highly romantic one, peopled with a lot of heroic characters who fought valiantly against the British using indigeneous weapons. This gives the dalits an opportunity to create heroic characters belonging to their community, who, despite their debatable authencity, can stir the imagination of people searching for heroes to identify with. The events that took place in the twentieth century are, on the other hand, very well documented, since the leaders of that period tried to build up a unified, homogeneous story of India's independence. This gave little space to the dalits since this story is dominated by upper-caste leaders. It is true that many people from the lower castes lost their lives in the Non-Cooperation, Quit India and other such movements, but the glory went to the upper-caste leaders who had organized them.

The 1857 movement was mainly confined to northern India, making it easier for the dalits of this region to invent and situate their heroes in paces with heavy concentrations of the lower-caste population, such as Awadh, Bundelkhand and Bhojpur. The events of 1857 are not just part of dalit memory but are also a part of the broader collective memory of the region, reflected in the songs, plays and other media of popular culture. This has enabled the dalits to invent heroes who could become both local heroes, revered across caste lines, as well as identity markers for the entire dalit community in its everyday struggle for dignity and self-respect. The dalit leaders knew that it was imperative to link themselves with the nationalists narrative and assert their role in the freedom struggle. However, they found it difficult to find space in the later phase of the freedom struggle because their leader Dr. Ambedkar had developed a rift with Mahatma Gandhi, the most important leader of this phase, after the struggle for dalit upliftment had picked up momentum. Thus, they had no option but to search for their heroes in the 1857 rebellion so as not to antagonize the Indian state, which legitimized the nationalist narrative as its own foundation. They could not afford to ignore the dominant nationalist narrative because one of the catalysts for the emergence of a dalit nationalist narrative was the dialogue with the state. But, neither they could negate Ambedkar nor his narrative of the nationalist movement. The need to strike a balance between the two led the dalits to search for their own heroes within the nationalist narrative. And the 1857 struggle was the event that gave them the spate to do so.

Another reason why the dalits found it crucial to link themselves with the 1857 struggle was to counter the allegations made by some intellectuals associated with the Bharatiya Janata Party (BJP) that the dalits were anti-national. According to these intellectuals, Ambedkar was against the mainstream nationalist movement led by Mahatma Gandhi and often supported the British. These ideologues try to belittle the dalits by stating that it was they who conquered India for the British, for example–the Dusadhs and Baheliyas fought for Lord Clive in the Battle of Plassey in 1757. In a bid to oppose the efforts of the dalits to write their own history and rupture the mainstream nationalist narrative, the *All India History Compilation Project*, formed by the Rashtriya Swayamsevak Sangh (RSS) for propagating history based on the RSS ideology, held a convention between 17 and 19 July 1999 in Allahabad. In this convention, Moreshawar Neelkanth Pingale opined that writing the history of Shudras, Gwalas and the tribals created hatred among sections of society and caused problems for an Indianised social life. Statements like these compeled the dalits to assert their role in the 1857 revolt which gives them an exalted position in the history of nation-building in India.

There is a difference of opinion among the members of the BJP-RSS is obvious when the governor of UP, Suraj Bhan, speaking at the same convention, rebuked those attempting to deny the role of dalits in the freedom struggle and underlined their contribution to the movement for independence. He added that Valmiki, the writer of the Ramayana, belonged to a dalit community and that we know about Rama and Sita because of him. He also mentioned the name of Jhalkaribai, who in the guise of the Rani of Jhansi, fought valiantly against the British in the First War of Independence.

Dalit politicians and dalit intellectuals use the history, memories and icons of 1857 in their discourses in various ways. One, when caste conferences are organized to facilitate identity construction, they publish posters and handbills in which the contribution of their caste heroes in the 1857 struggle is mentioned. Two, they justify their demands from the state as rewards for their role in the 1857 movement. Three, the BSP leaders highlight the contribution of those heroes of the 1857 movement who belong to the caste that they address during election campaigns. Four, the leaders of many castes publish posters and pamphlets in which they mention their role in the 1857 freedom struggle, in the course of mass struggles against the prejudices harboured by the state. Many castes are still considered 'criminal tribes' on the basis of old colonial legal Acts that the police continue to follow even after their abolition. **People from such castes say that when the upper castes were busy collaborating with the British to earn titles of *Rai Bahadur* and grabbing land that belonged to dalits, the dalits were fighting against the British rulers**. So the dalits earned the wrath of the rulers, who branded them as criminal tribes under the Criminal Tribes Acts of 1871, 1896, 1901-2, 1909, 1911, 1913-4, 1919 and 1924. Although these tribes have now been denotified, yet whenever a criminal activity takes place, the police, acting on preconceived notions, first arrests members of these tribes. As a protest against this kind of state atrocity, these communities organise protests and publish posters and handbills in which they mention their role in the 1857 movement.

Among the many heroes projected in the narratives of 1857, why did women warriors such as Jhalkarabai and Udadevi emerge as icons for dalit political mobilization in Uttar Pradesh? One reason might be that when dalit politicians, especially Kanshi Ram, set out to choose icons from among those present in the literature produced by dalit writers in the sixties to capture the mainstream nationalist narrative, they chose women icons on whom they could carve the image of Mayawati as a powerful mass leader of the community. Since a woman was to be projected as a charismatic mass leader, the icons chosen were also women who were brave and powerful and could provide symbolic power to Mayawati's image. The women were called *viranganas* (brave women), but in the narratives and visuals the womanly aspect was removed and only the bravery aspect highlighted. In popular parlance, the women warriors emerged as veers (brave men) to glorify Mayawati's masculine qualities. Mayawati is addressed as *Behanji* (sister) by her followers, but for them the world is more a term of honorable address rather than a sign of her femininity. These qualities have been glorified in religious texts and also in mainstream literature penned by authors like Maithilisharan Gupt, who wrote, *"Abala nari teri yehi kahani, achal mein hai doodh aur ankhon main ha pani"* (Vulnerable woman, this is your story – in your breast there is milk, and in your eyes there are tears).

The histories proposed by dalit intellectuals and politicians are not passive and unconcerned with the people. Unlike the histories written by academic historians, these are active in the memory of the people, full of power to influence dalits and mobilize them for the politics of making their future. Dalit political forces are successfully using the historical symbols invented in their electoral and political discourses for the mobilization of various dalit communities under one banner. The use of Jhalkaribai in the Bundelkhand region and Udadevi in the central region of UP are examples of this. Jhalkaribai, who was described as a maid servant of Rani Lakshmi Bai in the novel written by Brindavanlal Varma, was picked up by the dalits and given a larger-than-life image. They recasted her as one of their own heroes of the 1857 revolt and a symbol of their active role in the freedom struggle. The history, myth and memory of Jhalkaribai are being used by the BSP in their electoral discourse to mobilize dalits for their political empowerment in the Bundelkhand region.

In many parts of UP and Bihar one can find small shrines and memorial stones that are sacred to the people, especially the Dalits living around them. People throng there in large numbers to pray for the fulfillment of their wishes and for peace and prosperity in their families. These memorials were built in the memory of dalit heroes of the 1857 rebellion belonging to that region. These sites can be found in many parts of north India, such as Azamgars, Shahabpur, Arrah etc. The question arises: why have the Dalits, whose role in the revolt of 1857 was so gigantic, is not even acknowledged in academic history?

Deities and Histories in Daily Life

Majbauwa, Azamgarb

Majhauwa, a village in the Azamgarh district of UP, is predominantly inhabited by the Chamar, Pasi, Dhobi and Mali castes. Next to a narrow footpath inside a field in this village are four cemented stones. These are called *'Shabeed Baba'* by the villagers. The Dalits of this village regularly worship these stones, using red powder, pouring water on them and making offerings of home-made sweets like thekua. The village school master said that four villagers of the Chamar caste had laid down their lives during the 1857 rebellion. They started appearing in the dreams of the villagers, giving them messages that praying to the four martyrs would bring happiness to their lives. Since then they have become gods in the eyes of the villagers, who built shrines in their memory and began to pray to them for happiness and prosperity.

Shahabpur, Allahabad

In village Shahabput on the outskirts of Allahabad there is a high mound or *thaan*, where it is believed that the head of *Sangram Singh*, a hero of the 1857 rebellion, was buried after the British beheaded him. There is a tree on the mound beside which the villagers sacrifice goats to appease Sangram Singh. Dudhnath Pasi, the Pradhan of the village, who has taken a pond on lease, offers a lamb as sacrifice every year. No priests are called for this ritual but music bands are hired to play loud music during the ceremony.

Shahapur, Arrab

Around the village Shahapur in Arrab district of Bihar, *Ranjit Baba* is worshipped by some communities. His thaans (memorial stones) are usually found under peepal trees that are decorated with red loincloths, red flags, red powder marks, incense sticks, home-made sweets, etc. People of the villages pray for the fulfillment of their wishes at the thaans. It is said that Ranjit Baba became a martyr while fighting against the British during the 1857 rebellion. He then became a god incarnation.

The above cases tell us how martyrs of the 1857 rebellion belonging to the Dalits from various parts of northern India have become integral components of the lives of the lower castes living today in those regions. Contrary to the indifference of academic history to the role of the dalit martyrs, the fact that the Dalits themselves have given god-like status to their own heroes of the 1857 rebellion which reveals perhaps the wide gap between academic history writing people's history. Does the reincarnation of these rebel heroes as gods fulfill an existential need of the lower castes vis-à-vis the refusal of the so-called Indian mainstream to acknowledge their very existence? Has the memory of the 1857 rebellion become deeply ingrained in the collective psyche of the grassroots despite the claim that the rebellion was confined to kings and feudal lords and that the lower castes contributed to the struggle only as their soldiers, guards and stick-wielders?

Who was Ranjit Baba who is worshipped with so much devotion in the Shahabad region of the colonial period, which is now known a Arrah district in Bihar? A reference to Ranjit was discovered in the mail of Allen, dated 7 February 1855. The narrative of Ranjit Ram is as follows:

My name is Ranjit Ram. By caste I am a Gwala (milkman). I was a Havildar in the first company of the 40th Platoon and it was my job to distribute salaries to the soldiers. My father's name is Parasanram. I am a resident of village Shahapur, pargana Shahaput, district Shahabad. At this moment my age is 56 years. Since an early age I have been working with the East India Company. On 25 July 1857 I participated in the revolt in Danapur. Our first attempt was to capture Coilver Ghat and then move towards Arrrah. I stayed in Arrah for two hours. After that I told Sitaram Subedar that I wanted to go home and that I should be granted leave. I was granted leave and I spent six days in Shahapur, before going to the jungles of Jagdishpur. The very day that I reached we had to leave for Dulleut to combat the British army. But unfortunately we lost and a few of us had to stay on in the jungles while some went to Baraun and some others went to Piro. The next morning we all gathered together. Babuy Kuber Singh and Babu Amar Singh were our leaders. We went with them to Nokha and from there to Sararam, then to Tilaubhu in Pahariya and finally to the fort in Rohtashgarhg. We kept up our efforts to defeat the British. Negotiating the mountainous road we marched towards Riwa via Rapatganj (Robertsganj) and Daramadganj. But we were neither allowed to stay in Riwa nor allowed to leave. That was why we decided to go to Banda where we spent nearly one and a half months. At Banda rebel soldiers from other regions also gathered. The group included the soldiers as well as those who had come down from Fatehpur down the Grand Trunk road. There was also one company made up of Indian soldiers belonging to the 52nd Poltoon.

It is clear that a soldier of this name belonging to a lower caste had documented his personal experience of the 1857 rebellion. In another mail of Allen there is a description of the roles of Bhangi rebels belonging to the Arrah and Shahabad region. This fact about the four Bhangis also emerged from the narrative of one Barkandaj, whose evidence dated 31 May, 1858 is recorded in the Dumrao police station. His evidence states that four Bhangis who were active during the rebellion had given the British a very bad time.

Dalits of the Bundelkhand region highly revere the momory of *Jhalkaribai* who fought alongside Rani Lakshmi Bai of Jhansi while *Udadevi*, who was the companion of Begum Hazrat Mahal, is worshipped as a 'hero' in central UP. It is true that the stories of these dalit heroes are linked with those of queens like Rani Lakshmi Bai and Begum Hazrat Mahal, but it is nonetheless imperative to evaluate in the right historical context the roles of these brave Dalits warriors at a time when most of the kings and landlords were joining forces with the British to seek benefits from them. These examples testify that the dalit viranganas (brave women) played sterling roles in the rebellion against the British, along with the upper-caste kings, queens and landlords. Moreover, dalit historians cite many examples of lower caste heroes who were not associated with any upper-caste king or queen but fought against the British in their own capacity.

The 1857 rebellion ostensibly began when Mangal Pandey, Hindu soldier in the British army, rebelled at the Barrackpore cantonment, but in recorded history there is hardly any mention of Matadin Bhangi, soldier who provoked Mangal Pandey to rebel by pointing out that the cartridges which all the soldiers had to bite with their mouths were greased with the fat of cows and pigs. But the name of Matadin Bhangi figures in the list of soldiers who were arrested after the rebellion. In fact, Matadin Bhangi, who was also charge-sheeted, court-martialled and martyred, was the chief hero in initialing the 1857 rebellion. But, his contribution to the rebellion has remained only a footnote to the main text.

Matadin Bhangi was not a subordinate of Mangal Pandey but an employee in the British army, just like the latter. His participation in the rebellion was not one of being associated with an upper-caste person represented, on the one hand, his dissent against brahminical social order and, on the other, his protest against the British.

The 1957 rebellion, which came to be known as the First War of Independence, was an event that made deep inroads into the psyche of the people of North India, but is present more in popular oral traditions rather than in the written form. The rebellion was concentrated in the North India, but is present more in popular oral traditions rather than in the written form.

The rebellion was concentrated in the North Indian Gangetic belt that runs from Delhi to Bengal. It began in Meerut on 10 May, on 23 May in Etawah and Mainputi and on 27 May in Etah. In this way the rebellion moved to other parts of UP and Bihar like Kanpur, Awadh, Benaras, Azamgarh, Gorakhpur, Gonda, Bahraich, Sitapur, Ghazipur, Sultanpur, western Bihar and finally to Bengal. In North India it took the form of a turbulent agrarian upheaval gathering together a wide variety of discontents. The rebellion had not yet taken the form of an organized movement against the British but it commanded extensive popular support, especially in Awadh and throughout the North Western Provinces and western Bihar. Sepoy discontent was an essential ingredient of the rebellion but the mutiny derived its strength from the civil population. Peasants, political sadhus, local kings and, most importantly, the conservative sections of society, who had suffered greatly under British rule, became united against colonialism. The British government put up a stiff resistance. Their retribution was harsh and deadly. Villages were burnt down or hit with cannon balls. Thousands of rebels were hung from the gallows and an equally large numbers of dalit people were hung from trees as instant punishment. Although the rebellion ultimately failed, it did develop an anti-colonial consciousness within the people, especially in the Awadh region of UP, where the Rebellion was at its most intense.

It could also be said to be the beginning of a renaissance in the Hindi speaking belt. The rebellion left a deep imprint in the minds of the common people that is impossible to perceive from the scanty recorded history of the period. Recorded history only told the stories of the rich feudal landlords, and kings and queens like Rani Lakshmi Bai and Taantia Tope. The stories of the unsung heroes, who played their role behind the curtains of written history, were circulated only in oral history across rural North India. This gave the dalit intellectuals a lot of space to choose their own heroes of the 1857 movement and some of them for building up the image of Mayawati. It is interesting to note that the role of the Dalits in the 1857 rebellion has been negated by a few extreme-Ambedkarite and leftist journalists and scholars also, who try to link it with dissatisfied feudal lords, kings, soldiers and peasants.

References

1. Dinker, D.C. Swatantra Sangram mein Achhuto Ka Yogdan, Badhisatva Prakashan, Lucknow, 1990.
2. Biswas, A.K. Sepoy Mutiny (1857-58) An Indian Perfidy, Blumoon, New Delhi.
3. Briggs, G.W. 1920. The Chamars. Low Price Publication, Delhi: (reprinted, 1990).
4. Harit, B.L. 1995. Veerangana Jhalkari, Delhi.
5. Madan, G.P. Jhoothi Azadi, Bhartiya Baudh Parishad, Allahabad.
6. Nath, B.S.R.S. 1857 Ki Kranti Ka Janak: Nagvanshi Bhangi matadin Hela, Milan Prakashan, Allahabad, 1998.
7. Pasi, R.K. Bijli Pasi Ki Aithasikta. Pasi Subodh Kendra, Lucknow, 1992.
8. Badri Narayan, Women Heroes and Dalit Assertion in North India, Culture, Identity and Politics, Sage Publication India Pvt. Ltd. New Delhi, 2006.
9. Vidrohi, M.R. Dalit Dastavej, Satyam Prakashan, Delhi, 2004.
10. Yad, K.Y. Rajnaitik Satta, Bahujan Sahitya Sansthan, 2005.
11. Lokmat Samachar (Special Issue on Deepavali) Nagpur, 2005.
12. Namishray, Mohandass, Swantrata Sangram Kei Dalit Krantikari, 2003.

2

Role of Dalit Leaders in Ghadar Movement

The Ghadar movement, despite its brief duration, played a significant role in India's struggle for independence.[1] Among the very large number of those who joined the movement, over ninety five percent were Punjabi immigrants, mostly Sikhs. Amongst them, more than fifty percent were Dalits.[2]

Though it is yet to find its due recognition in the historiography of Indian nationalism, it can not be said to have remained 'an unwritten chapter' of that struggle. More than a dozen published accounts of the movement are already available; some of its major landmarks and characteristics have been briefly covered in a number of biographies and autobiographies and several other books relating to India's freedom struggle. Why then an important chapter on this movement, and what is its relevance to us today? An explanation may be necessary. That may also help in clarifying the themes chosen for the present study. The readers would acknowledge about the unsung dalits heroes, those who sacrificed their lives for the country.

The wave of emigration from rural areas of central Punjab to North America started in the conditions of economic distress at the beginning of the twentieth century.[3] Large numbers from the districts of Jalandhar and Hoshiarpur had earlier found their way to other foreign lands in search of employment.[4] They had worked as watchmen, policemen and caretakers in Malaya, Hong kong, Thailand, Sumatra, Shanghai and Manila. Some had even moved to East Africa and Australia. The discovery of better economic opportunities in North America in 1904 followed the encouragement given by the Hong Kong agents of the Canadian steamship companies.[5] According to Mackenzie King's report submitted to Dominion Parliament in 1908, the first of the Indians came in was induced by agents of Canadian Pacific Company.

The History tells us that only 45 Indians had entered Canada in 1905. Then the number swelled; 387 reached there in 1906; 2,124 in the following year and 2,623 in 1908.[6] All these immigrants came mainly from five districts of Punjab, largest numbers coming from those of Jalandhar and Hoshirarpur.[7] Other 75 per cent of them were Sikhs[8] out of which around 50 per cent were ex-soldiers who had served terms in the British Indian Army.[9] The Ghadar Movement which was founded on the Pacific Coast of America was manned mainly by men from amongst these immigrants from Punjab. These people had little political consciousness and nationalist interests when they arrived in North America. At the time when this emigration started, the Punjab was in a state of ferment. The Labourers and farmers were protesting against the Britishers particularly in the districts of Lyallpur, Lahore and Rawalpindi, sensed a whiff of '*nai hawa*'. They were exhorted to boycott government service and the courts, not to pay taxes and not to allow their grain to be exported.[10] The most notable influences for political development in the Punjab at that time were social reform movements, the Arya Samaj among the Hindus and the Singh Sabha among the Sikhs.

The movement for reassertion of their distinct identity inevitably took the form of de-Hinduising of Sikh community with obvious separatist repercussions. The pamphlet war–*Sikh*

Hindu Hai and *Hum Hindu Nahain Hai* – symbolished the contemporary polemics between the Arya Samaj and Singh Sabha.[11] A similar process had also been started among the Muslims. Kenneth Jones put it rather sharply:

By 1890 the Punjab was divided into a series of aggressive organizations, each possessing its own ideology, each containing a unique sense of identity. To protect that identity and its base became the most fundamental drive for educated and marginal Punjabis. [12]

There was the famous dalit social worker named *Mangu Ram* who was committed to independence as well as social justice. His idea was to unite the dalits under the institution. Later on he founded the Aadi Dharm.

Babu Mangoo Ram, Freedom Fighter and the Founder of Ad-Dharam Movement in Punjab[13]

Mangoo Ram was born on 14 January, 1886 in village Mugowal, Tehsil Garshankar, District Hoshiarpur. His father's name was Harnam Dass while mother's name was Arti. His forefathers were following the traditional occupation of tanning raw hides. Harnam Dass had left the traditional Chamar caste occupation of tanning and preparing hides but had started selling the tanned leather on commercial basis. Mangoo Ram's mother expired when he was only there years old. So his father began to depend heavily for assistance upon his three sons including Mangoo Ram. Since the leather trade required the knowledge of English language to read the sale orders and other instructions regarding the business, Harnam Dass was faced with great diffuculty. For the purpose of reading these sale orders etc. Harnam Dass had to seek the help of some other caste literates for an hour or so and in lieu of this he had to do some beggar (forced labour) for them. For this reason Harnam Dass was eager to have Mangoo Ram receive some early education to facilitate him in reading the papers relating to his leather trade. Mangoo Ram did not go to a regular school. But upto the age of seven, he was taught by a village 'Sadhu'; then he joined the village school and later a school at Mahilpur, a few miles away from his home. He also studied in a school in Dehra Dun for a short period where his elder brother had settled. In all these schools Mangoo Ram noticed that he was the only Chamer student and he always had to sit separate from other upper caste students. He listened to the teacher through open door. Even in high school, he was forced to stay outside the school building and listen to the class instructions through the windows. He used to take a gunny bag from his home for sitting purpose. Mangoo Ram recalled that once there was heavy hailstorm and when in order to safe himself he entered the room, a Brahmin teacher gave him severe beating and made him to put all the class room furniture outside in the rain so that the polluted furniture were washed and purified. Nevertheless, Mangoo Ram was a good student. He was placed third in the class in the primary school. Inspite of such discriminations and hardships Mangu Ram did not loose his heart. Mangu Ram went to the USA in 1909 in connection with his business. He got employment in California in a sugar mill.

Mangu Ram joined the Gadar Party founded by a nationalist Lal Hardayal in 1913. He worked at San Francisco under the leadership of Shri Sohan Singh Bhakna, a leader of Gadar Party in America.

The party consisting of five members including Mangoo Ram was sent to Los-Angles, where they boarded an intermediary boat after collecting their all personal identification. For the rest to this saga, Mangoo Ram was named as Nizam-ud-din, which was a Muslim pseudonym name.

The Gaddar party was publishing a magazine '*Gadar-di-Goonj*'. They had made a deal with the prime minister of Germany for support and they had sent a ship load of weapons 'the Kariamaru' to India, which was captured at Singapore. Mangoo Ram's intermediary boat took them to the Secrorro islands to join with the weapons boat but after 13 days a military ship from Sydney, 'the Man of War' discovered them. Only through the timely intervention of an American Warship they were spared. They went to Veracruz, Mexico to receive rations.[14]

There they finally connected with their weapons boat the 'Maverick', they joined the crew, took plenty of food and headed for India. They were halted again in Hawai, where Mangoo Ram alone with his companion witnessed the eruption of volcano. Free again, they advanced a bit further, perhaps to Jawa or to New Calecdonia. There the Japanese, on behalf of the British, imprisoned them for one year. Eventually, the British decided to hand them, but at mid-night, the night before they were to be hanged at dawn, fate intervened. The Germans spirited them away in the dark and all the five went in separate directions. Harnam Das and Charan Dass to Bangkok and the others including Mangoo Ram to Manila. Again fate altered their plans. A Typhoon appeared and their ship went to Singapore instead, where two British spies, (Bela Singh and Bhag Singh) apprehended them and handed over to the British authorities, who promptly ordered Mangoo Ram to be placed before a cannon and shot. The Germans again wishked Mangoo Ram and he was placed on a ship bound for manila. When Mangoo Ram arrived in Philippines he read a news report in the Manila Times indicating tht he had been executed for treason by the British in Singapore. In fact one of Mangoo Ram's captured colleagues who assumed his name to protect Mango Ram was shot dead in his place. This news of alleged death of Mangoo Ram reached Punjab, where his wife heard the report and promptly married his younger brother as per custom of the community.

In the meantime Mangoo Ram was kept in Series of hide-outs on various islands. Members of Gadhar Party were his benefactors. During this period they showed him hospitality and friendship. He was no longer an un-touchable but a comrade in distress.

The war ended in 1918 and Gaddar Party was no longer a threat to the British. Mangoo Ram decided to stay in Manila.

There he met an American Mr. Johnson of Marshal Field and Company (a department store in Chicago) who hired him to work in an Embroidery factory making shirts for the American market. Here while working in the factory his Gadar connections were discovered and he was interred for six months during the Prince of Wales visit to Manila in 1922. Mangoo Ram blamed the Marshal-Field for exposing him. Then, after six years work in the factory he decided to return to India.

Home-Ward Journey (Return to India)

Early in 1925, Mangoo Ram set sail. He arrived in Ceylone in the company of Christian missionary who had met him on board. After that he traveled through the sub-continent to the Punjab, visiting Madurai, Madras, Bombay, Poona, Sitara, Nagpur and Delhi. He observed enroute the social conditions as bad as any thing and particularly, the plight of the dalits and he was dismayed to see them. Mangoo Ram used to tell that the Gadar Party people in Francisco gave him clearance & designated him to work for the uplift of the untouchables in India. Thus in a new context the old revolutionary from San-Francisco continued the Gadar spirit.

As the political and social awakening knocking at their doors the new world was opening for them. The new comers generally sought jobs and settled near their relatives or the early comers from their villages. Most of those going to Canada settled in or around Vancouver city and Vancouver Island in the province of British Columbia, where the railway construction work provided opportunities of large scale employment.

While they were doing hard work, earning their livelihood and making money, the difficulties were waiting them. Indian labourers became victims of anti-oriental feelings.[15] The newcomers did not conform to the Euro-American culture. With their turbans, beards, dark complexion and different personal and social habits, they somewhat naturally aroused the curiosity of the white people. Another factor was the feeling of superiority in white man which emanated to a large degree from a heritage of aggressive colonialism.[16] An Indian was considered as belonging to inferior races. The Indian was characterized as a filthy beast.[17] The Indian immigrant was a colonized person of colour. Sucheng Chan observed that the world had by that time been categorized 'both by ideology and well-institutionalised practice into a system of social, cultural, political and economic hierarchies', so the Indian was considered as belonging to 'inferior races'.

Beginning of Political Consciousness

The political awakening among Indian in Canada and the United States rose with different types of activities revolving round three main factors: resentment and hostility against the white community for its prejudice and oppression, development of an ethnic identity[18], and nationalism directed against British colonialism in India.[19]

The encounter with white prejudice, anti-Asiatic riots and threats of exclusion and deportation of Indian immigrants, however, became a new powerful factor which tended to alter their orientation. The fears of deportation which were aroused during the last quarter of 1908 became a major reason for solidarity. When people are kicking you, as St. Nihal Singh wrote, 'you can not feel like affiliating with others of yours kin and country and pulling together.[20] So that Teja Singh started mobilizing and organising these people against the reported proposal of sending a number of Indians to British Honduras, the political tenor was conspicuously altered. Teja Singh talked in a profoundly spiritual idiom; most meetings were held in the Gurdwaras.[21] In 1907, Puri issued a lithographed propaganda sheet Circular-e-Azadi[22] (Circular of Freedom) in Urdu language which announced the formation of a Hindustan Association of San Francisco[23] with branches at Astoria and Vancourer.[24]

Guran Ditt Kumar[25], a native of Bhannu in the North West Frontier Province of India who came into contact with revolutionaries at the National College Calcutta (where he taught

Urdu for a short period) arrived in Victoria and setup a grocery shop there.[26] Harnam Singh of Sahri who was a *sowaar* (trooper) of the 4th Cavalary in India before 1904 also arrived in Victoria with Kumar in 1907.[27]

Taraknath Das started publishing from April 1908, a few days before he was dismissed from his job, an eight page periodical, *Free Hindustan in* English language.[28] So the political work of these nationalists appeared to have contributed a new element in the development of a political consciousness among their countrymen.[29]

What Har Dyal saw of the great potential material for rebellion in these Punjabi immigrants appeared to have revived his spirits and kindled in his heart hopes of translating a dream into reality. That he came up with Ghadar as the name for the propaganda paper was indicative of the form of political action he had in mind. This was further explained by him in his article 'Our name and Our Work', in the first issue of the Ghadar.[30]

On 1st November 1913, the first issue of the weekly Ghadar inaugurated a propaganda war. Sohan Singh Bhakna was elected as president of Ghadar Party. That issue was in Urdu. Hardyal described this beginning as 'a new epoch in the history of India, The mast-head of the paper carried a declaration as to its character, Angrezi Raj Ka Dushman (Enemy of English Rule), and an exhortation, 'O manly youngmen of India take to weapons quick'.[31]

The objective in starting the paper was made clear at the outset: 'Our name and work are identical'. An armed revolution was to be started in India, because the people could no longer bear the tyranny and oppression under the English Rule'. A big war between Germany and England was expected. That would be the proper time for starting a revolution in India.[32] As Har Dayal had told on audience at Astoria.

In the process, anti-Birtish feelings had been developed in the hearts of Gaddarists. Now they decided to bring out a newspaper called *Ghadar*. The task was, as the paper had already announced, to prepare the country for 'mutiny' until the time came, and that was to come 'soon', 'when rifle and blood will be used for pen and ink', and English rule would be destroyed.

The 'Wanted Columns' in the Ghadar occasionally contained the following: 'Wanted-Enthusiastic and heroic soldiers for organizing Ghadar in Hindustan.[33]

Remuneration	-	*Death*
Rewards	-	*Martyrdom*
Pension	-	*Freedom*
Field of Work	-	*Hindustan*'.

In the earlier issues of the newspaper, the Ghadar Party suggested some concrete measures for the overthrow of the imperial rule in India; sedition of Indian troops; murder of loyal (to the British) subjects and officials; hoisting of the revolutionary flag; breaking of jails; looting of treasures, thanas (police stations) etc.; propagation of seditious literature; union with the foreign enemies of the British; commission of dacoity; procuring of arms; manufacture of bombs; formation of secret societies; destruction of railways and telegraphs; and the recruitment of young men for revolutionary work.

Besides the Ghadhar, the party published important pamphlets including *Ghadar di Goonj* (echoes of rebellion), Illan-i-jang (declaration of ar), *Naya Zamana* (new age) and *The Balance-sheet of British Rule in India*. The Ghadar literature at first was puhblished in Urdu, Pubjabi and Gujerati. Soon the party attracted a large number of followers from Canada, the United States, the Philippines, Hong Kong, China, Egypt, Turkey and Germany. Their literature evoked the sentiments of patriotism, revolution, secularism, unity and independence.[34]

One of the regular features of the weekly was *Angrezi Raj ka kacha chitta* (A Balance Sheet of English Rule) consisting of fourteen points printed always on the front page.[35] The last point being fifty six years have passed since the Ghadar of 1857, now there is urgent need of the second one'. Another regular feature entitled *Ankon ki Gawahi* (Evidence of Statistics lit. figures) highlighted the destructive consequences of British exploitation in India. The British rule was characterized as an 'ulcer' and a plague on the nation. There could be no respite, it was argued, until 'this base, rascally, evil-doing, vicious government is destroyed.'[36]

The attention of the readers was then drawn to the war which Indian waged in 1857, 'the very name of which makes the English shiver'. That it did not succeed in the objective was attributed to lack of a complete unity amongst the countrymen. But it taught the English tyrant a lesson.

On every 10th May, the anniversary of the 'war' of 1857, a special issue of Ghadar was brought out, pointing the people to fallow the example of warriors of 1857.

Articles were also written in the Ghadar to inform the readers regarding 'similar' militant movements in Egypt, Ireland, Russia, China and the Earlier one in Maxico, suggesting propitious possibilities of support from the revolutionaries of those countries in the proposed fight against the British.[37]

A number of small pamphlets and tracts were published both in English and Indian languages, including the reprinting of articles published earlier. Prominent along those of early period were *Zulam*! *JGore Shahi Zulem* (Tyranny! Tyranny! *White Racial* Tyranny) in Gurmukhi etc.

More stirring of all the writings were a number of lyrical, poetical compositions in the language of immigrant workers. These were published in the Ghadar and also sung with a dash at various meetings of these people. Soon after, these were collected and published in book from entitled *Ghadar di Goonj* (Echo of Ghadar)[38] and distributed free of charge amongst Indians. These poems aroused the indignation of readers against British oppression. '*Zalam coolie pukaran sanoon* (Thses tyrants call us coolies) and *Zalam farangi lai gaye desh lutt ke'* (The tyrannous foreingers have looted away the country) were two of the oft repeated refrains in these poems. These poems also reminded the readers of their heritage of valour, their great heroes and their sacrifices; showered shame on the sluggish 'who defiled the great name of the Sikhs and stirred them to fight, kill the enemies and die bravely rather than live a cowardly life. One of these poems , for instance, read as under:

Why do you disgrace the name of Singhs
How come! you have forgotten the majesty of 'lion's
Had the like of Dip Sing been alive today
How could the Singhs have been taunted?
People say that the Singhs are no good
Why did you turn the tides during the Delhi mutiny?
Cry aloud: 'let us kill the whites'
Why do you sit quiet shamelessly
Let the earth give way so we may drown
To what good were these thirty crores born.[39]

The only need of the hour was to prepare for rebellion. '*Pray for the Ghadar*' was the chief exhortation; '*If you talk, talk of Ghadar*; *If you dream, dream of Ghadar; If you eat, eat for the sake of Ghadar*'. All else must wait. It was foolish to get absorbed in religious feuds or matters of the Vedas or the Koran, sang the poets.[40] Khushwant Singh termed it 'Zenophobic nationalism'.

All the literature thus published was distributed among the Punjabi immigrants in America and sent in bundles to contacts outside. Within a few months the Ghadar began to circulate among groups of Indians settled in Canada, the Philippines, Hong Kong, China, the Malay States, Singapore, Trinidad and Honduras and was also forwarded to India.[41]

A series of public gatherings of immigrants were addressed by Bhagwan Singh, Ram Chandra and Mohammed Barkatullah, among others. The biggest of these meetings was held at Sacramento. Prithvi Singh Azad who was present at that meeting described it as 'a gathering of true lovers of freedom where our every word and gesture was eloquent of the passion'. It was openly discussed as to what should be done on reaching India and how should they go about their work. That, however, says Azad, 'mainly expressed the fire and none of us had any clear idea of revolution.[42] A number of people in the audience were reportedly eager to leave for rebellion at once. *The Portland Telegram* flashed the news under a front page banner line: *'Hindus Go Home to Fight in Revolution'*.[43]

Some of the more impatient ones like Kartar Singh Sarabha, Raghubar Dayal Gupta and a few others had left earlier, without waiting for this meeting.[44]

Har Dayal was particularly inclined to emphasise the moral degradation of the Indian people causesd by subjection to foreign rule. In his article, *'The Social Conquest of the Hindu Race'* his argument turned mainly to the danger to Hindu tradition and moral order. He virulently decried the situation, whereby 'the beaf-eating Europeans', who were mere cobblers and coolies in England, had ousted high caste Brahmins and Kshatriyas from positions of leadership in the Hindu society. He, therefore, warned: 'If the social conquest is completed, there is no hope for our nation. On the other hand, the argument in another pamphlet, *Ghulamin Ka Zehar* (The poison of Slavery) which also focused on moral degradation, was basically secular in appeal. It was not only the British rule which was condemned but also the social system in which the native Raja and Zamindar were equally responsible for injecting the poison of slavery in the minds of the honest hard-working peasants and labourers.[45]

Party was divided into the wings: 'propaganda wing and action wing; the former working under Har Dayal and the latter under Khankhije himself. It is apparent in these accounts that to all these people Har Dayal occupied a central place in the Ghadar Movement and also that he appeared to them mainly as a powerful mobiliser.[46]

Harcharan Das, a close associate of Ram Chandra, who became an important approver for the prosecution during Second Supplementary Lahore Conspiracy Case (1971) and at the Sen Francisco Trial, referred to a detailed set of Seventeen Rules framed for a secret organization at the *Yugantar Ashram*. Important among these rules were that all fresh recruits were to be recommended by at least two members, that none was entitled to know all the party secrets until one has been a member for at least six months and that any one who revealed party secrets or misappropriated party funds was to be killed.[47]

The statement of Harcharn Das has been of a belief both in popular and academic works regarding a secret and planned organization of the party. Giles T. Brown described the *Yugantar Ashram Group,* referred by Das, as the 'inner circle' and further stated that 'with this Har Dayal hoped to control the activities of the larger association'.[48] There is, however, hardly any other evidence to corroborate the version given by Das. 'Tundilat' and Prithvi Singh Azad who were whole time workers at the *Ashram* at one time or another reported that there were no such formal rules of the organisaiton. According to them it was well understood by all those who worked there that they had to guard themselves against the 'spies', maintain essential secrecy and that embezzlement of funds by any body would be a serious crime punishable even by death. But no formal organization was rationally planned or established. Azad told the present writer for instance : 'As for the rules who should be taken and who should not be taken, it is not within my knowledge that any such rules were made; because I myself joined the *Ashram.* I required no recommendation. Nor any one asked me, who I was and where from I had come. I came and straight started working at the *Ashram.*[49]

The authority of the leaders was based, in practice, not on formal positions in the party hierarchy, but on the leadership qualities stereotyped in the minds of the followers. To some of them the *Ghadar* seemed to be the chief leader and the 'Red Book' for all they needed to learn and do. Most Ghadarities, as reflected in their evidence before the Special Tribunal at Lahore, seemed to carry exaggerated notions of the authority and leadership roles of particular individuals as also ignorance about the roles of many others. In what was a typical writing of Ghadar, it characterized the 'Ghadar Party', two years after its formation, in the following words. :

The People of this party cannot make the usual arrangements for organization, register, house etc..... Outside the country they wander thirsting, starving, clad in rags, but filled with great enthusiasm. Such is the sacred Hindustan Ghadar Party, which, though without any particular place for itself, has its soldiers ready everywhere and at everytime.[50]

Establishment of branches of the Ghadar party was said to be one of the important activities of its leadership. Sohan Singh Bhakna and some others toured different areas on the pacific coast of the USA for that purpose. According to him 72 branches were setup in USA alone within one year of the formation of the party.[51] By a branch he meant a group of Indians working in one mill, ranch or farm, who received the paper Ghadar and felt a concern for the country. Some of the branches he mentioned were, for instance, Astoria Mill, Monark Mill and Wina Mill.

As teachings of the Ghadar started reaching groups of Indian immigrants in various parts of the world or read out to them by priests in their Gurdwaras or in small congregations elsewere, they developed some degree of affinity and association with the Ghadar partriots. The first expression of that feeling was seen in the collection and contribution of funds and requests for Ghadar literature. These spontaneous groupings, known after the relatively more articulate amongst them, came to be called 'branches'. 'Branches spontaneously sprang up in Panam, Mexico and China', wrote Harjap Singh.[52] Prithvi Sing Azad also expressed a similar view: 'The Ghadar spread the ideas. The people themselves formed small bands and these of their own accord, started taking organizational shapes.[53]

Such grouping sprang up in large number of places, particularly in the province of British Columbia in Canada, Shanghai, Hong Kong, Manila and Penang, When questioned about the number of members in their branch, Gujjar Singh Bhakna, a leading Ghadarite from Shanghai said, 'we were four or five people'. That was the branch in china Town. America town had another branch, with as many Indians. 'We started working for rebellion according to directions received from the paper Ghadar, he added.[54] Where as such of the grouping as came up in the USA may have received occasional guidance from one or the other of the known central leaders, the groups in far-off places had to be completely on their own.

The contacts between these groups in the United States, were informal and indirect. Their activities on reaching Punjab, reflected more or less autonomous and separate group activity. These groups were referred to as Jathas, known after one or the othrer leader or an area e.g., Nidhan Singh's Jatha, Gujjar Singh's Jathas, Doaba Jatha, Majha Jatha etc. Some of these even announced the dates and places of starting a rebellion on their own.[55]

Even important leader seemed to carry conflicting nations of who occupied what formal position. The belief of the President of the *Hindi Association,* Sohan Singh Bhakna, that Harnam Singh 'Tundilat', and not Ram Chandra, become the editor of Ghadar after Har Dayal,[56] was a major case in point. Similarly, whereas Bhakna and 'Tundilat' believed that Santokh Singh became the Secretary and chief leader of the party after the departure of Har Dayal,[57] all other evidence indicated that the main leader was Ram Chandra.[58]

Such divergent beliefs pointed out not only to the absence of formal procedure of selection or nomination but also to the widely dispersed and diffused nature of decision-making authorities.

Prithvi Singh Azad

Prithvi Singh Azad was born on 15 September, 1892 at village Laldoo, Patiyal district. His family came to Punjab and settled there. During 1907-08 there was the National Movement in the name of Bangbhang. Sh. Lokmanya Tilak and Khudi Ram Bose both famous leaders had been arrested by British Govt. Sh. Prithvi Singh was influenced by these national incidents.

He was also influenced by the famous song "Pagri Sambhal Jatta", written by Sardar Ajit Singh.

When he was in America in 1912, he approached Lala Hardyal Singh. He was helpful for the extension of Gaddar Movement in Sanfrancisko. He also published the Gaddar Newspaper. When he was sailing in the ship alongwith his one hundred fifty freedom fighters, advancing to Calcutta, he was arrested on 7 December, 1914. In the court of Ambala he was sentenced Ten years imprisonment. After two years he was sent to Madras and kept in the jail. Then he was again sent to Calcutta and jumping throw the running train he ran-away, but caught. He again tried to run-away and succeeded.

Sh. Prathvi Singh Azad came near to Sh. Chander Shekhar Azad, who gave him his Automatic Mouser pistol. He was asked to visit and learn from Russian freedom fighters, how to start the movement in India. He accepted his challenge and stayed in Russia a few months.

Returning from Russia he came near to many freedom fighters in India. He also approached to Gandhi. In 1933 he was again arrested by the Britishers. He set free for a few months, again he was arrested by Bombay police.

Upto 1947 several times he was arrested. He bear hardships from Britishers. He was a true patriot. He wrote his own Autobiography named as "Kranti Path Ka Pathik". He was the President of freedom fighter organisation. He died on 5 March, 1989.

Udham Singh

Before long, Bhagat Singh became the hero of many legends, some of them true and some fond creations of popular imagination. Songs and poems about him could be heard wherever one went. His memory was enshrined in the heart of many a young man. Only a year after his death a young man was seen dancing in ecstasy with a miniature portrait of Bhagat Singh in his hands. The name of this young man was Udham Singh.[59]

Very little is known for certain about Udham Singh's early life. That, he belonged to Shahpur in Sunam is borne out by reliable evidence.[60] According to Giani Gurmukh Singh Musafir, Udham Singh's father was a Kambo by caste (dalit) and he worked for some time as a watchman on a level railway crossing.[61] The date of Udham Singh's birth is placed in December, 1899 and it has the merit of plausibility: there is hardly any doubt that he was born around 1900.[62] He himself stated in 1940 that his father had died when he was five or six years old.[63] There is a strong tradition, supported by the statement of Shiv Singh Johal, that Udham Sing was brought to Amritsar after the death of his father and grew up in the well known orphanage here. We are now certain that he joined the Khalsa Central Orphanage in 1907.[64]

Udham Singh left the orphanage after matriculation and with the indelible impressions of the massacre of the Jallianwala Bagh on his mind. Whether or not he was present there at the time of actual firing he appears to have personally witnessed the aftermath S. Swaran Singh tells us that in 1932 Udham Singh used to recall the episode with agony and anger. In 1940, enquiries were made to find out if Udham Singh's brothers or relations had been killed in the massacre. They had not been. In all probability, Udham Singh had referred to his countrymen as 'brothers', on the basis of which the enquiry was made. How clearly he had conceived the idea of avenging the death of his brothers in 1919, it is difficult to say.[65]

According to tradition, Udham Singh left India and went to America. There he came into contact with the Ghadarites who were continuing with their work of propagating the ideas of armed revolutions.[66] He stated revolutionary immigrants and to drive them to appointed places.[67] He is believed to have received a message from Bhagat Singh for returning to India and working here. Udham Singh returned with weapons. Before long, however, he was arrested by the police in Amritsar. On the charge of carrying arms without a licence he was sent to jail for four years. After his release he spent some time in Sunam.[68]

Udham Singh referred to Bhagat Singh in 1940 as his best friend. This was surely not an afterthought. In Kashmir, in 1932 he was seen carrying Bhagat Singh's portrait and occasionally referred to him as his *guru*. At this time Udham Singh was full of revolutionary songs, particularly the famous *ghazal* by Bismal which opens with the line: *'Now we are longing to wager our heads'*.[69] Whatever the duration and the nature of his contact with Bhagat Singh, Udham Singh was an ardent admirer of his young guru who was an embodiment of cool courage and selfless sacrifice, the traits which he himself cherished and cultivated.

In 1932, Udham Singh appeared to be occupied with some important but self-assigned task; he was full of confidence, he knew English well and spoke it fluently, he knew the work of a motor mechanic; he knew the work of a carpenter; and he knew how to change garbs. He stayed in Kashmir at least for a few months. Leaving India around 1933 he reached England sometime in the mid 1930s.[70]

Another deposition records that Udham Singh succeeded in leaving India and making his way to the West coast of North America. Major cities such as Vancouver, San Francisco and Los Angeles contained many people from ethnic minority groupsm particularly Chinese and Japanese. Sikh immigrants had arrived at the end of the nineteenth century and by their hard and business skill, they had established respectable communities on this continent of new opportunity.[71] Having experienced freedom not usually available in the land of their birth, they followed closely the changing political scene in India. It seems likely that Udham Singh was sponsored by the Ghadar Party to visit these communities, to give them a first hand account of the Jallianwala Bagh massacre, to promote the growth of local branches of the party, and to raise funds. It must be assumed that he was traveling under a false passport.

There is no evidence that he was issued with a British passport in his own name before leaving India. Leaving the western sea-board, he traveled to New York and took a ship for Europe. He was in the Baltics in 1926 and visited Germany and Poland. [72]

Yet other information shows that in the USA he made contact with the Ghadar Party. He worked for some time in a railway workshop. He addressed Indians on many occasions. At the workshop he only had to work for six hours. There he built his own party organization naming it the *'Azad Party'*, an off-shoot of the Ghadar Party. He dispatched revolutionary literature to India. [73]

Bhagat Singh and his associates were hanged by the British on 23 March 1931. Udham Singh came to know of this in the jail when he was making ropes and was saddened by it. [74] On release from jail on 23 October,1931,[75] he was met by his party associates and went to Amritsar to find out about the activities of his group. [76] After this, he visited Husainiwala for some days and paid tribute to Bhagat Singh.[77] From there he went to Sunam. He was wearing strange clothes: an English hat on his head, a coltly necktie and beautiful coloured glasses. He carried a small rod in his hand. So attired he resembled a British official. In his new clothes many people did not recognize him. He shared his jail experience with them.

At Broadcasting House, the editors for the BBC Home and Forces Service made a final check on their scripts and announced: "Sir Michael O'Dwyer, a former Governor of the Punjab, was assassinated this afternoon at a meeting in the Caxton Hall, London. Lord Lamington and Sir Louis Dane, also former Indian Governors, were wounded; and the Secretary for State for India, Lord Zetland was hit and slightly injured.[78]

"The meeting had been arranged by the East India Association to hear an address by Sir Percy Sykes. The shooting occurred at the end of the meeting when Lord Lamington rose to move a vote of thanks for Sir Percy and to Lord Zetland, who presided. The speech had just ended and the meeting was about to break up, when a short thick-set Indian made his way from the centre of a side gangway of the hall towards the platform. Four or five [in fact six] shots were fired. Sir Michael O'Dwyer was shot dead. Lord Lamington and Sir Louis Dane were both wounded in the arm. Lord Zetland was able to go home after treatment at St. George's Hospital; his only injury was a bruise on the ribs from a bullet which went through his jacket. Sir Percy Sykes was not hit.

"Immediately after the shooting an Indian tried to make a dash out of the hall but he was seized by members of the audience. The police took statements from every individual in the Hall. No one was allowed to leave for two hours.[79]

"Sir Michael O'Dwyer was 74, and he joined the Indian Civil Service in 1885. From 1908 to 1909 he was Acting Resident in Hyderabad, and from 1913 to 1919 he was Lieutenant Governor of the Punjab. It was during this period, on 13 April 1919, that the Amritsar shooting occurred. A mob had attacked banks and other buildings and Europeans had been killed. At the request of the Civil Authorities, troops were called out and a number of natives were killed. This shooting raised a great political controversy at the time, followed by a committee of inquiry, a parliamentary debate and action in the courts. Sir Louis Dane was lieutenant governor of the Punjab immediately before Sir Michael O'Dwyer's term of office. Lord Lamington is a former governor of Bombay."[80]

The shooting was reported on the front pages of newspapers around the world, particularly and for obvious reasons in the British and Indian dailies. The German newspaper hailed the 'Indian' as 'a Fighter for freedom' and the shooting as 'an expression of the pentup fury of the downtrodden Indian people'. A lucid account was given of the Amritsar massacre. The Berliner Zeitung called the murder 'the touch of the Indian fight for freedom', and said that "during the war Great Britain has tried to create the impression that Indians are complacent and unconditional supporters of Great Britain, and her war policy. In this fantastic picture crack now the shots of the courageous Indian who by his deed has made himself the spokesman of his fellow countrymen.[81]

That evening (14 March) the German broadcasting station commented again: 'The active resistance to Britain's Indian policy by the Nationalists of the country has recently taken a more concrete form in Sir Michael O'Dwyer's assassination at Caxton Hall by a Punjab Nationalist, Mohamed Singh Azad. Indians apparently have not forgotten that on 13 April 1919, Sir Michael O'Dwyer had 600 defenceless Indians executed in the province of Punjab. Sir Michael O'Dwyer was one of the most ruthless and bloodthirsty of the Punjab's governors. It was he who forced the Punjabis to shed their blood for the benefit of Britain during the last war. This assassination was a vendetta and a justified one at that. We realise that a widespread revolt is impending in India'.[82]

The entire press in England published details of the Caxton Hall shooting, with photographs of Udham Singh and others, including O'Dwyer,[83] Zetland,[84] Dane,[85] Lamington,[86] Sykes[87] and Bertha Herring. While giving the scenario, these newspapers linked the shooting with the massacre at Jallianwalaj Bagh.[88]

In India, the English-language newspapers carried editorials which deplored the murder, condemned the extremists and underlined the strong ties between India and Great Britain. The nationalist press was less emphatic in criticising the shooting and was at pains to point out the root causes of violent acts by the extremist fringe. In general terms, however, the Indian media expressed horror at what had happened. Prominent coverage was given to **Gandhi's reaction**. He told reporters : **The news of the death of Sir Michael O'Dwyer and the injuries to Lord Zetland, Lord Lamington and Sir Louis Dane has caused me deep pain. I regard this act as one of insanity...he hoped it would not affect Indian politics...he expressed condolence with O'Dwyer's family and congratulated Lord Zetland upon his escape**.[89]

Nehru stated that the assassination was widely regretted and hoped it would not have far-reaching repercussions on the political future of India.

The Times of India wrote: "The actions of the assassin, which are condemned by responsible Indians in London and India, show that the outrage was the act of a mad-man or a man crazed by virulent anti-British propaganda. The unhappy Jallianwala Bagh incident has been forgotten in the Punjab". The Tribune (the Congress Party newspaper) condemned the "outrage" in strong terms, and remarked on "tragic irony of fate".

O'Dwyer was already on his special list because of the executions of the Ghadar Party patriots, tortures during recruitments of the Punjabis in the World War-1, the massacre at Jallianwala Bagh, the atrocities committed during Martial Law in April 1919 and also his persistent and unabated anti-Indian venom. Louis Dane and Lord Lamington were supporters of O'Dwyer's doctrine of keeping India in a state of slavery with an 'iron hand' and Lord Wellingdon became responsible for execution of his patron Shaheed Bhagat Singh. Obviously he had been nursing a plan to assassinate some British officials connected with Indian political affairs and the above persons, having already earned Udham Singh's hatred, compelled him to resort to Caxton Hall protest.

On 13 March the much awaited opportunity by Udham Singh came and he reached Caxton Hall. He certainly knew the presence of O'Dwyer, Zetland, Lamington and Dane. He accompanied an unknown kind English lady to gain entry with a revolver in his pocket. The speeches made by the speakers were in defence of imperialism and the speech made by O'Dwyer was particularly racy in Character. In his speech O'Dwyer did not forget to mention his success in suppressing the Punjab rebellion of 1913-16, his efforts on the recruitment front during the war and the Jallianwala Bagh massacre. This may have infuriated Udham Singh beyond the point of endurance. When the meeting ended at 4.30 p.m. he took out his revolver and shot O'Dwyer, and wounded Lord Zetland, Lord Lamington and Sir Louis Dane. He was overpowered immediately and arrested.

In Udham Singh's utterances in the face of trial and death, there are ecohoes of Kartar Singh Sarabha who had died for the country twenty four years earlier. However, Udham Singh was consciously emulating another young martyr: Bhagat Singh. In one of his letters he refers to Bhagat Singh as his 'best friend' who had left him behind by ten years, adding 'he is waiting for me'. The portrait of Udham singh, more even than the legend that has grown around his person, clearly reflects the cool courage and firm determination which are associated with him.

Udham Singh has not been ignored by the writers of independent India, not in the recent past at any rate. His name is included in Giani Gurmuikh Singh Musafir's book on the martyrs of the twentieth century, in the Eminent Freedom Fighters of the Pubjab by Professor Fauja Singh, and in the Sardar by S. Kulbir Singh. The story of 'the heroism of Shaheed Udham Singh' has been publicized; he has been portrayed as 'the patriot who avenged the Jallianwala Bagh massacre'; and he has become the subject of a historical novel: Saheed Udham Singh by Kesar Singh. Search for the facts of Udham Singh's life has gone hand in hand with an imaginative portrayal of his personality. Still, the biographer of Udham Singh is faced with the paucity of factual information about him.

There is something in the modern outlook which places a high premium on 'what acrually happens'. Empirical evidence, therefore, has come to acquire a value it never proposed before. Search for factual information has come to have its own justification. The primary purpose of the present work is to publicise some significant facts of Udham Singh's life so that his personality is better appreciated by both laymen and historians.

Our information on Udham Singh comes from there important sources: oral evidence, archival material and a personal collection. S. Swaran Singh and S. Inder Singh Murari of Barath Sahib near Pathankot who wer connected with the Gurdaspur conspiracy case in the early 1930's came to know Udham Singh personally and have vivid memories of this impressive personality. They were kind enough to reduce their memories to writing for our purpose and they willingly answered all questions posed to them regarding Udham Singh. In a certain sense, their evidence has a unique value: Udham Singh comes alive through their lifelike portrayal of numerous small incidents of his life. We have used their evidence for the reconstruction of Udham Singh's life. Also, we have given the essentials of their evidence in the form of an appendix for the benefit of others. We are extremely thankful to these gentlemen for their enthusiastic cooperation.

In the National Archives of India, New Delhi, File No.77, 1940, Government of India, Home Department (Poll Secret) relates to : 'Desirability of securing that this trial of Udham Singh should be reported as unsensationaly as possible'. It contains very useful information on the reaction of the Governments in the United Kingdom and in India to the trial of Udham Singh. The precautions taken by both the Governments during the month of April, 1940, largely account for the absence of publicity which the trial of Udham Singh would have received in the normal course of things. Accession 292 of the National Archives of India contains papers relating to Udham Singh's trial. With the help of these records it is possible to reconstruct the incidents of March 13. They also reveal something of the feeling with which Udham Singh acted.

More important than either of these sources is a collection of document which was formerly in possession of S. Shiv Singh Johal, the best friend of Udham Singh in London in the late 1930s. Through the courtesy of Mr. M. S. Gill of the Indian Administrative Service, this collection is now with the Guru Nanak University. But for this collection, the present book would not have been published. It consists of 19 documents, 7 of which are Udham Singh's letters. Most of these letters were reproduced by Mr. M. S. Gill in an article on Udham Singh which appeared in The Illustrated Weekly of India in the beginning of 1972. They do form the most important part of this collection, not merely because they were written by Udham Singh but also because they can statute an extremely valuable source of information on him and afford an insight into his character and personality.

However, the remaining 12 documents are not without a value of their own. For one thing, like the letters of Udham Singh, they are all dated. Four of these twelve documents are mere receipts : one on a printed 'pad' of Bernard Linder & Co. Solicitors of North Wembely; another on a leaf of a printed receipt book of Robert Clayton & Co., solicitors of London; the third one on a small piece of ordinary paper; and the fourth on a sheet of rather good quality paper. The last two are also the receipts given by Clayon & Co. to S. Shiv Singh Johal. The contents of these receipts are significant. The first clearly shows that Shiv Singh engaged the solicitors concerned for the defence of Udham Singh a day before he was charged for murder. Before his trial, Shiv Singh engaged another, more expensive if not also more reputable, firm of solicitors. The third and the fourth show that Shiv Singh engaged the firm for 'appeal' against the judgment pronounced by the court on June 5 by paying 70 pounds. The value of these apparently useless pieces of paper to the biographer of Udham Singh is obvious.[90]

Equally valueable are the other eight documents. The document numbered VIII in this book reveals Shiv Singh's anxiety to see Udham Singh personally in the prison before his trial took place on June 4. Documents XII, XIII and XIV show that the chaplain of the prison in which Udham Singh was detained after his rial succeeded in getting 'Hindustani prayer books' from Shiv Singh only after writing to him a forma and rather forbidding letter. Udham Singh's own request, made earlier for a Gutka ('Sikh prayer book'), had been ignored by Shiv Singh. Documents XVI and XVII establish beyond doubt that Udham Singh had been executed before August 6. Further more, though the belongings of Udham Singh were sent to Shiv Singh, his ashes were refused. The last two documents indicate that Shiv Singh was keen to have a copy of the verdict given by the court on the appeal made on behalf of Udham Singh.

Turning to the letters of Udham Singh we find several points of interest. The first letter, written from Brixton Prison on March 15, 1940, bears the number 1010 which was given to Udham Singh by the prison authorities. **His name is given as M. Azad and he himself signs as Mohamed Singh Azad.** His real name at this time was known to all concerned but he persisted in keeping up the pretence. The letters, U and S appear as a sort of sign at the top right corner of the letter, written probably by Udham Singh himself. The letter is addressed to 'Mr. Singh Sahib' of the Gurdwara Sri Guru Singh Sabha, 79 Sinclair Road, Shepherds Bush, London, W. 14. There is hardly any doubt that this letter was meant for S. Shiv Singh Johal, but Udham Singh does not like to disclose his former association with him.[91]

Why should Udham Singh write to an unknown person? The contents of the letter must be analysed with this question in mind. He says at the very outset that he does not know the 'full name' of the addressee and immediately asks for a favour: books, to keep him busy: books in Urdu or Gurmukhi to be sent by post. Udham Singh's idea was to establish contact with Shiv Singh without bringing suspicion or blame on him. 'I do not know you', he goes on to say; but he knew Mohan Singh, formerely in charge of the Gurdwara, who would have sent some books to him. Udham Singh harps on books as his most obvious need in the prison. He was not allowed to write in Hindustani, he says, but still 'you will understand the sort of 'book' I want. In 'revolutionary' code, the 'book' referred to a revolver or a weapon. Having made the suggestion, Udham Singh hastens to qualify : 'some books about history or Indian news papers'. Towards the end he suggests that Shiv Singh 'will be appreciated' for sending books but he should not incur too much 'expence' (risk?).

The letter is by no means grim. Udham Singh does say at one place that he would 'be born again', for he was most likely to be sentenced to death. But he adds that he had waited for this case for many years. However there are statements in this letter which reveal his sense of humour. 'I am looking forward to go some better castle', he says at one place; 'I am having many body guards and I am well looked after', he says of his position in the jail; 'I am guest of the H. M. the King George now', he adds in a 'note'. It must be added that these humouous 'asides' were meant as much for the consumption of his sensors as for the addressee.

The second letter, dated March 20, is addressed to Mr. S.S. Johal, Secretary Khalsa Jatha, 79 Sinclair Road, London, W.14. By now 'Mr. Singh' of the first letter has responded and, therefore, Udham Singh has come to know him as it were. Udham Singh is thankful for the books sent to him and refers to the forthcoming 'examination' which would enable him to receive the 'highest degree' one can obtain in life. Had books been the real nee, or the only need of Udham Singh in prison, this letter could have ended where it ends. But there is a postscript to this letter which is longer than the letter itself. The contents of the postscript are indeed very interesting. Udham Singh refers to 'a gentleman' who visits him daily in the hope of converting him to Christianity. Since the gentleman was wasting so much of 'his time and my time also', Udham Singh suggests that he may accept Christianity and might get some good position in government 'when I will go back'. Not that he was really tempted, because he uses this whole statement as a spring board for the one that follows naturally: 'I have written to Moslim Mosque Puteny about Quran Sherif I like to Read'. He did not hope for any response, which did not matter; he was Mohamed Singh nonetheless. Furthermore, Udham Singh says that priests are allowed to the inmates of the prison and, therefore, he would like to meet a Sikh priest From contact through post to a personal meeting with Shiv Singh, that was the purpose.

There is a post-postscript to this letter. Udham Singh refers to Mohan Singh now as 'that dirty pig' but only because he had left London and the new priest was not known to Udham Singh. For any Sikh priest, nevertheless, he would bring his two hands together and say' Sat Sri Akal'. He asks again for Urdu books and in the 'note' makes a very significant suggestion: 'I have given Quran Sherif in English to some one in the East. If you go that side please ask. I think there is one Liabrary in where they keep Indian books'. The Quran Sherif of Udham Singh was obviously something quite different from the sacred book to which the words normally refer. In order to allay possible suspicion he lastly adds that he had left his God in India and did not understand the English Sod; he ate cows and pigs because they were European. To take Udham Singh literally in these letters would be the surest way of misunderstanding him.

The third letter, dated March 30, issued by the authorities in the name of 'U Singh' is addressed to 'Mr. Jahal Singh', Secretary Gurdwara, 79 Sinclair Road, London, W. 14. This 'Dear Mr Jahal Singh' is only Shiv Singh Johal. By the use of the letter a in pace of o, Udham Singh has made his friend as ignoramus (jahil) : Shiv Singh had failed to see the import of Udham Singh's letters. At any rate, the books sent by Shiv Singh are being returned and Udham Singh asks for more books. He had enjoyed reading and he was enjoying his stay in the prison as 'a guest of Royal Faimley', putting on weight. Udham Singh had learnt how to die cheerful and, therefore, he needed no solicitor or counsel. He was looking forward to be married with 'execution' and he wished people not to trouble themselves for his sake. There is a clear reference to Bhagat Singh in this letter : 'I am not a soildier of my country (.) it is since ten years when my death I will see him as he is waiting for me'. The letter ends with an emphasized request for books, including one prayer book. We wish we knew the code.[92]

In the fourth letter, dated, April 6, Udham Singh is 'still looking forward to having books'. He was happy in prison, eating rice and curry and having a lot of rest. But he was 'short of Indian books' and did not know 'whom to write to get the books'. The letter this time is addressed to 'Dear Friends through the Secretary, Khalsa Jatha, 79 Sinclair Road, London, W. 14. In the postscript he asks for Hir Waris Shah for taking oath in the court.

Waris Shah (who sang of immortal love) was Udham Singh's priest now. He had been formally charged for murder and knew that his real identity was known to his prosecutors. 'They have changed my name in the House of Commons', he says; adding, 'Mrs Chamberlain gave me the name Udham Singh'. The reference no doubt is to Lord, not Lady, Chamberlain.

In the fifth letter, written on April 14, Udham Singh complains that he is being 'maltreated' in the prison. But all that he means is that whereas others were allowed religious books he was not. The prison authorities were getting more vigilant and strict. Udham Singh tells his friend that the Governor of the prison is 'a though guy' and changes his mind every five minutes'. At any rate Shiv Singh did not receive any letter from Udham Singh for more than four weeks. The sixth letter was written on May 20; it is addressed to the secretary of the Sikh temple in Shepherds Bush. What is most significant about this letter is its directness and its smooth and correct English: 'Do you think that you could find time to come to see me before I go to the Old Bailey, as after the trial I may not be able to see you'.[93]

The letter of May 20 turned out to be virtually his last letter. He was tried on June 4 and sentenced to death on the day following. His letter of June 7 was written out for him by some official connected with the prison; he only signed it. This letter contains a brief, formal request for the Sikh prayer book (Gutka). Henceforth Udham Singh's contact with the world outside the Pentoville Prison ceased for ever.

References

1. Harish K. Puri, Ghadar Movement, ideology Organization strategy, Guru Nanak University, Amritsar, 1983. p.1.
2. *Ibid,* p. 3.
3. *Ibid,* p.16.
4. Report, Census of the Punjab 1901, p. 14.
5. Huge Johnstone, The Voyage of Komagata Maru : The Sikh Challenge to Canada's Colour bar (Delhi, OUP, 1979), p. 2 Also confidential report of W.E. McInnes, 15 November 1907, secret agent in the employment of the Department of interior, Government of British Columbia, Correspondence, Colonial Office Records, 886/I, p. 138.
6. Das, *op. cit.* pp. 4-5
7. S.A. Waiz (ed.), Indians Abroad (Bombay : The imperial citizenship association, 1927), p. 648.
8. Report of Daddy S. Burjor, Official 'Hindu' interpreter of the US Immigration Department, Government of India, Commerce and industry department, emigration A, Proceedings No. 4.
9. *Ibid*; also Sohan Singh Josh, Baba Sohan Singh Bhakna (Bombay : PP.H, 1970), p.14 Harnam Singh 'Tundilat' believed that 75 per cent of all Indians on the pacific coast were ex-soldiers. Unpublished Account. p. 15.
10. Extract from the diary of Superintendent Police, Lahore, Home Political A, Proceeding August 1907, Nos. 148-235, Appendix-B.
11. Ghadar movement, Ideology Organisation Strategy. p. 20.
12. Kenneth Jones, Arya Dharm : Hindu Consciousness in the 19th Century Punjab (Delhi : Manohar Publications, 1976). P. 315. For an excellent analysis of why did Sikhs suddenly develop this fetish for separate cultural boundaries see Harjot S. Oberoi, 'From Ritual to Counter-Ritual : Rethinking the Hindu-Sikh Question, 1884-1915', in Joseph T. O.' Connell, Milton Israel et al. (eds), Sikh History and Religion in the Twentieth Century (Toronto : University of Toronto, 1988) pp. 136-158.

13. The research paper by K.C. Shanmar, Ex. I.G. Jailer, Punjab. Ad- Dharam Movement in Punjab, Babu Mangoo Ram the founder of Ad-Dharam Movement in Punjab, Dr. B.R. Ambedkar.
14. *Ibid*, p.2.
15. According to G.H. Lowes, The Sikhs began arriving in British Columbia in 1904 and almost immediately became the victims of anti oriental feelings, the Sikhs of British Columbia p. 13 St. Nihal Singh wrote that, 'when the Indian immigrants began to arrive in knots of 20 or more – the cry of the 'Hindoo peril' was raised – British Columbians became hysterical believing that the Indians would despoil their country as did the Huns...........' 'Indians in America', Modern Review, March 1908, pp. 206-207.
16. Sucheng Chan, 'Overseas Sikhs in the Contentx in Internatioonal Migrations', in Mark Juergensmeyer and N.Gerald Barrier, eds., Sikh Studies: Comparative Perspective on A Changing Tradition (Berkeley: Graduate Theological Union, 1979), p.194.
17. According to Tundilat, while those coming from the army had taken to the European dress, the rural (sic) Punjabis generally wore their own dress, some of them would go to the bazaar dressed in dhoti. Unpublished account, p. 11 G.H. Lowes, *op. cit.* p. 54.
18. Lowes, *op. cit.* p. 1.
19. Ghadar movement p. 43.
20. St. Nihal Singh, 'The Triumph of Indians in Canada', Modern Review, August 1909. p. 105.
21. Mystery and Power of Teja Singh; The Vancouver Daily Provinece, 12 December, 1908, p.1, Also Swayne's Memorandum, *op. cit.*
22. Home Political A, Proceeding, July 1908 Nos. 137-139.
23. Swayne's Memorandum, *op. cit.*
24. Cited from Joan M. Jenson, 'The "Hindu Conspiracy" 'A Reassessment', Pacific Historical Review, Vol. XLVIII, No. 1 (February 1979). p. 71.
25. Bose, Indian Revolutionaries Abroad, pp. 49-50. See also Ker, *op. cit.* p. 227.

26. History sheet of G.D.Kumar, India office records L/P & J/6/1137 of 1912.
27. Ker, *op. cit*. p. 217.
28. Ghadar movement. p. 48.
29. *Ibid*, p. 52
30. *Ibid*, p.72.
31. *Ibid*, p. 77.
32. Reported in the Ghadar, 6 January 1914, see also Judgement L.C.C., Home Political A, Proceedings, October 1915, No. 91, p. 71.
33. Navtej Singh, Challenge to Imperial Hegemony The life story of A great Indian Patriot Udham Singh, Publication Bureau, Punjabi University, Patiala, 1998, p. 14.
34. S.C. Mittal, Freedom Movement in Punjab, 1905-29, Delhi, 1977. pp.73-7.
35. The fourteen points (thirteen in Gurmukhi edition; point
36. Ghadar movement. p. 79.
37. In an article, 'A storm is about to burst in Egypt, Drizzling has already started', the awakening of Egyptians was said to be highly auspicious for India; the 'Key of the Suez Canal is in their hands'. Similarly Indians were also advised to learn lesions from and to evince interest in the revolution in Mexico and the struggle going on in Russia. Ghadar, 1 November 1913.
38. The first such collection of 22 Baints, 9 Kabits and some Korara Chhands running into 28 pages was printed in a book form in April 1914 (Sen Francisco : Ghadar Press, n.d.)
39. Ghadar di Goonj, No. 1 poem 8.
40. No pundits or Mullahs do we need
    No prayers or litanies we need recite.
    These will only scuttle our boat.
    Draw the Sword; 'it is time to fight'
    Ghadar di Goonj, No. 1 poem 4, trans. Khushwant Singh.
41. Home Political A (Secret), Proceedings, September 1914 No. 210.
42. Prithvi Singh, Kranti Path ka Pathik, pp. 980-81.
43. The Portland Telegram, 7 August 1914, See also Ker, *op. cit*, p. 224.

44. Tundilat, op. cit., p. 82.
45. Ibid.
46. Bhupendra Nath Datt, Aprakashit Rajtnitik Itihas, Appendix V. Also Dharmavira, LAla Har Dayal and Revolutionary Movement of His Times, p.196.
47. Evidence of Harcharan Das, Second Supplementary L.C.C, Home Political B, Proceedings, May 1917, Nos. 542-43 . File. pp. 150-51.
48. Giles T. Brown, 'The Hindu Conspiracy and the Neutrality of the United States, 1914-1917, p. 7.
49. Azad, interview with the author, 10 March 1973, see also 'Tundilat' op. cit., pp. 42-43.
50. Ibid.
51. Sohan Singh Bhakna, Jeewan Sangram, p 46.
52. Harjap Singh, 'Meri Pardes Yatra' (Urdu), unpublished diary, Gujarat Jail, dated 19 September 1943), p. 106.
53. Azad, interview with the author.
54. Gujjar Singh Bhakna, interview with the author.
55. Ibid.
56. Sohan Singh Bhakna, op. cit. p.48; 'Tundilat', op. cit., p. 38.
57. Prithvi Singh Azar, interview with author. See also Chenchiah, op. cit, Part II, p. 13 and evidence of Hrcharan Das, Second Supplementary Lahore Conspiracy Case, Home Political B, Proceedings, May 1917, Nos. 542-43.
58. Amar Singh believed that after Har Dayal, the chief leaders at the Yugantar Ashram were Barkatullah, Bhagwan Singh and Amar Singh himself. Lahore Conspiracy Case, Home Political A, Proceedings, October 1915, No. 91, File p.70. Nawab Khan and Mula Singh, two important leaders of groups in India, gave conflicting statements. Mula Singh believed that Sohan Singh Bhakna was President of a revolutionary society in Oregon state; Har Dayal was secretary of (all) Indian revolutionary societies. Home Political A, Proceedings, October 1915, No. 91, File p.89. In the same case, Inder Singh told in his confession that there was a society in San Francisco of which Har Dayal was President and Ram Chandra was Vice-President. Evidence in Lahore

Conspiracy Case, op. cit., p. 385. see also Giles T. Brown, op. cit., p. 26 and Bose, Indian Revolutionaries Abroad, pp. 61-62.

59. J.S Grewal and H.K. Puri, Letters of Udham Singh., Guru Nanak University, Amritsar, 1974. pp. 37.
60. See, for instance, Appendix, Below.
61. Gurmukh Singh Musafir, Vihween Sadi de Shaheed, 1. See Also, Kulbir Singh, Sardar, 275.
62. December 26, 1899, is the date of birth given by Fauja Singh, Gurmukh Singh Musafir and Suba Singh. However, according to the report of the prosecution, Udham Singh was 37 in April 1940.
63. The statement of M.S. Azad (Udham Singh). 'Trial of Udham Singh', National Archives of India, Accession 292 f. 25.
64. Udham Singh and his elder brother were admitted to the Khalsa Central Orphanage, Amritsar, on October 24, 1907 vide C.No. 121-221 of the register of admission, 118: quoted, Suba Singh, Inqilabi Yodha Udham Singh, 11n.
65. The reply to the enquiries made was sent to the commissioner of Police, New Scotland Yard in a letter dated 30 May, 1940 : Additional Secretary's note of June 19, 1940, Serial No. 5 File No. 77, Government of India, Home Deptt. Poll Secret, National Archives of India.
66. This is based on the evidence of S. Inder Singh, See. Appendix, below.
67. Ibid.
68. Gurmukh Singh Musafir, Vihween Sadi de Shaheed, 2; Kulbir Singh, Sardar, 276.
69. M.S. Gill, 'Udham Singh : The Patriot who Avenged the Jallianwala Bagh Massacre', The Illustrated Weekly of India, 30 January 1972, 36. The words of the original are : Sarfaroshi ki tamanna ab hamare dil mein hai.
70. Letters of Udham Singh, p. 39.
71. Ibid.
72. Roger Perkins, op. cit. pp. 130-131.
73. Navtej Singh, Challenge to Imperial Hegemony, The Life Story of A Great Indian Patriot Udham Singh, Punjabi University, Patiala, 1998, p. 65.

74. Ibid, p. 120.
75. Secret Letter, dated 15 March 1940, File No. P&J(S) 466/36.
76. J. N. Sandhey, op. cit, pp. 120-21.
77. Gurcharan Singh, op. cit. pp. 131-32.
78. Navtej Singh, Challenge to Imperial Hegemony, The Life Story of A Great Indian Patriot Udham Singh, Punjabi University, Patiala, 1998, p.127
79. Ibid., p.128.
80. Ibid., pp. 15-17.
81. The Times, 15 March 1940.
82. Challenge to Imperial Hegemony, The Life Story of A Great Indian Patriot Udham Singh, p.132.
83. O'Dwyer was born in Tiperrary in April 1864. In 1885 he entered the Indian Civil Service. By 1896 he had risen to be director of the Department of Land Records and Agriculture in Punjab. He was successively Settlement Officer for the States of Ulwar and Bhurpore, Revenue Commissioner for the North-West Frontier, and Acting Chief Commissioner. After acting as Resident in Hyderabad for a year and Agent to the Governor General in Central India from 1910 to 1912, he was appointed Lieutenant Governor of the Punjab in 1913. In that year he received his Knighthood. His term of office, which lasted till 1919, in which year, his term having ended, he retired, covered a stormy period in Indian affairs. Of this he gave an account in his book India As I Knew if, and defended his action during the disturbances following the passing of the Rowlatt Bill. It was always his contention that the leniency shown towards rioters in Delhi early in 1919 aggravated the situation, which culminated in the Amritsar shooting in April 1919. The Hunter Committee subsequently appointed condemned General Dyer's action at Amritsar, and declared that O'Dwyer's procedure would have been more wise if before approving that action he had ascertained the facts more fully. O'Dwyer replied that the Government had asserted its intention 'to prevent by all means, however drastic, any recurrence of these excesses'. In 1924 he again was in the news in conflict with Sir Sankaran Nair over his book 'Gandhi and Anarchy'. In 1933 O'Dwyer said that the White Paper proposals had the effect of reducing Britain's

position in India from that of managing director to that of mere 'watchman'. In fact since his retirement he had consistently opposed any change in the form of the Administration in India, believing that a democratic constitution would be unworkable. See, The Manchester Guardian, 14 March 1940; The Daily Mirror, 14 March 1940; Daily Herald, 14 March 1940 and Roger Perkins, op. cit., pp. 6-7.

84. Lord Zetland had been Secretary of State for India since 1935 and was one of most influential men in Neville Chamberlain's government. He was a able politician and administrator, had travelled extensively in the Orient and was a former governor of Bengal. See, the Daily Mirror, 14 March 1940 and Roger Perkins, op. cit., p. 4.

85. Louis Dane had spent nearly 40 years in India. He joined the Indian Civil Service and then spent most of his life in north west India helping the English to administer their imperial possessions. His final appointment had been that of Lieutenant Governor of the Punjab between 1908 and 1913. The Daily Mirror, 14 March 1940 and Roger Perkins, op. cit., p. 4.

86. Lord Lamington was Governor of Bombay from 1903 to 1907. See The Daily Mirror, 14 March 1940.

87. The Brigadier General Sir Percy M. Sykes had spent nearly thirty years in some of the primitive areas of Central Asia. By 1905 he had arranged himself to be appointed Consul General at Khorasan (Persia). For the next nine years he operated as diplomat and gatherer of military intelligence. Leaving the army in 1920 he embarked upon as successful career as author and commentator. See Roger Perkins, op. cit., pp. 1-4.

88. See, The Daily Mirror, 14 March 1940; The Manchester Guardian, 14 March 1940; Daily Herald, 14 March 1940; The Guardian, 14 March 1940; The Daily Telegraph, 14 March 1940 and The New Statesman, 16 March 1940.

89. Roger Perkins, op. cit., p. 22 and Suba Singh, op. cit., pp. 35-3.

90. Letters of Udham Singh p. 12.

91. Ibid, p. 13.

92. Ibid, p. 16.

93. Ibid, p. 17.

3

Bengal from Swadeshi to Non-cooperation, c. 1905-22 in the Context of Namasudras

I

The study of Bengali caste-Hindus bhadralok groups attracts and draw various questions. This brings up to the queries what was Bhadralok's attitude to the British rule as well as to the Dalits? According to the testimony of Sandford Arnot, his English Secretary (whose moral scruple and veracity have been questioned), Rammohun Roy used to tell his English friends that India would need British rule for anothrew forty or fifty years. The point of this testimony was that Rammahun Roy was moderate in his political views. What was no howeverw equally stressed was his assumption that the British rule would be an agency of India's social, political and economic modernization, One may say that this wa an act of faith.[1]

Since the Hoogly town Calcutta had been flooded much ideas. The elite group was realizing the sentiments of mass and their own duties towards the British Empire.

If we sit idle, and hesitate to rise till the whole population are goaded to desperation, then we shall continue idle till the end of time ... Without blood, O patriots! Will the country awake?' *Yugantar, 26* August 1907.[2]

As per the confidential official report on Non-Co—operation and Khilafat in Bengal, 1924..."The events of the first quarter of 1922 confirmed the fear that the movement had gone beyond the control of the leaders ... The spirit of violence and contempt of all authority, which now began to show its head, was not of the leaders, but of the masses.'.[3]

The title of the chapter indicates an interesting contrast between the Swadeshi movement in Bengal (1905-8) and the Non-Co-operation-Khilafat upsurge in the same region (1919-22) from the point of view of the nature, extent and consequences of 'subaltern' participation in nationalist politics. During the anti-Partition agitation the masses appeared irritatingly inert to the more radical activists, despite the formulation of a theory of 'extended boycott' or 'passive resistance' which demanded popular participation and often anticipated the methods of Gandhism.[4] The movement in practice seldom went beyond the confines of *bhadralok* groups. The politics of mass contact soon became transformed into revolutionary -terrorist activity by a handful of educated youth. Non-Co-operation- Khilafat in sharp contrast revealed a picture of masses outstripping leaders, particularly in the winter of 1921-22, and popular initiative eventually alarmed leaders into calling for a halt. C. R. Das may have been unhappy about the timing of Gandhi's Bardoli retreat[5] but Calcutta and district newspapers had become nervous about the radical social implications of the upsurge months back.[6] The *Amrita Bazar Patrika*. a newspaper with a radical-nationalist reputation, explicitly praised the clauses in the Bardoli resolution which gave assurances to zamindars as helping to remove the misunderstanding 'that the movement of Mahatma Gandhi is aimed at the destruction of the rights of all property-owners.'[7]

This contrast forces us to make an analysis of the conditions and nature of subaltern militancy which was, infact, an anti-imperialist movement. Certain preliminary points about concepts and methods require clarification here. The categories of 'elite' and 'subaltern' have aroused some misgivings as allegedly assuming a simplistic two-fold division of society, and as a departure from the familiar digits of Marxist class-analysis.

Despite much talk about the need for mass awakening, the Swadeshi Movement of 1905—8 seldom got beyond the confines of caste Hindu bhadralok, groups-students, journalists, teachers, doctors and lawyers who very often had a link with rentier interests in land in the form of zamindari or intermediate tenure-holding. The main centres of the upsurge reveal a strong correlation with the presence of large numbers of educated Hindu gentry : Barisal (Backergunj), Madatipur, Vikrampur, Kishoreganj, the Brahmanbatia subdivision of Tippera, as well as of course Calcutta with its heavy bhadralok concentration."[8] The peasant seldom if ever appear in Swadeshi plays:"[9] The volunteers in Mukunda Das' *jatra Palli Seva* declare that they all have some land and hence do not have to worry about (mere rice and *dal*'[10] and police statistics about the social origins of Samiti members in Backergunj finely establish the link with intermediate tenure-holding."[11] A few Calcutta lawyers with nationalist affiliations did develop an interest in the labour movement, and Aswinikumar Dutta's *Swadesh Bandhab Samiti* could briefly acquire some kind of mass base in Barisal villages through sustained humanitarian constructive work. Yet the limits remain very evident, particularly in comparison with Non-Co-operation-Khilafat days. The strikes led or unions formed were mainly of white-collar employees of printing presses and railways or of Bengali (and seldom Hindustani) workers in jute mills. The plantations and mines were entirely unaffected and, with the exception of something like a hartal on 16 October 1905, there were no instances of political strikes. [12] Even Barisal village samitis consisted 'of the bhadralok of the village' [13] and an Anushilan militant turned Communist has recalled in his memoirs how peasants were occasionally mobilized for swadeshi meetings, shy and silent participants in loin cloth roped in by the well-dressed babus to prove Hindu-Muslim unity.[14] And evidence about the considerable use of caste, religious and class pressures by the patriotic Hindu gentry to enforce the boycott in the countryside is really far too extensive to be dismissed as official or Muslim propaganda.[15]

So far as labour is concerned nationalist leadership generally entered the scene well after 'spontaneous' initiative had led to a strike. Patriotic barristers like Aswinikumar Banerji or Apurbakumar Ghosh began their brief careers as labour leaders only when in the autumn of 1905 arrested clerks and tram workers sought legal help.[16]

If Islam provided the key vehicle for Muslim peasants in the expression of their socio-economic grievances, one could expect caste movements to perform somewhat similar functions for rural Hindu society.[17] The first two decades of the twentieth century in fact witnessed a large number of 'Sanskritizing' caste movements and association in Bengal. The most significant among these were the movements among the Mahishyas of Midnapur, Howrah, Hooghly and 24 Parganas, the Rajbansis of Jalpaiguri, Rangpur and Dinajpur and the Namasudras of Jessore, Khulna and Faridpur-the three major castes below the level of the bhadralok in a province otherwise marked by unusually great fragmentation among intermediate and low castes.[18]

The Mahishyas of Midnapur and the Rajbansis of north Bengal included large numbers of gentry and jotedars as well as peasants. The Namasudras in contrast were overwhelmingly cultivators or sharecroppers subordinate to bhadralok zamindars or tenure-holders.[19] The movements organized by the *Bangiya Mahishya* and *Rajbansi Kshatriya Samitis* consequently remained confined to claims to higher caste status and 'Sanskritizing' changes in surnames or social customs; agrarian issues were hardly ever raised.[20]

Among Namasudras of Jessore however a conference in 1908 which discussed educational and social improvement and set up a structure of village. union and district committees financed by weekly rice collections was followed up the next year by moves 'not to work as menial servants' in upper-caste houses in Narail sub-division and a refusal to cultivate lands of the latter in Magura. The Jessore Namasudras got some support from Muslim cultivators occupying a similar socio-economic position, and in 1909 Muslims in a village of Sadar sub-division 'combined not to cultivate *the* lands of their Hindu landlords, unless the latter agreed to allow them to retain a two-thirds share of the produce instead of a half-share'-fascinating evidence of an anticipation of the *tebhaga* demand of the 1940s.[21] A Madaripur pleader in June 1909 reported similar refusals to cultivate *barga* lands and render menial services on the part of the Namasudras of Faridpur.[22] At Telak village near Khulna town in May 1908 a Namasudra-Muslim combination allegedly challenged Brahman control over the local festival of Kali in a conflict which quickly led to a confrontation with the police on the Sherpur pattern. Three years later, in a contrast which once again reveals the interpenetration of diverse issues, Namasudras and Muslims along the Jessore-Khulna border came into conflict with each other, with riots and looting affecting eighteen villages. Details of both incidents unfortunately do not seem available.[23]

A Government of India unpublished 'Note on serious disturbances and political trouble in India from 1907 to 1917' provides interesting confirmation of the distance of mass upheavals from the world of organized national politics during this entire period. The section on 'political disturbances' is confined virtually to a survey of revolu-tionary-terrorist activity, while the only incidents with something like a mass character included in the list for the Swadeshi years in Bengal are the Mymensingh riots of April- May 1907 and the Calcutta clashes of October 1907. For the years from 1908 to 1917, apart from the two Namasudra disturbances already mentioned, the only other Bengal reference is to a communal riot at Titagarh and Serampore on the occasion of Bakr-Id in January 1909.[24]

The two recurrent and salient features seem to be the potential strength of peasant solidarity in East Bengal and of mill hands and casual labour in and around Calcutta, and the extreme volatility of popular sentiments and actions. The Praja movement throughout its history would combine in ever-varying proportions anti-zamindar class sentiments with appeals for Muslim solidarity, and the Kamariarchar conference presaged both aspects by its expression of purely agrarian demands though a meeting in which all the speakers were Muslims. In the riots of January 1909, following a clash over cow-slaughter at Titagarh, 'Muhammadan emissaries' were able 'to get their co-religionists in all the mills on the right bank of the Hooghly to march together and cross the river to wreak vengeance on the Hindus', while 'a large number of Muhammadan workers in the Calcutta mills as far south as Garden Reach struck work and commenced to march in various bands on Titagarh.[25]

Ismail Husain Siraji, Mujibur Rahman, Moniruuaman (all three with Swadeshi backgrounds, incidentally) and Muhammed Akram Khan were co-operating actively with extremist veterans like Krishnakumar Mitra and Shyamsundar Chakrabarti, and some radical Hindus of Telinipara and Chandernagore were allegedly employing an agent named Hyder 'to preach a regular Jehad against the British ... among all the Mussalman mill hands belonging to the mills on both sides of the river between Hooghly and Calcutta.[26] The September 1918 riots again saw 'the coolie class ... giving trouble ... a large crowd of coolies made incessant attempts ... to break through from Garden Reach and obtain entry into Calcutta.[27] Though ultimately directed against Marwaris, the riots had been preceded by bitter anti-British propaganda in the course of which Fazlur Rehman, one of the principal non-Bengali agitators involved in the affair, had even 'eulogized the action of Kshudiram Bose and other revolutionaries'. Governor Ronaldshay in his diary juxtaposed the provocation offered by the alleged insult to the Prophet in the Anglo-Indian journal *Indian Daily News* with memories of the Shahabad riots of 1917, the 'misfortunes of Turkey, the internment of Indian Muhammaden leaders, and the high price of cotton cloth during the past winter to a considerable outbreak of hat-looting .. .' as causes of the riots.[28]

The reference in Ronaldshay's diary to cloth-prices is a reminder that economic-determinist explanations of popular outbursts have been fairly common. They have been put forward by contemporary officials and later historians alike as supplements to or sometimes alternatives of the interpretation in terms of mobilization from the top alone, and pride of place in such analysis has usually gone to price-fluctuations. British officials often tried to relate bhadralok involvement in Swadeshi and terrorism to the impact of the post 1905 price rise cutting into relatively inelastic and sometimes in adequate incomes from fragmented zamindaris, tenure-holdings and services, while the link with the labour upsurge of 1905-8 appeared obvious.

Official files and private papers make abundantly clear that what really alarmed the authorities and made of Non-Co-operation Khilafat a movement vastly different from that of 1905—8 was the large scale adoption of such 'other methods' through popular initiative and not anything deliberately worked out by Gandhi or the Calcutta leaders. The vast range of such initiatives extended from sporadic hat-looting[29] through a massive labour upsurge to jail-breaks. resignations by policemen, non-payment of chaukidari and Union Board taxes, hostility to settlement operations, no-rent, and virtually total disavowal of British authority by peasants fired by a conviction that Gandhi raj was coming or even already in existence.

Throughout 1920 and even part of 1921 the correspondence of the Governor of Bengal indicates that labour unrest evoked maximum official concern, followed by the Khilafat agitation (itself connected with the presence 'of a very large Muhammadan labour force employed in the jute mills');[30] specifically Gandhian Non-Cooperation came as a poor third.[31] In a telegram to the Secretary of State, Chelmsford attributed the unprecedented countrywide strike wave primarily to economic factors: soaring prices and the 'general shortage of industrial labour' due to post-war industrial expansion and the influenza epidemic. But he also mentioned as contributory elements the growing awareness 'that capitalists, millowners in particular, are making very large profits', the impact of 'world-wide political unrest ... frequent reports of labour trouble in England and Europe', and 'to some extent' encouragement 'by political agitators in India'.[32] The Bengal Committee on Industrial Unrest listed 137 strikes in the province in the nine months starting from July 1920, while the annual administrative reports chronicle 150 strikes involving 265,000 workers in 1921 and 91 strikes involving c.160,000 next year.[33]

Once again, the Swadeshi Labour turmoil was on top of the agenda and a number of Labour Unions were coming-up in many parts of this country with the prominent leaders such as I. B. Sen, S. N. Haldar and N. C. Sen. But, this time, these labour unrests were communal in nature since these were promoted by Khilafat agitators like Muhammed Osman and swamis or 'political sanyasis' which made British officials nervous.

Initiative from below however remained far more important than organizarion through outsiders in the strike wave of 1919-22. The Committee on Industrial Unrest statistics reveal the striking fact that labour unrest was at its height in the last quarter of 1920,"[34] i.e. before the Non-Co-operation-Khilafat Movement really got into its stride in Bengal. Political agitation and labour militancy followed parallel but largely separate paths, intermingling only on two occasions: the East Bengal railway and steamer strikes following the belabouring of tea garden coolies at Chand pur in May 1921, and the use of mill hands as volunteers courting arrest in Calcutta in December 1921-January 1922. Yer sratements that leaders like J. M. Sengupta 'brought *off*'[35] the East Bengal strikes grossly oversimply a more complex reality. These began really as a more-or-less spontaneous protest against Gurkha atrocities taking place 'before the very eyes of the railway employees'.[36] The strikes were no doubt encouraged by the Bengal Congress decision to provide 'advice and financial help',[37] but they continued mainly on the basis of specific labour demands for strike pay and recognition of the Assam-Bengal Employees Union.[38]

Though most strikes took place on specific economic demands, other dimensions were not entirely absent. Racist insults and assaults at Jhajha and Tundla provided the immediate occasions for the two EIR strikes in early 1922. At Kumardhubi in January 1921 the men left work after a similar incident, and when the management tried to layoff some of them declared 'that they would either go back to work in a body or not go back at all.[39] In November 1921 in a striking demonstration of working class solidarity tramwaymen were 'joined by mill hands from neighbouring mills' in picketing Belgachia depot (north Calcutta) and in subsequent clashes with the police.[40] 5,000 Calcutta dock labourers went on strike on 14 December after an officer had removed a man's Gandhi cap; they demanded the immediate release of C. R. Das and the right to 'shout Gandhi Maharaj Ki Jai while working on board.[41] And in a fascinating combination of patriotic millennial rumours and hardheaded collective bargaining jute mill workers in the last week of December 1921 demanded an end to the common practice 'to keep three days wages in hand while paying a week's wages. The reason of such a demand is, we are told, that the workers are in the belief that they will get Swaraj on the 24th.[42]

The rumour of imminent swaraj in fact worked wonders repeatedly during 1921 and early 1922. Apart from the famous exodus of 6,000-7,000 coolies from Chargola tea estates in May

1921,[43] the most spectacular instance was probably the jailbreak by 669 prisoners from Rajshahi on 24 March 1921. This had been preceded by rumours that Gandhi was coming to Rajshahi on 25 March to end the British raj. The prisoners before breaking out 'bound *rakhis* or threads on their wrists as a sign of unity'. thus reviving the symbolism of 1905 in a totally different context, and marched openly in a body through the streets of the town after overpowering their guards.[44] Smaller jail breaks occurred or were attempted at Sirajganj, Netrokona, Dinajpur, Rangpu, Midnapur and Barisal.[45] Even more serious from the government point of view was large scale disaffection among the police with thirty Calcutta Muslim constables and head-constables resigning after a Maidan meeting of 200 policemen on 13 November 1921, pro-Non-Co-operation sentiments among upcountry constables in Howrah, and reports of police unrest flowing in from Noakhali, Rangpur, Mymensingh, Khulna, Bogra, and 24 Parganas.[46] A Hindi newspaper quoted a moving statement by one disaffected constable: 'We shall all go home giving up our service and till land and spin charkha and pass our days happily. Mahatmaji has opened our eyes.'[47]

From the point of the rural movements, a social ostrasization had been started in the country-side. The British offices, including Tehsildars and revenue officers, were shown boycott placard and other signs. A wave of boycott of settlement operations was under the process in many parts of the country.

In Midnapur the district Congress urged paying up of chowkidari taxes once the Union Board had been withdrawn in December 1921, but there were still widespread refusals in regions like Contai, Panskura in Tamluk, Daspur in Ghatal, Debra in Sadar and Gopiballbhpur in Jhargram sub-divisions. The SDO of Ghatal reported that 'the masses absolutely refuse to listen to' local Congress committees, using the argument that payment to the Swaraj Fund exempted them from all other claims, while Santals of Gopiballavpur claimed 'that the chaukidari tax had been abolished by Gandhi Maharaj's order'.[48]

Meanwhile in semi-tribal north-west Midnapur (Jhargram sub division) Santals and Mahatos (Kurmis) went about looting haats, destroying liquor shops amidst shouts of 'Gandhi Maharaj Ki Jai', searching for foreign cloth but taking 'all kinds of cloth indiscriminately', and forbidding the export of paddy but (interesting evidence of some sort of underlying 'moral economy') not 'taking any away' ... 'everyone at Silda, including the non-co-operators, was very much afraid', and there was panic in Jhargram on 29 January. The Santals had been inflamed also by a dispute with the Midnapur Zamindari Company over 'wood for houses and agricultural purposes.' No additional police was ultimately required for Contai but Jhargram had to be pacified by a route-march of the Eastern Frontier Rifles.[49] There was also a spate of dacoities, thirty-three in Midnapur district in January 1922 out of a total of 111 in the province that month.[50]

At Madarihat in Jalpaiguri district on 21 February, following a market quarrel between a Marwari shopkeeper and a Santal coolie, police attempts to arrest some Santals led to an attack by a crowd wearing Gandhi caps which 'demanded the release of the prisoners, shouting all the time that they were immune from bullet wounds as they were wearing Gandhi Maharaj's caps.'[51] Three Santals were killed in police firing. No-rent movements developed in neighbouring Rangpur, affecting the estates of Maharaja Manindra Nandy of Kasimbazar in Kurigram sub-division.[52] Marwari and Shaha merchants and moneylenders became principal targets along the Rangpur-Assam border, and in Batashan pargana the District Magistrate persuaded the zamindar to give concessions to his tenants as there was 'some danger that that Raiyats' Samiti might be captured by the non-co-operators.

The Non-Co-operation, which had been abruptly called off by the Congress Working Committee at its Bardoli session on 12 February 1922, was followed by a wave of looting and law violation. Gradually, the situation mainly in the rual areas got aggravated and a confrontation between the Zamindars and the farmers and workers was surfaced. At many places, the Zamindars were assaulted.

Bargadar *movements* seem to have developed earlier in Jessore, Khulna, or Faridpur, where Namasudras confronted upper caste jotedars, then in Midnapur where Mahishya caste ties helped to keep the countryside more united for a time. In north-west Midnapur in 1923 the Santals blamed newcomer 'Bengalis' for their troubles and displayed a loyalty towards the dispossessed Pratap Dal in preference to the zamindar of Jamboni who had recently taken over the Dalbhum estate from the former.[53] As the protests were usually against what were felt to be new developments, evocations of earlier norms tended to be extremely common, at times developing into golden-age myths. Peasant rioters in Mymensingh in 1906 recalled an old pargana rate of rent,[54] while Santals in 1923 'believed that they were simply carrying on an old tradition', bringing back a 'golden age' when 'all jungles were free'.[55] A nice sense of discrimination was sometimes displayed in actions conditioned by such memories.

Examples of the first type include the refusal of enhanced rent in the Swadeshi period by tenants of patriotic zantindars like Brojendra-kishore Roychaudhuri of Mymensingh, the Muslim attacks on Hindu gentry in 1906-7 fired by rumours that officials were on their side, and the beating-up of Swadeshi babus by plebian elements in Calcutta in October 1907. In the Sherpur incident of September 1907 we meet the alternative version too: the Muslim crowd attacking the police shouted 'that the nine-anna zamindar [a Hindu, and quite a 'well- behaved' one] had ordered them to beat the police and loot their quarters.' The local Superintendent of Police drew 'a rather apt parallel between the shouting of the crowd and the cry of the Musalman rioters in the Dewanganj and other looting cases that the Government and the Nawab [of Dacca] had ordered them to loot the Hindus. It is quite probable that the mob had as little foundation for the one cry as for the other ...'[56]

II

During the nineteenth century, the members of the Namasudra caste had emerged as a settled peasant community by taking advantage of reclamations in the vast marshy and forest tracts of eastern Bengal.[57] This process of physical transformation from an amphibious existence to the status of settled agriculturalists and social mobility had also differentiated them in terms of economic condition and social status, though they were not as yet very sharply divided in class terms. In many respects they all still shared a common experience of deprivation and degradation and were closely knit by affinal and kinship ties and geographical location. This shared experience created a congenial ground for the construction of a collective self based on an ideology of protest that would subsume the inchoate class distinctions within the group and set it against its Other.

The essence of this new collective self of the Namasudras was an ever-growing sense of self-respect and what had contributed to its development, apart from their constant encounter with an unfriendly physical environment, was their contact in the eighteenth and the nineteenth centuries with a number of libertarian social influences.[58] Their first organised endeavour at self-affirmation started in Faridpur-Bakarganj region in late 1872, when in official documents they were still being referred to as Chandalas.

The Chandala leaders, as it appears, thus tried to invoke the notions of conununity solidarity as an alternative source of power. The initial set back impressed upon the Namasudra leaders the necessity of a more effective social organisation that would both bind the community together and give them self-confidence to assert themselves as a collective against the hegemonic elites of the local Hindu society. This emotional need of the community explains the growing popularity of the *Matua* sect, which had emerged and spread among the Namasudras of Faridpur also in the 1870s.[59] The sect was started by a man called Harichand Thakur, who was born in a Chandala or Namasudra family in 1811 (or 1812) in a village called Safaladanga in Gopalganj subdivision of Faridpur district.[60] He and his family had been Vaishnavites for generations. His grandfather Mochanram was a devout Vaishnava and was known in his locality as Thakur Mochairam. Mochanram's eldest son Jasomanta was a Vaishnava devotee as well, and he too inherited the title of 'Thakur' and it was from his lime that the family abandoned its original surname Biswas.[61] So Harichand started gathering a following. Immediately after this he started organising his men, the Dalits, more and more of them flocked around Harichand.

In order to vindicate the irreverent image of his sect, Harichand turned the ridiculous epithet ('*moto*') into a symbol of protest; he called his sect '*Matua*', a word that could not be found in the elites' lexicoo. The sect gradually grew in size as it became the rallying point for all the untouchable and lower caste people in the region - the Namasudras, of course, constituting an overwhelming majority of them. Harichand died in 1878, but the sect expanded further under his son Guruchand Thakur, born in 1846.[62] The latter formalised the doctrines of the sect to suit better tbe needs of an emerging peasant community.

In 1901 the Namasudras of the districts of Dacca, Faridpur, Bakarganj, Mymensingh, Jessore and Pabna once again appealed to the government. Bhishmadel Das and several other members of the Namasudra Association of Orakandi sent a representation pleading for the designation of Namasudra, with the old despising name 'Chandala' being dropped. In support of their claims they also submitted copies of *vyavastha* or opinion of several *pundits* of Bengal.[63] What is more important, although the high-caste Bengali population of the region ridiculed them for putting forward such a demand,[64] the local officials such as the Collector of Dacca, the Officiating Magistrate of Bakarganj or the Magistrate in charge of census work in Faridpur, all supported them and recommended the use of the new term 'Namasudra' in the census returns.[65] The situation made the political matrix very clear to the Namasudras, with the local caste Hindu elites opposing their social aspirations and the colonial state.

On 4 July 1905 it became publicly known from the Secretary of State's statement in the House of Commons, that the final sanction had been given to the long debated scheme of partitioning Bengal. Four days later the Government Resolution was published in the Calcutta papers. Early in August, Congress in Calcutta called for the boycott of English piece goods and other imported articles and advocated the use of their *swadeshi* substitutes. The movement rapidly gained sympathy of the educated community all over Bengal. Soon the zamindars took it up and through their *naibs* (agents) and peons, began to forbid the use of European goods by their *raiyats*[66].

Namasudras were also thinking along the same lines. In 1905, on behalf of the Dacca Namasudra Hetaishini Samiti, Nagarbasi Mazumdar and Raghunath Sarkar met Sir Bampfylde Fuller, the Lieutenant Governor of the new province of Eastern Bengal and Assam. They apprised him of the socio-economic condition of the Namasudra community and demanded similar political rights as those granted to the Muslims.

The nationalists seemed to have been aware of the developments and sufficiently conscious about the necessity of doing something to mobilise these people. The *swaraj* which the educated elites were talking about, asked in an article in *Navyabharat*, was it comprehensible to Dinu Mandal or Hamir Sheikh? If it was not, then it had no meaning and unless the confidence of these people could be gained the struggle for freedom was bound to fail.[67] A Namasudra, even when a graduate, could not sit beside a higher caste; was it any manifestation of peoples' love for the country, asked Sudarshan Biswas, a nationalist leader from east Bengal. Until this community was not properly respected, he thought, the *swadeshi* movement was not going to succeed.[68] The wisdom of the existing Congress policy that social reform could wait until political freedom was achieved, now came to be seriously questioned by men like Dhirendranath Chaudhuri.[69] To salvage the situation, therefore, the nationalists in 1908 made renewed attempts to mobilise the Namasudra community and the eighteenth resolution of the Bengal Provincial Conference held at Pabna in February, spoke of giving 'social privileges to the Namasudras, such as use of barbers, washermen and bearers'.

In the second meeting as well, he made similar appeals which were 'reported, however, to have had little effect on the people more particularly addressed'.

Similarly in Bakarganj, the Swadesh Bandhab Samiti through its 159 village branches had been constantly trying to bring the Namasudra peasants into its organisation. This particular problem received special attention during the deliberations of the Barisal District Conference held on 17, 18 and 19 August 1908. On the second day, Sricharan Sen moved the fifteenth resolution which ran as follows: 'This conference considers it necessary to spread education among the Namasudras whereby to improve their social condition.

It was in 1917 that an all India Depressed Classes Association had been formed and this had inspired many in Bengal as well, the Namasudras being the foremost among them. The first concrete initiative to establish such a common forum in Bengal was taken by a Paundra Kshatriya leader, Manindranath Mandal, who was from the very beginning in close contact with prominent Namasudra leaders like Mukunda Behari Mullick and Rebati Mohan Sarkar, the editor of *Namasudra Hitaishi*. His idea was to have an association which would follow the 'principles and policies' of the Muslim League. Through his initative, a conference of all the depressed classes of Bengal was held at the city College hall in Calcutta on 5 February 1922 - ironically the same day of the Chauri Chaura incident. It was presided over by the Namasudra leader Bhishmadeb Das and was addressed among others by the two Mullick brothers, Mukunda Behari and Nirod Behari. In this conference the Bangiya Janasangha or the Bengal Peoples'

Association was formed as a formal organisation of the depressed classes. It was meant to fight for their social and political rights, particularly to secure for them adequate representation in the self-governing bodies, in the legislative council and in the public services.[70]

It is said that the Namasudra movement, until about 1937, remained alienated and distanced from the so-called nationalist movement under the leadership of the Indian National Congress. But it is not true. Thousands of freedom fighters belongs to Dalit, had taken important role in the history of freedom.

So far as the Namasudra leaders were concerned, while a handful of them stuck to their demand for a separate political identity and traditional alignment with the Muslim League, others, and who gradually came to constitute the majority, joined the Congress by the beginning of the 1940s. This meant a complete reversal of a political stand consistently maintained for more than three decades. This integrationism was also a trend observable in general in the entire Scheduled Caste movement to which, at least at an organised level, and the mutual jealousies notwithstanding, the Namasudra movement had now effectively merged. This integration of the Scheduled Castes into the most powerful structure of national politics was, however, rooted in the logic of their own movement. Their aim, ultimately, had never been to isolate themselves from the national life, but to gain a position of power within the political nation. For the leaders at least this appeared to have been achieved in the years following the election of 1937 and therefore the time for integration had also arrived. But this process of integration was not without its accompanying tensions and conflicts.

With the death of Guruchand in March 1937, the major influence that had kept the Namasudra movement away from Congress politics was removed. Then the Calcutta Scheduled Caste League, formed later that year, emerged as a new and vital link between the Congress and the Namasudra leaders. Among the latter, those who were associated with the new organisation included such prominent personalities as P.R. Thakur, Rasiklal Biswas, Jajneswar Mandal, and Jogendranath Mandal who later became its president in 1940.[71] The occasion that can be regarded as a turning point in the direction towards a new political alliance was the meeting held at Albert Hall in Calcutta on 13 March 1938 to commemorate the first anniversary of Guruchand's death. It was presided over by J.C. Gupta, the Chief Whip of the Congress legislative party in Bengal and was addressed by fourteen other prominent leaders of the province, including the Congress president Subhas Chandra Bose. The latter in his speech paid glowing tributes to Guruchand and described him as 'a superman' who had 'regenerated the Hindus of Bengal by infusing new life into them'. He had 'elevated the status of the Scheduled Castes who have been able to fall in line with the caste Hindus in social and political life.[72] In other words, what Bose tried to emphasise was that their upliftment had already been accomplished through the initiative and endeavours of Guruchand and therefore the moment of their integration into the social and political mainstream had also arrived.

This integration now took place at an astounding pace. On 16 March 1938, i.e., three days after the Albert Hall meeting, about twenty Scheduled Caste legislators, including a number of prominent Namasudras, assembled at the residence of Subhas's elder brother Sarat Chandra Bose and decided to co-operate with the Congress party and withdraw their support for the coalition ministry.[73] They formed a new legislative party, known as the Independent Scheduled Caste Party, with Jogendranath Mandal as its Secretary.[74] This new party decided 'to work in cooperation with the Congress.

Accordingly, Scheduled Caste leaders like Satyendranath Das held meetings in predominantly Namasudra areas and urged them to join the Congress and strengthen the fight against imperialism.

Thus during the 1940s the majority of the Namasudra leaders, along with their other Scheduled Caste colleagues, conveniently integrated into the dominant political structure in the country.[75]

The Namasudra protest movement hereafter developed through a different channel. We find two different levels of protest mentality, one of the elites against low ritual position and continuing exclusion from the sources of wealth and power, and the other of the peasants against social humilation and economic exploitation.[76] The Namasudra peasants also showed remarkable signs of integration, but in striking different ways.

References

1. S.. Bakshi, Raja Rammohan Rjoy, Pathnak of India, Om Publications 2783, Bhagat Singh Gali, Chu Mandi Pahar Ganj, New Delhi, 2001, p. 25.
2. Sumit Sarka, The Conditions and Nature of Subaltrn Militancy: Bengal from Swadshi to Non-Co-Oparation, c.1905-22.

   Report on Native Papers (Bengal), hereafter RNP (B), week ending 28 August State Archives (hereafter WBSA).
3. Government of Bengal, Political (Confidential), hereafter GOB Poll (Conf.), History of the Non-Cooperation and Khilafat Movements in Bengal, p. 13, WBSA.
4. This was developed above all in Aurobindo Ghosh's famous articles in Bande Mataram, 9-23 April 1907, later reprinted as Doctrine of Passive Resistance (Pondicherry. 1948), See also Sandhya, 21 November 1906: 'if.... The chaukidar, the constable, the deputy and the munsiff and the clerk, not to speak of the sepoy, all resign their respective functions, feringhee rule may come to an end in a moment. No powder and shot will be needed, no sepoys will have to be trained...........'... RNP(B), 1 December 1906, WBSA.
5. A compromise on favourable terms, possibly including a Round Table Conference to discuss more constitutional concessions, had been blocked in December 1921 by Gandhi against the wishes of Das and others, Reading to Montagu, telegrams of 15,

17 and 18 December 1921 (Redding Collection, India Office library, hereafter IOL, MSS Eur. E.238/4).

6. '.......... once the masses raise their heads, we do not know what will happen to us Babus', Nayak, 3 September 1921, The Hitavadi of 25 November 1921 warned of the 'grim shadow of Bolshevism' due to 'the manner in which the swarajists are exciting the labourers.' The Nayak of 1 December 1921 complained that 'in Dinajpur it has become difficult to maintain zamindaries' and that, Tippera Guide of Comilla of 24 January 1922 and the Rarh Dipika of Rampurhat of 8 February 1922 sounded similar notes of alarm. RNP(B), weeks ending 10 September, 3 December. 10 December 1921 and 4 and 18 February 1922, WBSA.
7. Amrita Bazar Patrika, 25 February 1921.
8. For details about the location of the Swadeshi movement, see my Swadeshi Movement, pp. 26. 72. and Chapter 7.
9. A good example would be Amritalal Bose's play Sabash Bengali. in which Pashdanga village never becomes quite as real as the scenes of Calcutta life. No peasant appears on the stage and the village movement is presented as a matter of school-boys led by their patriotic headmaster, ibid., p. 300.
10. Ibid., pp. 358-9.
11. Thus in Sarupkhati police station of Backerganj 'nearly half the volunteers are said to be talukdars, that is to say. persons with a tenure-holding interest in the land', Government of India Home Political Deposit (hereafter GOI Home Poll Dry.) October 1907, No. 19. National Archives of India (hereafter NAI), quoted in ibid., p. 72.
12. For details , see Swadeshi Movement, Chapter 5.
13. Resume of Affairs in Backerganj for 1907, para 27, GOI Home Poll A April 1908, No. 24. NAI.
14. Satis Pakrashi, Agni Diner Katha (Calcutta 1947), recollecting his boyhood days in a village in Dacca.
15. Swadeshi Movement, Chapters 6, 7, and passim.
16. As when Banerji and Ghosh in September 1905 defended a clerk arrested for assaulting a strike breaker at Burn Company.

Next month they were reported as appearing for two tram conductors in a similar case, ibid., pp. 201-2.

17. In a recent article Partha Chatterji has made the interesting point that East Bengal Muslim landholding peasants behaved in many ways like intermediate castes in other pans of the country, with the difference that religion permitted easier extensions of the movements both upwards and downwards to include Muslim gentry and the Muslim landless or poor peasants. 'Caste and Politics in West Bengal', in Teaching Politics: Special Number on Land, Caste and Politics in Indian States (Delhi, 1982).

18. See Chatterji. 'Caste and Politics in West Bengal'. See also Census of India 1931 Volume V (Bengal and Sikkim) Part I, Statement XII-10. giving the district wise number per mille of the five most numerous Hindu castes: Brahman, Kayastha, Namasudra, Mahishiya and Rajbansi.

19. The proportion of Brahmans, Kayasthas and Baidyas per mille of the Hindu population in 1931 was 184 in Faridpur, 141 in Jessore, 118 in Khulna-but only 71 in Midnapur, 51 in Rangpur, 28 in Dinajpur and 27 in Jalpaiguri. Census 1931, Chapter 12, Statement XII-8.

20. Hitesranjan Sanyal, 'Congress Movements in the Villages of Eastern Midnapur, 1921-1931' in Asie du Sud: Traditions et Chdngements (Paris, 1979). For information about Rajbansi caste movements I am indebted to Ranajit Dasgupta's unpublished 'Nationalist and Left Movements in Bengal Jalpaiguri 1905-1947'.

21. O. Malley (ed.), Jessore District Gazetteer (Calcutta, 1912), pp. 50, 83. Tanika Sarkar in her unpublished thesis has already drawn attention to anticipations of tebhaga in 1909 and again in the 1920s, see 'National Movement and Popular Protest in Bengal, 1925-J4' (Unpublished thesis, Delhi University, 1981), pp. 111-21.

22. Binod Lal Ghosh (Pleader, Madaripur), 'What can be Done for the Namasudras', Modern Review, June 1909. Ghosh pleaded

for bener treatment by upper caste Hindus of Namasudras on the social plane, as well as efforts to start schools and dispensaries, but remained characteristically silent about remedies for agrarian tensions.

23. There are very brief references to both incidents in GOI Home Political Deposit February 1918, No. 31. The GOI files on the 1908 affair are not available, that on the Namasudra Muslim riots of May 1911 (GOI Home Poll B July 1911,76-83, NAI) are not particularly illuminating. See also RNP(B), week ending 6 June, 13 June and 20 June 1908 for some scattered information about the Telak village incident. WBSA.
24. GOI Home Poll DeP. February /9/8. No. 31. NAI.
25. Officiating Chief Secretary, Bengal to GOI Home. 4 January 6 January. 9/10 January 1909, GOI Home Police A February 1909. Nos. 149—55. NAI.
26. Extracts from Intelligence Branch Secret Reports for weeks ending 12 March, 30 April, 23 July 1913; Chief Secretary, Bengal to Presidency and Burdwan Divisional Commissioners, 8 February 1913. GOB Poll (Conf.) F.N. 66/1913.
27. Bengal Diary of Governor Ronaldshay, entries for 10 September 1918, Zetland Collection, IOL. MSS Eur. D. 609, NMML microfilm.
28. Bengal Diary, undated, ibid.
29. 'Haat'-the indigenous term for village or small town markets, usually held on a specific day in the week.
30. The 'proximity' of this labour force to Calcutta, Ronaldshay argued. was 'the chief danger', for the Muslim worker 'if aroused is capable of serious rioting as our experience in September 1918 showed.' Ronaldshay to George V, 12 May 1920. Zetland Collection.
31. 'Gandhi's non-co-operation movement still falls flat in Bengal' (Ronaldshay to Montagu, 5 July 1920). 'Apart from the activities of Kalam Azad and half a dozen of his tools in Calcutta, the situation in Bengal is entirely satisfactory', ibid., 19 July 1920. An earlier letter to Montagu (6 April) had identified some of

these 'tools' with 'the group of Calcutta pan-islamists which gave us trouble in September 1918'-yet another indication of the interpenetration of logically very different forms of political activity.

32. Telegram from Viceroy to Secretary of State, No. 8C, 25 October 1920, in reply to a query from the Secretary of State dated 16 October, GOI Home Poll B November 1920, No. 281. NAI.
33. Report of Committee On Industrial Unrest (Calcutta, 1921). p. 2; A Report on Administration of Bengal, 1920-1, p. xi and 1921-2, p. xi.
34. Of the 137 strikes listed by the Committee on Industrial Unrest, 11 percent took place in the third quarter of 1920, 65 per cent in the last quarter of the same year, and 24 per cent in the first quarter of 1921. Quoted in Sanat Bose, 'Industrial Unrest and Growth of labour Unions in Bengal 1920-24', Economic Political Weekly, Special Number, November 1981.
35. Rajat Ray, p. 367.
36. Statement of J.M. Sengupta at Chandpur, 14 July 1921, Mussalman, 22 July 1921. Following the Gurkha attack on the night of 20 May, sympathy strikes began among Chandpur and Laksham railway staff on 24 May; the decision for a general strike was taken by the Chittagong-centred Assam-Bengal Railway union next day. The steamer strike began on 27 May, following the arrest of the Secretary of the Sarangi Association, Abdul Majid. Indian Annual Register, 1922, p. 144.
37. Each station staff should go to the nearest Congress Office for advice and financial help.' Statement by J.M. Sengupta, Mussalman, 17 June 1921.
38. J.M. Sengupta's statement of 14 July pointed out that the railway employees were 'holding out on three points'-strike pay, no break in service, recognition of their Union (of which Sengupta was President). Mussalman, 22 July 1921.
39. Swami Biswanand in his speech to Kumardhati and Kulci workers at Barakar on 17 January 1921 emphasized this dimension: '... although mere w;iS need for food in this world.

there was also need for honour ... ', GOI Home Poll Dept. February 1921, No. 5. NAI.

40. Viccroy to Secretary of Statc, t4 November 1921, R~ading COllf.'CTion.

41. Muss.:/man, 16 December 1921.

42. Amrita B.:zar Patrika, 23 December 1921.

43. The Chargola labourers demanded large pay increases 'with shouts of Gandhi-Maharaj ki jai', and then left the plantations in a body. Viceroy to Secretary of State, 21 June 192 I, R~ading Collution. The Sanjivani complained on 7 July that the tea coolies were rejecting offers for agricultural employment in Bengal ... 'unfortunately the idea has bccome rooted in their minds that Gandhi has become king of their province and that his Raj is free from sorrow and want. They are not therefore prepared to go anywhere but their native villages.' RNP(B) forwf.'~k mding 16July In/. WBSA.

44. Official! account of the Rajshahi jail-break, published in MUHalm4Jn, 20 May 191\.

45. Report on Adminut Tation of Bengal, 1920-21, p.

46. Reports on Political Situation (Bengal), GOI Home Poll 18/ November /92/, 18/December /921. Note by D.I.G. Intelligence Branch, 31 December tnt-GOB Poll (Conf) 39/137/1921. In February 1922, two Nepali women were reponed as spreading disaffection among Gurkha annoo policemen in Calcutta. 'I beg to point out that it is now impossible to deal with these women', cumplaim'd the Deputy Commissioner of Police. GOB Poll (Conf) 14/21-)0/1922. WBSA.

47. Hindustan, 16 November 1921-RNP(B) for weak ending 16 November 1921.

48. L. Birley to Divisional. Commissioner, Burdwan, 27 January 19Z2, pleading for additional. punitive police for Conw and Daspur thanas, GOB Poll (Conf.) F.N. 87 (1-8) 1/22. WBSA. It is interesting thu many of these areas were to figure very prominently in later militant movements—Daspur in 1930 (the Chechuahat incident-see Tanika Sarkar, pp. 212-17), Conta..i

and Tamluk in 1942, Dcbra and Gopiballavpur in the Naxalbari days.

49. L. Birley to Burdwan Divisional Commissioner, 25 January 1922; A. W. Cook. District Magistrate. Midnapur, to Burdwan Oivisional Commissioner, I February 19Z!. ibid.

50. History of Non-Co-operation "Movement in Bengal.

51. Mussalman, 10 March, 1922.

52. Additional Superintendent of Police, Rangpur, to Deputy IG of Police, lntelligence Branch, Bengal. 12 February 1922-GOB Poll (Conf.) F.N. 14(21-30)/1912. WBSA.

53. Bengal Chief Secretary to GOI (Home), 10 May 1923, endosing extract from repon of Deputy Commissioner, Singhbhum to Chief Commissioner, Chotanagpur, 28/29 April l92J, GOB Poll(Conf)F.N. /811/91J.NMML.

54. Before and during the Iswarganj rioes of May 1906. there were 'wild and extravagant expectations' that rent would be reduced to Rs. 3—6 as per ara (a local unit of about five bighas). An identical demand had been raised in the same area way back in 1882-3. and the Dacca Commissioner felt that this was 'a reminiscence of a former pargana rate.' Swadeshi Movement, p. 458.

55. Report of Deputy Commissioner, Singhbhum. GOB Po" (Conf.) [./It.,/81/ /91hrNMM1

56 Telegram from Commissioner of Dacca Division, Jamalpur. 24 September 1907; letter of District Magistrate, Mymensingh to Commissioner. Dacca Division, 10 October 1907, Government of Eastern Bengal and Assam, Poll (Con!.) F.N. HJ(1-22)/1907. WBSA.

57. Sekhar Bandyopadhyay, Caste, Protest and Identity in Colonial India. The Namasudras of Bengal, 1872-1947 Curzon Press, St. John's Studios, Church Road, Richmond, Survey, TW92QA (Printed in Great Britain by TJ International, Padstow, Cornwall) 1997, p. 30.

58. Jogeschandra Pal, 'Bangalar Hindu', (The Hindus of Bengal), Bangabani, Vol. 5.

59. Emergence of such popular religious sects among the protesting Dalit was not a very unusual phenomenon in colonial India.

60. Parmananda Haldar, Matua Dharma Darshan, (Philosophy of Matua religion), (Thakurnagar, 1393 BS): 47; Nityananda Haldar, Srihari Darshan, (Philosophy of Horichand), (Faridpur, 1392 BS): 54.
61. Caste, Protest and Identity in Colonial India, p. 36.
62. Nityananda Haldar, Matua Dharma-Tattwa-Sar, 90.
63. G.B. General (Miscellaneous), File No. 10C-4, B. August 1901, Prog. No. 1.
64. Kedarnath Mazumdar, Dhakar Bibaran, (A description of Dacca), (Mymensingh, 1910): 36.
65. Caste File No. 111: 100, 104, 115, Mss. Eur. D191, 902.
66. Caste, Protest and Identity in Colonial India, p. 36.
67. Jogendranath Gupta, 'Prajasaktir Abhyuthan; (The rise of the subject people), Nabyabharat, Vol. 26, No. 5, Bhadra 1315 BS: 275-276.
68. Sudarshan Chandra Biswas, 'Jatiya Jibaner Udbodhan, Nabyabharat, Vol. 25, No. 11.
69. Dhirendranath Chaudhuri, Bartaman Abastha Sambandha Aro Dui Ekti katha.
70. Caste, Protest and Identity in colonial India, p. 36.
71. Amrita Bazar Patrika, 21 November 1973, 13 August 1940; Hindustan Standard, 12 April 1938.
72. Amrita Bazar Patrika, 15 March 1938, Hindustan Standard, 13 March, 15 March 1938.
73. Hindustan Standard, 18 March, 19 March 1938.
74. Naresh Chandra Das, Namasudra Sampraday O Bangladesh, (Namasudra Community and Bengal), Calcutta, 1368 BS): 58.
75. Caste, Protest and Identity in Colonial India, p. 208.
76. Ibid, p. 241.

4

The Role of Dalits in Chauri Chaura

The event of Chauri Chaura is very important in the freedom struggle movement, specially about the role of dalits, those who were hand to mouth they had decided to uproat the British empire. Here we are giving a few chapters from the report of Shahid Amin. His essay "Approver's Testimony, Judicial Discourse: The Case of Chauri Chaura"[1] was published in subaltern studies.[2]

I have earlier suggested that the attack on Chauri Chaura *thana* on 4 February 1922 was rooted in a paradox: popular ideas about the 'powers' of Mahatma Gandhi were not only at variance with those of the local nationalist leadership, they clashed with the basic tenets of Gandhism itself.[3] My study of the major historical source of this 'well-known riot' has brought another paradox to the fore: the displacement of the rebel in the judicial discourse of the event. In the records of the trial the silences of the peasant-accused are superimposed upon and given meaning by the instrumental 'speech' of the rebel turned Queen's Evidence Mir Shikari, the 'Chief Approver'.

We search in vain within the judicial proceedings for the views of the protagonists rebels against the local coercive state apparatus at the important market town of Chaura. The court proceedings largely record and reconfirm the silences and denials of the 200 odd peasants accused of burning the thana and killing the gendarmes of that precinct. We are confronted instead with the long testimony of the approver. There is no running away from the figure of Shikari by turning to the pages of the judgment; the balancing exercises of the judges at Gorakhpur and Allahabad are shot through with recurrent recourse to the testimony of Shikari, the approver. The fact that my access to 'Chauri Chaura' was simultaneously barred and made possible by the approver's testimony and judicial discourse suggests that this set of texts cannot be brushed aside in a search for the rebels' view of the event: the problem demands a certain recognition in its own terms.

It is I feel, quite important for any historian of the subaltern classes to investigate the discursive practices within which statements by the police, administration, judges, and by the accused themselves, are produced.[4]

As for the approver, he is nothing but a rebel (in fact that is his primary qualification as approver)—but he is a rebel who has shifted his locus within the event from protagonist of rebellion to agent of counter-insurgency. By slipping into the cloak of approver, Mir Shikari transformed himself from a malik [5] of the local peasant 'volunteers' to being a servant of the prosecution, one who even while speaking of the rebels' past spoke so on behalf of his masters. Shikari was then both an 'accomplice' to the crimes committed and an 'approver' of the prosecution's view of those crimes: in this reconstruction his speech is more important than his person.

In what follows I have not tried to discover textual clues to an internal explanation of the act of reneging on Shikari's part: in the absence of sufficient .evidence that must remain an open question. I have not been looking out, either, for crucial portions of truthtelling interspersed with patches of falsehood: that would leave unposed the problem of the structuring of his testimony. My effort has been, rather, to analyse how the testimony of the approver is constructed and constituted, and how it functions as materiel for judgment the official pronouncement on the event. This is a necessary first step towards listening to the silences of the peasant-accused of Chauri Chaura.

1. The Making of the Approver

'An approver should be examined first and not after all the witnesses who are supposed to corroborate his evidence are examined'. It is thus that a certain priority is accorded to the approver's testimony in the latest edition of the classic handbook on the law of evidence in colonial and post-colonial India.[6] True to this form, Mir Shikari, twenty-seven year old cultivator from chotki Dumri, a village owned by the Majithias of Dumri Kalan and joined to the thana by a mile-long stretch of dirt-road, was ushered in as 'Prosecution Witness No. 1' in the Chauri Chaura case.

In the course of his approver's testimony (AT), which engaged the attention of the judge for the better part of a week. Shikari covered considerable ground and went over it with exemplary thoroughness. Some of the motifs Shikari's AT (reproduced in Appendix B) etched and elaborated in the district court at Gorakhpur included the formation of a mandal at chotki Dumri, the enrolment of volunteers, the organizational network and channels of communication in tappa Keotali and the surrounding Hata tahsil, the participation of local volunteers in bigger Khilafat-Non-Cooperation meetings, the decision to picket liquor, meat and fish shops, the altercation with the thanedar of Chaura, the deliberations to assert volunteer-strength at the thana and the bazaar, the organization and proceedings of the meeting preparatory to the march to the thana, the clash with the police and the burning and killing at the precinct.

This substantive piece of testimony was offered by the prosecution, through the approver its instrument to the judge as materiel for his own discourse: the judgment. The Sessions Judge had, however, on his records two other statements by Shikari, magisterially recorded in March and April respectively. The purely instrumental nature of the AT is clearly brought out in Shikari's statement of 5 April 1922:

I am an approver in this case./ I mentioned many men as being joint with me in the crime./ I identified one of my accomplices today./ This is Kalu or Lalu Chamar. He was with us in the sabha; he raised his hand in the sabha; he accompanied us up to Chaura; he was crying jais; and he dismantled the thana tiles in the course of the riot. I know accused from before. He lives in Rakba.[7]

Before making these revealing disclosures during the course of the committal proceedings Shikari had also produced a confession', soon after his arrest on 16 March, which had been duly recorded by Deputy Collector Thakur Mahendra Pal Singh.[8] The legal position is that such confessions are considered 'voluntary' statements if recorded with procedural safeguards by a competent magistrate, and are inadmissible as evidence in a court only if 'the making of the confession appears to the Court to have been caused by any inducement, threat or promise, having reference to the charges against the accused person, proceeding from a person in authority [e.g. the police]'.[9] If, for example, the confession were extracted by the police holding out the promise or hope of obtaining pardon for the accused (and making him a witness for the prosecution), such a confession would be inadmissible in court.[10] Technically it is the Committing Magistrate and not the police or the prosecution who can confer the status of approvership and the accompanying pardon, but there is nothing, apart from a possible retraction in court, to prevent the police from inducing such confessions and extracting vital pieces of evidence at the preliminary stages of the investigation. The onus of proving that such a 'confession' was not made voluntarily rests on the accused.

There was of course little prospect of Shikari retracting his earlier confession on the grounds that it was extracted by the police with the use of torture or the lure of reward failed approvers might have done this.[11] The significance of his confession lies in revealing, at an early stage of its career, the purely instrumental nature of the authorial voice of the approver, where the 'I' of 4 February 1922 is at the service successively of the police, the prosecution and the judges at Gorakhpur and Allahabad. This is achieved not by contingent factors whereby a certain number of policemen confront a particular accused-to-be-made-approver. It is the consequence of the requirements that the AT must fulfil to be admissible as good enough evidence in court: the potential approver must implicate himself as an accomplice the I/We of the narrative of the event must consistently be used as an instrumental voice which helps bring everybody named by it (apart from the first person singular) nearer judicial penalty. The following portion of Shikari's confession brings this out rather well:

Then violent pelting of kankars began. I also threw kankars. . . . As soon as they [the constables] came out at the door, we, all those whose names I have mentioned to have been present at the gate of the thana, we killed them . . . , I too set fire to the dewanji's house.[12]

The significant characteristic of Shikari's confession is that it bears clear traces of certain essential markers of the AT, so much so that it qualifies decidedly as a proto-AT text. To be sure, there were two other potential candidates, Bhagwan Ahir and Ramrup Barai, for the role of approver. All three were kept in the kotwali in separate cells—away from the other accused locked up in the district jail— for it was 'thought that one of these three might be made an approver'.[13] The legal requirement was that they should not see the accused before formally identifying and implicating them in court.

In his confession Bhagwan Ahir, a demobbed soldier turned drill master of Dumri Mandal, recounts his altercation with and the subsequent beating by the thanedar of Chaura the immediate spark that set the thana on fire. He also dwells upon the confabulations, deliberations and organization for the gathering at Dumri on 4 February to question Gupteshar Singh, the thanedar, and picket Mundera Bazar. He provides an account of the Dumri sabha and recognizes some two dozen volunteers. In his narrative of the riot he names persons who brought kerosene and burnt the thana, and a few others who killed a constable and the thanedar. But, interestingly, Bhagwan Ahir stops short of implicating himself directly in the riot: he shies away from revealing his true accomplice self. He attempts rather to highlight his good deeds during the riot and underlines the inherent dangers of his liminal position as a government pensioner/volunteer one who fell outside the rigidly polarized theatre of violence at the Chaura thana. His narrative of the riot is broken by his having to go some distance to relieve himself. After this break the thread is picked up by Bhagwan Ahir, not to implicate others by implicating himself but to establish his role in the rescue of the thanedar's widow and her children to stress, in short, his increasing distance from the rioters:

All the people were ready to kill the wife of S.I. Dudhai Bhar had a sword in his hand and proceeded to kill the S.I.'s child. I took up the child in my arms and requested Dudhai Bhar to spare the life of that child. Bhar [w] then proceeded to kill the other child. I took up that child too in my arms .... Then a large number of people whom I do not know fell upon her. I entreated these fellows also. Then I took the S.I.'s wife up to the field of Naipal .... Then Inderjit Hajjam said 'This man gets pension beat him . . . The Sub Inspector's wife will be witness for him'. Then Karia struck me two blows with a patti. Ramdas also beat me.[14]

But all this is to bark up and snuggle against the wrong end of the judicial stick, for an approver-to-be is subsequently pardoned not for his occasional good deed during the crime to which he testifies. His testimony must be that of an accomplice,[15] and it is here that Bhagwan Ahir fell short of procedural requirements. One gets the feeling that he was shortlisted as a potential approver not because his confession was first-rate AT material but because as an important personality from the pre-history of the event his transformation into Queen's Evidence would have been a major political and psychological victory for the prosecution over the accused. Bhagwan Ahir suggests himself as a pawn in the unfolding politics of the trial, but as one who was worsted before he could cover enough ground to be imbued with a certain power. Just three days after his confession Shikari came up with a more complete and legally sustainable story. The half chance of freedom available to the renegade was thus not properly grasped by this subaltern of the Mesopotamia campaign. He died on the gallows in the summer of 1923.

Ramrup Barai, the panwala from Mundera Bazar, was arrested quite early in March and provided a very full story in his 'confession' before the magistrate.[16] Ramrup's statement is full of authentic details about the prehistory of the riot and the actual clash outside the thana on the afternoon of 4 February. An idea of the inversion brought about by the power of local volunteer organizations is conveyed by the verbal abuse directed at the thanedar of Chaura. When Bhagwan Ahir, Ramrup Barai recalled, was cornered by Gupteshar Singh in Mundera Bazar on 1 February for being a *'namakharam'* government pensioner turned 'volunteer', Bhagwan Ahir replied with an abusive, 'Lund se' (my penis (to you))! This four-letter retort proffered to the local thanedar in the presence of other 'volunteers' in the Bazar was largely responsible for Bhagwan Ahir being beaten up by Gupteshar Singh a significant link in the chain of events leading to 4 February 1922. But the betel-seller from Mundera Bazar was not just recalling the pre-history of 'Chauri Chaura', expletives and all; his 'confession' was that of a potential approver. Clear impressions of the directions given by the police are to be found in two types of statements: the characteristic self-implication in 'joint crimes', and the way Ramrup interrupts the narrative of micro-sequences to identify the accused at each and every stage of their march towards the thana. I have tried to highlight this latter feature by a schematic table of Action and Identification. This basic structure, fulfilling the requirements of a full-fledged AT, was far too precious to the police to have been created by the mere recollection of an arrested rioter.

Action 1: Gathering at Mundera Bazar on 1 February 1922 to picket the Bazar.

Identification: 'Among the volunteers who were there I recognized Bengali Bhar of Bhartolia, Lal Mohd., Ramdas Kalwar, Bhagwan Ahir, residents of Chaura, Shikari and Nazar Ali, residents of Dumri. I did not identify others. The remaining others were of Raghuapur, Bale, Dumri and Chaura. I do not know their names'. Action 2: Deliberations in Dumri on the 1st night and 2nd morning, when letters were drafted to gather at Dumri on 4 Feb. (to question the S.I.) Identification 'Bengali Bhar, Lal Mohd., etc... were present there . . . When I reached there [the next morning] all the persons who were present the previous night were sitting at that time.[17]

When Ramrup comes to the actual clash with the police we get such statements as, 'Then all turned... towards the thana and began to throw kankar from the [railway] line: I also threw kankar from the line'; Then myself, Nazar Ali, Shikari and a Sain and many others pulled out the thana gate and broke it'; 'We all, i.e. myself, Bhagwan Ahir and a Muhamadan of Chaura whose name I don not know went to the market and asked for kerosene oil'.

This *panwari* from Mundera bazaar then produced for the police and the prosecution a first-rate 'confessionl, and he had only to wait in hopeful solitary fonfinement at the kotwqali for summons to appear as a approver in the makeshift court the Committing Magistrate had set up in the middle of the districty jail compound. Ramrup's prolonged absence in the kotwali had created a strong suspicion among the accused of his having been pardoned. Dwarka gosain of Chaura, when faced with an adverse mention in Ram rup's confession, replied: 'Ramrum Barai and I havfe no enmity. He names me as he ha been given a pardon and had appeared as a witness'.[18]

But the fact was the Ramrup had been pipped at the post by Shikari and wa now in the same boat as Dwarka Gosain; except that while Dwarka survived a fourteen-year stint in the Andamanas to be released in 1938, Ramrup Barai, partly because he had implicated himself in the hope of being pardoned, wa convicted of murder and hanged.

Taking a cue from 'Chauri Chaura' one could say that in every case of mass peasant rioting the AT is the usual precondition for the judicial process to take its course. Khan Ashfaq Hussain was almost axiomatic on this point: In every big case an approver is put up, therefore . . . I and the DIG consulted as to who should be made approver . . .', he told the Session's Judge in September 1922.

Faced with the considerable task of successfully pressing charges against the 225 accused of joint crimes committed during the riot at Chauri Chaura, the prosecution's main concern was to get hold of a connected narrative a chain of events leading up to and ending with the 'occurence' itself. No amount of rummaging by the police through confiscated Congress and Khilafat papers at Gorakhpur could do away with the need for 'hard' evidence about the background to the riot from Chaura, chotki Dumri and tappa Keotali generally.[19] The AT was not the only narrative to have been produced from this ilaqa in the court: others agents and karindas of neighbouring landlords, peons and khidmatgars at the thana and the neighbouring railway station, constables and chaukidars who survived the massacre were no doubt summoned and testified to the crime and its pre-history.[20] But much of this evidence was fragmentary and did not cover its entire course. As for the accused, none of them came forward to make a programmatic or political statement.[21] Even the 'ring leaders' proffered only different sorts of denials and alibis, ranging from Nazar Ali's plea of mistaken identity with his namesake. Shikari's uncle, to Lal Mohammad's claim of having been knocked down unconscious by buckshot before the thana was stormed.[22] Speech of this kind in the court-room was mostly evasive: these were attempts by the accused to dissociate themselves from the events being narrated most minutely by Shikari—so as to escape punishment.

However, fear of punishment, while it makes the accused 'economical of truth',[23] also yields the figure of the approver: the peasantaccused turned renegade, who, protected by the law (and goaded by the prosecution) speaks of the pre-history and the actual occurrence of the event in a historical, systematic and accusatory mode. Punishment thus generates reticence and disclosure at the two ends of the spectrum. Judicial discursive practice ideally requires both these; in fact in the case of a mass trial it banks on the disclosures of the approver to strike the reticent accused down with fear of punishment. Shikari's was a 'competent' testimony against the Chauri Chaura accused, forged from an early stage to feed and fit into the production of judicial discourse.[24]

The narrative, a connected chain of events leading to the 'occurrence at the thana' is broken up into micro-sequences relevant to the crime, and at each juncture Shikari is made to pause and remember the names and faces of those whom he now 'recognizes' as those accused of involvement in the riot. Some of the more important of these appear below.

Action 8: Dumri Sabha on the morning of 4 February, marching on oath to the Thana (para 17)

Identification: 'I noticed carefully. Everyone was ready to go, no one drew back.... All the men of my village raised their hands. That is all the accused of my village who are present. Also Ramrup Barai, Thakur Ahir (approver), Nepal Mallah, Ganesh Bania the Chaura accused whom I have indentified: all these persons were among those who raised their hands. And

Sham Sunder accused, and Meghu Tiwari accused, and Dwarka Pandey accused, and Abdullah alis Sukhi accused and Jaglal Kewat accused, and Kalu alias Lalu accused (Chamar), and Baran Bania accused; and many persons whom I do not remember. And I 'recognized by face' several others.'

While the defence has a well-defined strategy towards the AT what about the accused themselves? What do the court records tell us about their perception of the approver and his damning testimony? In reply to the question, 'Shikari identifies you as among the rioters. What do you say to this?', the accused could either think of no good reason why their ex-comrade should betray them so, or they dug into their common past to come up with what in most cases the court described as 'frivolous and undocumented enmity'. The first type of response is typified by the comment of Gobardhan Pasi, a self-confessed 'volunteer' of Dumri: 'Shikari is of my village. I have no enmity with him. I cannot say why he entangles me' [humko kyon phansa raha hai][25] Dudhai of chotki Dumri on the other hand had this to say:

We Chamars had bought a pig for sacrifice a year ago. It entered Ilahi Musalman's house and then into Shikari's field. Shikari quarrelled with us at this. The Mukhia came and separated us. The Musalmans stopped our water. We dug our own well and take water from it.[26]

Bikram Ahir, the ex-chaukidar of Dumri turned 'active volunteer' who lost his brother Surajbali chaukidar in the riot, pleaded personal enmity of a different sort:

Shikari is my enemy. When I was chaukidar, I challaaned his father over 20 years ago for theft; and about 5 years ago I challaaned his mother and sister for theft. All three were convicted. I identified the corpse of Shikari's wife when she was cut by the train. So he names me.[27]

And to complete the series, Kauleshwar Kurmi, a labourer from the nearby village of Jungle Mahadeva (in the middle of the forest that had till the 1890s skirted Dumri itself) thought of the time when 'Shikari wanted subscription' for the Tilak Swaraj and Khilafat funds from him, and he refused.[28]

A related feature is that the final, true construction of the narrative and the fixing of its meaning is effected fairly early at the sessions trial. At the highest level says, The High Court, the question is not so much whether the master narrative of the lower court is true or false, for the 'facts of the case' are no longer at issue; it is questions of culpability and 'just' punishment which are under consideration. But what is the 'true' narrative of a riot like Chauri Chaura, where an estimated 6000 people were involved, 1000 suspects listed and 235 put on trial? A judicial master narrative in a case such as this has to tackle two issues: (1) whether the accused arraigned did participate in the riot, and (2) re-present the pre-history of the 'occurrence' in an intelligible fashion, as leading the accused to riot outside the thana on that particular day in February 1922. But precisely because 'Chauri Chaura' was a mass phenomenon which happened at a certain distance from the 'organized' world of district politics.[29]

Para I : I pay Rs. 34-7-0 rent a year; I know Lal Mohammad. Lal Mohammad Sain sold announcements in Urdu; he said they were Gandhiji's papers. Their price was 2 as. And 4 pice. They had been sold for two months before January (1922). I bought a paper. When he sold it to me he told me to take the paper and returned it when Ghandhiji asked for it. I know Nazar Ali and Abdullah. Abdullah is also called Sukhi. They enrolled volunteers. In Mundera and Satrih and Pipraiya and Dumri and Raqba and Rajdhani.

Para 2: In January on the Thursday Na Ali told me that Lal Mohammad Sain would next day bring a hakim from Gorakhpur and I was to become a volunteer tomorrow. I said I was the only member of my household and the work was too much how could I become a volunteer. He said that persons who refused to become volunteer4s would have their homes and fields taken from them after swaraj had been obtained. And then they would be sent overseas. I said nothing then. On the Friday Lal Muhammad came with the bhakim to my door in

Dumri. There were 3 or 4 men of Gorakhpur with the hakim. The hakim sat on my cot under a nim tree in front of my door.

Para 3: About 50 men of Mundera came in front of my door. And men of Chaura came. And Brahman whom I have identified here, a tallish man. Perhaps his name is Dwarka. And many men came with him. Abdullah of Rajdhani alias Sukhi, and with him 10 or 15 men, and a Pandit of Rampurwa, whose name I know now to be sham sunder; I learnt his name when I identified in court. Nazar Ali alco came; and all the men of my village were present. Ganesh Bania of Mundera and Chedi Bhar of Chaura and Sampat alias Badri (or Badri) of Chaura, and mahadeo of Chaura and Bhagan Ahir and subha and Lal Muhhammad and Sham Sunder and Dwarka and Abdullah, Nazar Ali, Sadho; I do not remember who else was there. Some of the names – most of them- I learnt before the lower court. The rest I knew before. In all 150 or 200 poeople collected at my door.

Para 4: West of my house, 4 or 4 bighas, is a grove. The hakimji went off there and every one followed. The hakimji gave a lecture there. He told us to suw cotton. And to make yarn and spin cloth. And wear it. And he told us to settle any quarrel amonst ourselves and not to go to the thana. And not to go to the zamindar. And to give up toddy and spirits. And not allow anyone ot drink it. And when there was swaraj we should pay 4 and 8 annas a bigha. So we should become volunteers. Lal Muhammad Sain was appointed secretary (by him), and Bhagwati Bania, 2nd secretary and treasurer. And I was made 3rd secretary. And Nazar Ali was made deputy assistant manager. With the hakimji was a Pandit and he wrote down Ramrup Brai's name and told him to go and work as a volunteer. We were told all to collect subscriptions (chanda and chutki). Chutki means rice or flour, a fistful. Many men there said they would become volunteers. Then we went to the Chauri Chaura stateion with the hakimji. He told Lal Muhammad, Nazar Ali and me to make over to Bhagwati the subscriptions collected by us. He told us to be subject to Lal Muhammad and Nazar Ali and obey their orders. The hakimji went off and we went home.[30]

References

1. Subaltern Studies V, ed. Ranjit Guha, Oxford University Press, Delhi, 1987.
2. I am grateful to Habib Ahmad, Dipesh Chakrabarty, Partha Chatterjee, Veena Das and, specially, Ranajit Guha for several discussions preceding this essay. A special word of thanks is due to David Hardiman for locating and supplying me with a copy of the reminiscences of Judge Theodore Piggott. I have also benefited from the criticisms made at the Second Subaltern Studies Conference held at Calcutta in January 1986. A long session with Professor Upendra Baxi, though quite late in the day, has helped me plug some of the legal loopholes in the argument. For those which remain I would have to blame myself.
3. Shahid Amin, 'Gandhi as Mahatma: Gorakhpur District, Eastern UP, 192102, in Ranajit Guha, ed. Subaltern Studies III: Writings in South Asian History and Society (Delhi, 1984).
4. Cf. Guha, 'Criticism must therefore start not by naming a bias but by examining the components of the discourse, vehicle of all ideology, for the manner in which these might have combined to describe any particular figure of speech'. Ranajit Guha, 'The prose of Counter-Insurgency', in Subaltern Studies II (Delhi, 1983), p. 9.
5. 'Malik' was the term used by both elites and subalterns to characterize the leader/s of the volunteer force which had marched from the nearby village of Dumri to the Chauri Chaura thana.
6. Woodroffe and Ameer Ali's Law of Evidence (14th edition), edited and revised by B.R.P. Singhal and Narayan Das (Allahabad, 1981), Vol. iv, p. 3338. Unless otherwise stated. Ameer All, Law of Evidence, refers to the fourth edition of this classic work compiled by the original authors.
7. Committal Proceedings, 5 April 1922. The records of the Court of Sessions in the Chauri Chaura trials nos. 44-5 of 1922 (District Records, Gorakhpur) will be referred to as Trial,

followed by page number; the records of the Committing Magistrate will be referred to as (date of evidence/exhibit no.) Comm. Progs.

8. Sections 164 and 364 of the Cr. P.C. contain provisions for the recording of such 'judicial confessions'. Any magistrate, not being a police officer, may record a confession made to him, while the case is under investigation by the police, or at any time afterwards, before the commencement of the enquiry (preliminary to committal to the court of sessions) or trial. Such confessions are to be recorded and signed in the manner prescribed under sec. 364. Section 25 of the Indian Evidence Act categorically rules out the admissibility of a confession made to a police officer.
9. Indian Evidence Act, 1872, section 24.
10. Ameer Ali, The Law of Evidence (4th edition, c. 1908), commentary on section 24.
11. Sections 25 and 26 of the Evidence Act only rule out confessions made to the police. They do not prohibit the police from extracting the story out of an accused and then getting it duly recorded before a magistrate. In fact, section 29 lays down that if 'a confession is otherwise relevant, it does not become irrelevant merely because it was made under a promise of secrecy, or in consequence of deception practised on the accused person for the purpose of obtaining it, or when he was drunk, or because it was made in answer to questions which he need not have answered, whatever may have been the form of these questions, or because he was not warned that he was not bound to make such confession, and that evidence of it may be given against him.' Emphasis added.
12. Statement under section 164 of IPC of Shikari, S/o Mir Qurfaan, age twenty-five years, resident of Dumri Khurd, P.S. Chaura, 16 March 1922, exhibit no. 138, Comm. Progs. Emphasis added.
13. Evidence of Khan Bahadur Saiyid Ashfaq Hussain, Trial 679-80; cf. Appendix B, para 26.
14. Statement of Bhagwan, Ahir, 13 March 1922, exhibit 226, Comm. Progs.

15. Ameer Ali, pp. 835ff.
16. Statement of Ramrup . . . Barai, 6 March 1922, exhibit 225, Comm. Progs.
17. Ibid.
18. Subaltern Studies V; p.174. (Memo of examination, 28 May, 1922, Comm. Progs.
19. The Sadr Kotwal raided the Congress and Khilafat offices the next day and carried a cart-load of papers (forty files, nine bundles of pledge forms, both signed and unsigned, a dictionary and even a one-maund weight!) to the kotwali. These papers were gone through by the DSP to extract lists of volunteers of the Chaura thana. See, Trial 791-4, and exhibits 17—122, Comm. Progs.
20. See for Instance the evidence of Sadhai, the syce of the darogha, Autar, the washerman of the thana, and of Siddiq, the only surviving constable from the thana, before the Sessions Judge. 22 Cf. section in below.
21. Cf. Section 111 below.
22. See inter alia, the statement of Nazar All and Lal Mohammad, 6 June 1922, Comm. Progs.
23. Judgment, High Court.
24. The relevant section in the Law of Evidence states: 'An accomplice shall be a competent witess against an accusea person; and a conviction is not illegal merely because it proceeds upon the uncorroborated testimony of an accomplice'. Section 133. Of course there is a 'rule of prudence' (section 114, illustration (b)) which requires judges not to convict on the basis of such uncorroborated testimony, but legal pundits recognized that the raison d'etre of section 133 was the 'impossibility' of bringing 'the principal offenders to justice.... Without recourse to such evidence'. Cf. Law commission of India. 69th report on the Indian evidence act, 1872 (Delhi, 1979) chapter 73.
25. Memo. of Examination, Gobardhan, S/o Ram Baksh, Pasi, 31 May 1922, Comm. Progs.
26. Memo, Dudhaiee, s/o Debi Deen, Chamar, 27 May 1922, Comm. Progs.

27. Judgment, High Court, p. 33.
28. Memo, Bikram, S/o Sheocharan, Ahir, 25 May 1922, Comm. Progs.
29. Memo, Kualeshwar, S/o Janki, Kurmi, 2 June 1922, Comm. Progs.
30. Subaltern Studies V. p. 190.

5

Dalits and Massacre of Jallianwala Bagh

The 13th of April was the day of Baisakhi festival – the New Year Day of Hindus. On this auspicious day the great Guru Gobind Singh Ji had founded the 'Khalsa', an organization of the 'pure and faithfuls' dedicated to the service of humanity, that took a heroic stand against religious tyranny and oppression by the mighty Moghul power. This very day was destined to witness another historic event in 1919, which further heightened its sanctity and significance.

From time immemorial Baisakhi has been celebrated in North-Western India with great enthusiasm, and more so at Amritsar, the city being a sacred place for Sikhs and Hindus alike. On this day thousands of men, women and children come to Amritsar from far and wide, take a dip in the tank of Nectar (Amritsar), and after having darshan of Har Mandir (Golden temple), return to their homes. The practice of holding a Horse Fair on the eve of Baisakhi had also come to stay.

This time (13th April, 1919) Amritsar was in the throes of an unusual political turmoil. The city had been observing a continuous haartal for the 4th day. Every day saw funerals of martyrs, who had succumbed to their injuries sustained on the 10th April, as a result of firing at the hands of the military.

As already pointed out at the end of the last chapter, an announcement was made on the 12th April that a meeting would be held on the next day, i.e., the Baisakhi day, in the Jallianwala Bagh.

The Bagh being so near the Golden Temple and the day of the meeting being that of the Baisakhi festival, it was expected that people in very large numbers would attend the meeting. The British chose it to be a suitable occasion to take revenge upon the patriotic Punjabis by opening fire on them.

On the 13th morning, General Dyer again marched through the streets of Amritsar, exhibiting his arm and strength in order to overawe the people. It was arranged like some sort of ceremonial parade. At its head were City Inspector Ashraf Khan and his Sub-Inspector Obeidulla, mounted on horses. Behind him came Malik Fateh Khan, the Naib Tehsildar, seated in a bamboo cart, with a man beside him beating a drum. Then came the contingent of white troops. They were followed by two cars – General Dyer and Irving seated in the first and Rehill and Plomer in the second. After them marched the Indian troops. Starting from the Ram Bagh headquarters, the procession crossed the railway line at Hall Bridge, passed through Hall Gate and came down to Hall Bazar. Five times it stopped between Hall Gate and the Post Office (Town Hall). The drum was beaten and people were given time to flock. A proclamation was read twice or thrice in Urdu and then again in Punjabi at every stoppage. Handbills were also distributed at some places carrying the text of the proclamation in Urdu. The proclamation declared that every assembly of the people would be dispersed by force of arms. In vernacular this was explained as ... "Golee se chittar-bittar dega"

The procession passed through various streets and chowks, and at 19 places the proclamation was read in the manner indicated above, and handbills were also distributed at these places. The original English version of the proclamation is reproduced below:

"It is hereby proclaimed to all whom it may concern that no person residing in the city is permitted or allowed to leave the city in his own or hired conveyance or on foot without a pass. No person residing in Amritsar city is permitted to leave his house after 8. Any persons found in the streets after 8 are liable to be shot. No procession of any kind is permitted to parade the streets in the city or any part of the city or outside of it any time. Any such processions or any gathering of 4 men would be looked upon and treated as an unlawful assembly and dispersed by force of arms, if necessary."

On the heels of Dyer's procession, or shortly thereafter, a counter-proclamation was made by a group of boys, beating an empty kerosene-oil-container that a meeting would be held at the Jallianwala Bagh at 4.30 p.m. at which Lala Kanhya Lal (A senior Lawyer aged 75) would preside and give valuable advice to the people.

At 12.40 p.m., while Dyer was still in the city along with his procession, he was told that people were not in a mood to obey his orders. They were least impressed by his show of arms and in defiance of his proclamation, the meeting, as decided, already, would be held in the Bagh. This news was surely an 'unexpected gift of fortune' for General Dyer. About the meeting he already knew from the intelligence reports, but he was having a doubt in his mind lest his marching through the city and making the proclamation referred to above should discourage people from attending the; meeting, in which case the golden opportunity which had presented itself to British administration would be lost.

General Dyer had deployed all the available troops carefully at every strategic point, both inside and outside of Amritsar City, and even then he was left with a striking force of about 400 strong.

Feeling very hot in the city, Dyer returned to his headquarters at 1 p.m. Thereafter he was receiving news about the meeting at regular intervals.

People had started pouring into the Bagh after 2 p.m. At 4 p.m. Dyer received the news that a large number of people had assembled there. The news was given to him by no less a person than Mr. Rehill, Superintendent of Police. Immediately thereafter the news was confirmed by Mr. Lewis, Manager of Crown Cinema, who had come through the city disguised as an Indian. (He was most probably working as special spy during those days.) Dyer at once gave orders to his striking force to fall in. He told his company commanders to their surprise that "they would not be going with him". "If there is anything to be done," he said, "I will do it alone."

The General set out for the most important journey of his life, leaving behind a strong contingent to guard his headquarters and taking the rest with him. He had his favourite Captain Briggs beside him in the car. Behind him came the two armoured cars, followed by the police car with Rehill and Plomer. Miles Irving did not accompany them since he had more urgent engagement in the Fort.

As the column marched along, five pickets, each of forty soldiers, were dropped on the way to take positions at strategic points. The contingent which accompanied the General right up to the Bagh was wholly Indian and comprised fifty soldiers armed with rifles and forty Gurkhas armed with only *khukris*.

In 1919, Jallianwala 'Bagh' was no 'garden', but a desolate piece of land – a rectangle of irregular shape, about 250 yards long and 200 yards wide. (Originally, however, it had been laid out as a garden in the middle of the nineteenth century by its original owner, Pandit Jalla, after whose name the garden came to be popularly known as Jallianwala Bagh. Later on, the garden fell into disuse, and, still later, became desolate.) Long before 1919, houses had been built all around the Bagh with their back walls towards it. Only on the southern side, for a small length, there was no house, and, instead, there was a small stretch of low boundary wall, about five feet high. There were only four or five narrow lanes leading into the Bagh – each hardly three or four feet wide. The Bagh contained one small 'Samadh' (tomb) towards the southern side, with four small trees growing near it, and an open well of quite a big circumference towards its eastern boundary, with three trees growing nearby. It is also a note-worthy point about the Bagh of those days that the level of its land was not even. A small strip of land near the entrance from the Jallianwala Bazar side was on a higher level, while the rest of the land was at a lower level below.

Dyer had never visited the Bagh before. He was relying on the map and the guidance from Rehill and Plomer. The party proceeded to the Bagh from the Jallianwala Bazar side. After entering this bazaar, they found that a very narrow passage led from there into the Bagh. It was not possible to drive the armoured cars into this passage; therefore, they had to be left behind. Dyer then entered the Bagh along with his soldiers. He saw a vast crowd collected there. Before his arrival eight speakers had spoken. No person was elected as chairman of the meeting. Instead a portrait of Dr. Kitchlew adorned the Presidential chair. The meeting was, at the time of Dyer's arrival, being addressed by a man standing on a platform. As already pointed out, the strip of land near the entrance was on a higher level. Dyer and his troops stood on this strip, so that they could have a better view of the crowd. The meeting was going on in a perfectly peaceful and orderly manner. People from the horse fair had also come to the meeting on hearing that a 'jalsa' was being held there. Some boys and women were also present to witness the usual tamasha on such occasions, particularly when such meetings was the order of the day.

General Dyer had nothing to wait for. He had gone to the Bagh with a fixed mind and an iron determination. He turned to Captain Briggs and asked him about the number of people assembled there. Briggs estimated the number around five thousand. But, in fact, about 20,000 persons were present in the Bagh at that time. Dyer did not think it necessary to give any warning to the people. He at once deployed his troops – twenty-five riflemen on the right and twenty-five on the left. All this happened within thirty seconds. The general then instantly ordered them to open fire.

Some of the crowd, seeing the armed soldiers behind them, shouted excitingly *"A gaye, A gaye"* (They have come, they have come) and people got alarmed. Hans Raj, one of the active workers of the Congress, however, from the rostrum assured the gathering that there was no cause for fear and they should sit down. Meanwhile the troops opened fire. Again shouts of *'Phokian', 'Phokian'* were raised by some ones, but the illusion ended soon, when the bullets began to take toll of lives.

Now it was a panic-stricken crowd. People realized at once that they were caught in a death-trap. Within no time the vast crowd rose in a wave, and rushed madly on all sides to escape from the hail of bullets. There were also present in the midst of the crowd some retired soldiers who had faced many such occasions while on active service. They shouted at the running people to lie flat on the ground instead of exposing themselves to bullets by running, but few fortunate persons paid head to their valuable advice. Others continued rushing hither and thither only to be hit by bullets at the next step. On all sides, however, the tide of human wave was dammed back by the house-wall barriers. People who knew about the few small exits rushed in hundreds towards each of them. Seeing this, Dyer directed his soldiers to fire at those points. Many people died at the mouths of these exits as a result of firing, while many others were trampled by onrushing crowds. Many people attempted; to jump over the five-foot high small piece of boundary wall on the opposite side to escape, but only a few could do so, while many others were hit by bullets and fell back, dead or wounded. Many children and the old lost their lives by being trampled over by the crowds. Many people also ran in the direction in which the well was situated, and, blinded by terror and unable to check their momentum some fell into the well, which, unfortunately, had no protection-wall around it in those days. (Many dead bodies were recovered from the well later on.)

Some of the soldiers fired in the air in the beginning at which General Dyer shouted: "Fire low. For what else have you been brought here?"

The scene of horror may better be described in the words of Arthur Swinson:

"Towards the exists on either flank, the crowd converged in their frantic effort to get away, jostling, clambering, elbowing and trampling over each other. Seeing this movement, Briggs drew Dyer's attention to it, and Dyer,.........directed the fire of the troops straight at them. The result was a horror; men screamed and went down, to be trampled by those coming after. Some were hit again and again. In places the dead and wounded lay in heaps; men would go down wounded, to find themselves immediately buried beneath a dozen others.

"The firing still went on. Hundeds, abandoning all hope of getting away through the exists, tried the walls which in places were five feet high and at others seven or ten. Fighting for a position, they ran at them, clutching at the smooth surfaces, trying frantically to get a hold. Some people almost reached the top to be pulled down by those fighting behind them. Some, more agile than the rest, succeeded in getting away; but many more were shot as they clambered up, and some as they sat poised on the top, before leaping down on the further side.

"Twenty thousand people were caught beneath the hail of bullets: all of them frantically trying to escape from the quiet meeting place which had suddenly become a screaming hell."

The firing continued for ten to fifteen minutes; 1650 rounds were fired, i.e. 33 rounds per rifleman. The firing ceased only after the ammunition ran out. Dyer admitted later that if more ammunition had been available, that too would have been spent on the people. Not only that but had he been able to take machine-guns into the Bagh, he would also have fired straightaway from them and exhausted them on the assembled people.

General Dyer left the Bagh, along with his force, at about 5.30 p.m. leaving behind a scene which was like a hell on earth. At least 2,000 persons lay in the Bagh, either dead or wounded. Piteous and heart-rending cries were rising from the lips of hundreds of wounded people simultaneously and every one of them was crying for water. But there was nobody to give them water or any kind of relief or assistance. Hundreds of people were in the throes of death, and, here and there, every minute, people were giving up the ghost. No doctor entered the Bagh to render medical assistance to the people. Even those residents of Amritsar, whose kith and kin had come to attend the meeting, did not dare to enter the Bagh for quite some time to search for their dear ones and take them away in case they had died or been wounded.

Many of the wounded tried to crawl out of the Bagh and with great difficulty reached the lanes and streets, but, unable to move further, they fell here and there and quite a large number of them died in the streets "in pools of their own blood."

After some time, residents of Amritsar, whose family-members, friends and neighbours were known to have gone into the Bagh to attend the meting, took courage and entered "the hell" to search for their dear ones. By then, darkness had descended on the Bagh, and the dead and the injured were scattered all around throughout the area and there were heaps of them at many places. It was, therefore, not easy for the residents to search out their dear ones. Moreover, people knew of the order of Dyer that nobody was to remain out of his house after 8 p.m. On account of all these factors, only some persons or parties were able to search out their dear ones and they took them away hurriedly. But near about 8 p.m., all search parties left the Bagh and the remaining wounded were left to the mercy of God. It is estimated that more than 1,000 wounded persons remained lying in the Bagh throughout the night, besides hundreds of dead bodies. Many of the wounded died during the night on account of heavy bleeding. A considerable number of those who had been taken away by their relatives also died at their homes during the night before the eyes of the helpless members of the family, since no doctor would come to their assistance on account of the terror of Dyer's order that anybody coming out of his house after 8 p.m. would be fired at.

All walks of people participated in the gathering at Jallianwala Bagh, majority of whom were from the dalit and backward communities. A list of persons killed in the Jallianwalan Bagh massacre is given below:

List of Persons Killed in the Jallianwala Bagh on 13th April, 1919

Sr. No.	*Name and Parentage*	*Caste*	*Age*	*Residence*
1.	Hardiyal	Kamboh	45	Amritsar City
2.	Gian Chand S/o Kirpa Ram	Kamboh	15	Amritsar City
3.	Harnama S/o Viroo	Barber	30	Amritsar City
4.	Mohd. Sharif S/o Mohd. Ramzan	Mason	12	Amritsar City
5.	Barkat Ali S/o Ajahi Bux	Turkhan	32	Amritsar City
6.	Imam Din S/o Murad Bux	Lohar	50	Amritsar City
7.	Khuda Bux S/o Vasao Shah	Fakir	40	Amritsar City
8.	Mohd. Bux	Mason	36	Amritsar City

(Contd.)

(Contd. Table.)

Sr. No.	*Name and Parentage*	*Caste*	*Age*	*Residence*
9.	Nathu S/o Gulab	Kamboh	8	Amritsar City
10.	Miraj Din S/o Ladha	Kharasi	20	Amritsar City
11.	Waris S/o Chirag Din	Arain	30	Amritsar City
12.	Palla S/o Gurditta	Sweeper	40	Amritsar City
13.	Bal Mukand S/o Mangal Chand Nohria	Nohria	25	Amritsar City
14.	Nur Mohd. S/o Jhandu	Teli	30	Amritsar City
15.	Khair Din S/o Mangtu	Teli	30	Amritsar City
16.	Feroz S/o Sher Mohd.	Zargar	25	Amritsar City
17.	Ram Chand S/o Saran Das	Kargar	34	Sathiala (Amritsar)
18.	Bhagat Salig Ram S/o Sant Jawala Singh	Sadh	60	Amritsar City
19.	Sobha Singh	Tarkhan	55	Amritsar City
20.	Chatroo	Sadhu	60	Amritsar City
21.	Arur Singh S/o Roda Singh	Tarkhan	20	Vadala, Amritsar
22.	Viroo S/o Mian	Jalaha	20	Makhanwind, Amritsar
23.	Mul Singh S/o Kan Singh	Ramgarhia	40	Amritsar City
24.	Bibi Har Kaur W/o Hardit Singh	Jatni	40	Lopoke
25.	Viroo S/o Nathu	Bharal	29	Amritsar
26.	Naina S/o Kunun	Mehra	29	Vanchari, Amritsar
27.	Vir Singh	Kamboh	29	Devidass Pura, Distt. Amritsar

(Contd.)

(Contd. Table.)

Sr. No.	*Name and Parentage*	*Caste*	*Age*	*Residence*
28.	Karim Din	Lohar	30	Sohian Kalan, Distt. Amritsar
29.	Kanshiram S/o Motiram	Saini	21	Bahlopur, Distt. Gurdaspur
30.	Mangal Dass S/o Diyaloo	Bairagi	25	Chabhal, Teh. Tarn Taran
31.	Madho S/o Raja	Barber	22	Narowal, Distt. Sialkot
32.	Hussi S/o Sikkandar	Zargar	22	Amritsar City
33.	Ismail S/o Miran Bux	Zargar	22	Amritsar City
34.	Ibrahim S/o Imam Din	Zargar	25	Amritsar City
35.	Jagan Nath S/o Bal Kishan Mehra	Zargar	25	Amritsar City
36.	Kashmir Singh	Zargar	25	Amritsar City
37.	Kaka Singh S/o Nihala	Chimba	23	Amritsar City
38.	Miraj Din S/o Nabi Bux	Kharasi	18	Amritsar City
39.	Mul Singh S/o Mana Singh	Carpenter	20	Amritsar City
40.	Madho	Barber	20	Amritsar City

References

1. Ghadar Movement, Ideology Organization Strategies, 1983.
2. Udham Singh : The Patriot who Avenged the Jallianwala Bagh Massacre.
3. Letters of Udham Singh.

6

Congress and the Dalits

The birth of the Indian National Congress in 1885 was the most important political development in the country since the mutiny of 1857. For more than twenty years after its foundation it completely dominated the political life of India. "It is difficult to think of any age or country in which a single political institution played such a dominant role for more than fifty years in the liberation of a country from foreign yoke". The birth of the Congress "crystallized for the first time the new political forces in India, which till then had been located and scattered. It created a sense of common brotherhood based on common aims and grievances, bringing together people from Calcutta to Madras and from Lahore to Bombay". The London Times declared: "For the first time, perhaps since the world began India as a nation met together.[1]

The Indian National Congress, which was destined to play a dominant role in India's struggle for independence, was formed at a national convention held in Bombey in December 1885, under the presidency of W.C. Bonnerji. A retired British civil servent, A.O. Hume was crucially involved in this process, as it was he who toured across the subcontinent, talked to prominent political leaders in Bombey, Madras and Calcutta and persuaded them to meet at a national conference that was initially supposed to meet at Poona.[2]

But what ever might been the historic significance of this first meeting, Hume's involvement in it gave rise to a lot of controversy regarding the origin of Congress. The 'safety-valve theory' or the conspiracy theory, which was deduced from this simple fact, was for a long time subscribed to by all shades of historians.

The theory originated from William Wedderburn's biography of Hume published in 1913. Weddberburn, another ex-civil servant, wrote that in 1878 Hume had come across seven volumes of secret reports which showed that there had been seething discontent among the lower classes and a conspiracy to overthrow British rule by force. He became disturbed, met Lord Dufferin and together they decided to establish an organization with educated Indians. This would serve as safety valve by opening up a line of communication between the rulers and the ruled and would thus prevent a mass revolution. The Congress was in this way the creation of British rule. This safety-valve theory was believed by the earlier nationalist historians; the imperialist historians used it to discredit Congress and the Marxist historians developed a conspiracy theory from this. R.P. Dutt, for example, wrote that Congress was born through a conspiracy to forestall a popular uprising in India and the Indian bourgeois leaders were a party to it.

In the 1950s these safety valve or conspiracy theories were proved to be wrong. First of all, those seven volumes of secret reports have not been traced in any of the archives either in India or London. Historians argue that given the structure of British information system in the 1870s, it was highly unlikely that so many volumes of secret reports could have existed. Except in Wedderburn's biography of Hume, nowhere else any reference to the existence of such reports could be found, and he too mentioned that they were supplied to Hume by religious gurus, and were not procured from any official sources. Then the opening up of Lord Dufferin's private papers in the late 1950s cleared up the confusion by exploding the myth of Dufferin's sponsorship of the Congress or Hume.[3]

The venue of the Conference was shifted from Poona to Bombay on account of Cholera.[4] Its name was also changed to the Indian National Congress. The first session of the Congress began on 25 December, 1885, at Bombay. It was attended by nearly one hundred delegates of whom 72 were non-officials.[5] Two leading Muslims of Bombay, R.M. Sayani and A.M. Dhararnsi also attended the session. The largest number of delegates - 38 in all-came from the western (Bombay) presidency and six different centres. The southern (Madras) presidency sent 21 delegates from 13 different centres. Bengal sent three representatives all of whom were from Calcutta. W.C. Bonnerjee atrributed this small contingent from his home province to "a series of misfortunes, deaths, illness and the like".[6]

Seventy-two non-official Indian representatives included people apparently from various walks of life, or belonging to "most classes", as claimed by the official report of the Congress. There were lawyers, merchants and bankers, landowners, medical men, journalists, educationalists, religious teachers and reformers. If we look at their regional distribution, thirty-eight came from Bombay Presidency,[7] twenty-one from Madras. Apart from the Presidencies, seven representatives came from the four principal towns of North-Western Provinces and the Awadh and one each from the three towns of Punjab.[8] In other words, it was, despite lofty claims, a gathering of professionals, some landlords and businessmen, representing primarily the three presidencies of British India. In their social composition too, the members of the early Congress belonged predominantly to the high caste Hindu communities and this pattern continued unchanged for more than two decades of its existence. This limitation of participation did not fluster the member of the congress, as they complacently claimed to represent the whole nation; but it obviously put some constraints on their programmes.[9]

We were confronted with sharp and categorical formulations made by the Communists on the nature of the Congress-led mass movements against imperialism.[10] 'Even Dange's book *Gandhi vs Lenin,* which sought to differentiate between the historical reality in Russia and India, did not make any analysis of India's colonial reality specifically; it only discussed some issues comparatively.[11]

Thus began our quest to learn what the Congress Movement against imperialism was all about and how one was to understand the Gandhi-led mass movements in colonial India. From an empirical study of the communist 'party policy' the focus shifted to studying the relation of the party to the surrounding society.

A major source of inspiration were the writings of Antonio Gramsci and as he put it...

The history of a party can only be the history of a particular social group. But this group is not isolated; it has friends, kindred groups, opponents, enemies. The history of any given party can only emerge from and complex portrayal of the totality of society and state. The historian, though given everything its due importance in the overall picture, will emphasize above all the real effectiveness of the party, its determining force, positive and negative, in having contributed to bringing certain events about and in having prevented other events from taking place.[12]

This work is neither intended nor claims to be a 'complex portrayal' of colonial India's society and the state. It only takes this methodological approach as its point of departure to raise some question and discuss a few aspects based on an empirical study of Indian political life during the period 1920-47. This is in the hope that the path towards a more complex treatment of the subject can thus be opened up historiographically.[13]

One question constantly rose to the surface throughout the course of this work : if Marxism is the theory–the 'science'–

of historical reality, then what was the nature of the Marxism upheld by the Communist Movement in India?

This central preoccupation with the Marxism of the Communist movement logically led to a large emphasis being placed on the role of ideology and the politico-ideological implications of a national liberation struggle against imperialism for class politics, organization and consciousness. Class was not a self-sufficient category in colonial India; it was still in a process of formation.

The history of the Indian people's struggle against imperialism was ideologically over-determined because of the fully structured colonial ideology of the ruling power and the corresponding evolution of a nationalist ideology which sought to replace it – aiming at overthrowing colonialism. The ideological over-determination was even more pronounced due to the fact that the struggle between the Congress-led mass movements and British imperialism was fought on the terrain of 'hegemony' in which ideology was bound to play a major part. 'Ideology' not in the sense that it is superimposed on economic reality and 'objective forces', but in the sense in which ideology is itself a material force and an objective basis for political action.

A.K. Gopalan, who started as a Congressman and later joined the Communist Party of India (CPI), gave a moving account of how the congress movement broke the even tenor of so many lives and captured the imagination of the people.[14] However, during the course of the national movement the communists did not acknowledge this.

It is only that some communists in India, grudgingly acknowledged the 'reality' of the anti-imperialist struggle which overwhelmed the consciousness of different classes. However, it is of crucial significance that this reality of anti-imperialist nationalism is still identified with 'peasant consciousness' and the working class is meticulously excluded from it. B.T. Ranadive writes:-

How is it that despite a blatantly reactionary class policy the Congress succeeded in getting the masses and forcing the

British to retreat? How is it that the vast numbers from the peasantry, consisting of diverse lower castes, joined the Congress? The appeal of nationalism and anti-imperialism attracted the peasant who found no difficulty in identifying his misery with foreign rule. This was the new class reality- the unity forged by imperialist exploitation – which the congress fully utilized, and those who pitted themselves against it were inevitably routed. [15]

An anti-imperialist, popular national movement of the type led by the Congress in India needs to be analysed at various levels. Gramsci's method of historical analysis can prove very useful. [16]

Now Roy concluded, the masses were politiciesed mass and straining at the Gandhian leash which prevented mass militancy. He wrote that there was '*an undeniable existence in India of a widespread feeling of national solidarity, of national enthusiasm and desire to end the present system of government*. .....' that being the case, the masses were ready for a radical programme. [17]

The masses of the Indian people('s) .... consciousness must be aroused first of all. And the cause for which they fight must include their immediate needs. What does the man in the street need? The only aspiration of his life is to get two meals a day........... The abstract doctrine of national self- determination leaves them passive [18]......

Considering the fact that Roy was an 'inspired' student of Lenin and the Russian Revolution, it is inexplicable why he did not remember that this 'abstract doctrine' was a major force in the oppressed areas of the Tsarist empire and the recognition of this contributed significantly to Bolshevik success. Roy's *Manifesto* in fact contains a near denial of the role of nationalist ideology by saying : 'The cause of this awakening......... is to be looked for in their (masses') age-long economic exploitation and social slavery. *The mass revolt is directed against the propertied class, irrespective of nationality.* It is simply deluding oneself to think that the great ferment of popular energy.......... is the result of the non-cooperation agitation.

Reviewing the 'Revolt of Labour of India' at the beginning of 1922, Roy revealed his shallow or careless use of the term 'consciousness'. He wrote : 'Indian labour may be illiterate........... (but) they feel in every moment the lash of the exploiters. *Torture and stomach pangs are enough to awaken them to class-consciousness* and mass politicization flowed his 'exposure theory' - expose the leaders and win over the masses.

The most of the leaders of India's freedom struggle were helped in their careers by the bounty of both nature and circumstances. Like Jawaharlal Nehru and Subhash Chandra Bose. They were either scions of semi aristocratic families with leisure and learning at their door-steps. Or like vallabhi Patel and Rajagopalachari, whose paths to political eminence were eased by ready recognition by Mahatma Gandhi. Indira had the advantage of being the darling daughter of Nehru. Above all most of them belonged to the new urban middle class or more aptly the 'bourgeoisie' with Metropolitan centres, like Bombay, Calcutta, Madras or Ahmedabad as the base of their operations.[19]

Congress and Jagjivan Ram

Jagjivan Babu, who belonged to grassroot, lacked all the traits of a class leaders who had inherited from their vintage. He was born and brought up primarily in a poor family without a varitable back ground. He had his education not at Harrow and Cambridge, not even at Delhi or Madras, but in a small village. He started his political career not as an idol of the masses or as a romantic revolutionary but as a worker for the masses of the people of the who were down-trodden and neglected and that too at the time when service to such people was not in vogue. It is by the sheer strength of his character and independence of his spirit that Jagjivan Babu has worked his way up to the present status.[20]

He passed his I.Sc. examination in 1928 and went to Calcutta for further studies and joined the Vidyasagar College. In Calcutta he came into contact with various men, some of them from the backward classes. He helped in setting up various Ravidas Sabhas. His initial success was encouraging.[21]

In Calcutta he began to wear khadi; but he was not a regular user of khadi till 1932. while in Calcutta he took to the charkha but because of his various other activities both as a student and as a leader he could not spin much. But in five or six months he had enough yarn to make a 4½ yards dhoti. He found time for spinning, for meeting various types of leaders and for political and social activities, for organizing Ravidas Sabhas and reading literature. He organized a conference in willington park which made him a known man in nationalistic circles. The conference was great success, nearly 10,000 persons attending it.[22]

Some senior members of the Dalit Sudhar Sabha, which was started by the congress attended the Wellington Park Conference. They began to take an interest in him. Among them were J.M. Sen Gupta, Subhas Chandra Bose, B.C. Roy and P.C. Ghosh,; they took notice of him and encouraged him in his activities.

Mani Mukherjee was one of the pioneers of communist thought in Calcutta. He was a school teacher and lived in a house at the corner of Bow Bazaar and college street. He used to distribute cyclostyled communist literature to the young men of Calcutta. Jagjivan met him and had many discussions with him. Mani gave him the communist manifesto drafted by Marx and Engels which Jagjivan read. He became interested in the labour movement in the country for the first time.[23]

In the meanwhile the commission headed by Sir John Simon arrived in Bombay on February 5, 1928. "Simon go back" shouts rent the air in various cities of India. Jagjivan organized bid demonstrations in Calcutta. It was the time of the Bardoli Satyagrah under the leadership of Sardar Patel. In Punjab,

Lala Lajpat Rai was injured in lathi charge, later on he died. A police officer, Saunders was shout dead by Bhagat Singh, Raj Guru and Sukhdev.

Those were the years, particularly 1924 to 1928, when Mahatma Gandhi confined his attention to khadi and communal peace. The ghastly communal riots of that year would have daunted a less ardent sprit. Mahatma Gandhi wrote lengthy articles on communal peace in the pages of his paper *Young India*. He chided the Hindus roundly for this great disfigurement of a fair land. He had faster in the house of a Muslim in a symbolic effort to promote harmony between the two communities, he wanted them to come together for fighting the common enemy, the British.[24]

It was at the Calcutta Congress in December 1928 that Jagjivan saw Mahatma Gandhi for the first time. But he saw him then only from a great distance; there was no possibility of a talk.[25]

Gandhi laid stress on spinning and he was listened to by a great number of persons all over the country. His sphere of influence was widening and growing fast. Even Jawaharlal Nehru who had a Western outlook on most of the things listened to Gandhi with respect and took to spinning and khadi which he called "the livery for freedom".

Mahatma Gandhi's ears were tuned to the beating of the hearts of the countrymen. His appeals always struck a note of harmony in the ears and hearts of common men. His greatest concern he said at Calcutta was the hardness of the hearts of the educated in particular. He called spinning "the gateway of our salvation." The inspiring example of the Mahatma made young Jagjivan vow to devote himself to the masses.

At the same time as the Congress was being held there was an All Party Conference at Calcutta. Jinnah attended it and spoke demanding one-third of the seats for the Muslims in the Central Legislature, reservations for the Muslims in the Punjab and Bengal and vesting of residuary powers in the

Provinces in a Federal Constitution and the unconditional separation of Sind. This attitude of Jinnah was also later emphasised at a meeting in early 1929, presided over by the Aga Khan. At this meeting were made demands of a more inflexible nature which opened the path for the later partition of India.

Jagjivan was one of those who saw clearly the character of the Muslim League from the earliest and he exposed it fearlessly in many meetings he organised in Calcutta in 1929.

Mahatma Gandhi gave a call to the nation for the boycott of foreign cloth and liquor. The Viceroy saw trouble ahead. He wrote in a letter to his father in January 1929: "We have got a lot of tiresome shoals and storms around us - communists and people who are preaching Independence and political agitators, of all this in a country where antigovernment agitation is apt to be taken at its face value and where there is little public opinion or judgment by which the extravagance of such things can be weighed. In short, I look forward to a stormy year; and in the present temper of the Indian politicians, I do not see any great prospect of easily getting things back to smooth waters at present."[26]

Irwin considered Nehru, Subhas Bose and some other young Congress leaders as communists. The intelligence despatches from Calcutta about Jagjivan described him as a young man who had strong leftist leanings, Irwin himself belonged to the Conservative Party in England and disliked any utterance that smacked even remotely of the radical. By this time he could now very well anticipate the dimensions of the struggle ahead in India.

In March 1929, a number of Trade Union leaders, some of them communists, were brought to trial in what has to be known as the Meerut Conspiracy case. Commenting on it Mahatma Gandhi observed: "The Government is giving the usual periodical exhibition of its red claws which usually remain under cover." Jagjivan organised a meeting in Calcutta consisting mostly of students and roundly condemned the trial of the Trade Union leaders.

The Government introduced a Public Safety Bill in the Central Assembly. Sir John Simon also was witnessing the proceedings of the Assembly one day when Bhagat Singh buried a bomb from the public gallery. It fell near the Treasury Benches, Irwin described it in a letter to his father: "Two men in the public gallery proceeded to throw two bombs at the Government Benches. Luckily, partly owing to the bomb being bad and to a combination of fortuitous circumstances, they did practically no damage and everybody concerned had a most miraculous escape. Having discharged the bombs one of the men proceeded to shoot with a revolver, which again luckily jammed after the first two shots had missed. There were the usual hair-breadth escapes of the people who had moved a yard or so away one way or the other, who must have been killed if they had stayed where they were. Anyhow the whole thing was a Providential deliverance. The Assembly was immediately adjourned."

Soon after this incident, there were a large number of arrests in Delhi, Punjab, Uttar Pradesh and Bengal. Jagjivan accommodated in his house some young revolutionaries of Bengal and made arrangements for their stay later in Bihar. [27]

On 12th March, 1930 at 6.30 in the morning Mahatma Gandhi left his Ashram and began his 240 miles march to Dandi.

Eighty satyagrahis followed him, old persons and teenagers, harijans and mill workers, scholars and editors. Mahatma carrying his long bamboo stick led at so brisk a pace that even the young men found it difficult to keep up. The dust on the path was strewn with yellow leaves.

On the 6th April Gandhi reached the sea. There he picked up some salt left by the waves and by this simple gesture broke the British law which said that it was punishable for anybody to possess salt not obtained through Government monopoly agencies. Sarojini Naidu who had sought to stay his hand now stood by his side. He had walked for 24 days and the eyes of the entire nation were on him. There were picketings and hartals throughout the country; processions were taken out in large numbers. The atmosphere became tense. At Peshawar the 39th Garhwal Rifles were asked to fire on a peaceful large procession. The sepoys refused and some of them were later courtmartialled.[28]

At Dharsana Salt Depot the peaceful satyagrahis were beaten up mercilessly by the police. United Press Correspondent, Webb Miller wrote: "In eighteen years of reporting in twenty two countries, I have never witnessed such harrowing scenes as at Dharsana. From where I stood I heard the sickening whack of clubs on unprotected skulls." But Irwin in a letter to King George V described the incident as minor injuries to a few persons.

Jagjivan was in Arrah in the summer of 1930. He organised many secret meetings in the town. The friends he met agreed that the organisational work for a big demonstration at Patna should be entrusted to him. His efficiency at organising was generally admired. After organising an impressive demonstration in Patna, he returned to Calcutta.[29]

In Calcutta there was a huge procession to protest against the beating of satyagrahis. Jagjivan Ram was one of the young men who organised and led this procession. All the jails in India were full to overflowing. In Calcutta there were many police atrocities; peaceful satyagrahis were beaten up. Some revolutionary suggested that Jagjivan should not court arrest as he might be able to do good work by remaining outside at this time of stress. Jagjivan avoided being arrested. But when he was leading the procession he received some blows from the police lathis.

The first Round Table Conference was opened by the King on 12th November, 1930. Mahatma Gandhi was in jail and none of the Congress leaders took part in the R.T.C.

deliberations. In June, Motilal Nehru had told the Government of India that negotiations were possible only if the Government would support the demand for full responsible government of the country subject to the terms of agreement as to transfer of power necessitated by India's special needs and position and which could be discussed in the R.T.C. Sapru and Jayakar requested the Viceroy's permission to interview Mahatma Gandhi in Yerawada jail and confer with him in an effort to bring about understanding and to induce the Congress to be represented at the R.T.C. No decision was reached in the meeting between them and Gandhi. Then they took themselves to Naini jail for another conference, this time with both the Nehrus. Sapru wanted to have a meeting jointly with all the leaders. The Viceroy permitting, the Nehrus were removed to Yerawada jail. Vithalbhai Patel and Sarojini Naidu were also brought there. But the leaders would not budge from their demand for independence and a transfer of all powers, political as well as economic.

A big youth rally was organised in Patna. Jagjivan Ram was the chief speaker. Nearly seventy thousand persons attended the rally. Jagjivan spoke for an hour demanding the immediate release of Mahatma Gandhi. He observed in the course of the speech that the spirit of India could not be crushed by bayonets and bullets.[30]

Jagjivan Ram had during the year 1930 plunged into national activities. His health was impaired – he had borne the brunt of many lathi charges and he was ailing for many weeks and found that he could not sit for his B.Sc. examination. In March and April 1931 there was comparatively less political activity and Jagjivan thought he would sit for the final degree examination. He passed securing high marks.[31]

Early in his youth he took up congress work and when occasions demanded, he courted imprisonment along with others. When in 1937 there was talk for the first time of having congress miniseries in provinces and Mahatmaji laid down the condition that the congress would form ministries only when an assurance was given that the Governors will run the government with the advice of the ministers. But the governors refused to give such assurance in the first instance. Many provinces then has a congress majority. Therefore, no cabinet, which did not enjoy the support of the congress, would function constiututionally. Still the governors in accordance with the central policy tried to form Ministries in all the provinces. [32]

Somehow or the other, certain attempt was made in Bihar to form independent ministry and Mr. Yunus formed an interim Ministry. Jagjivan Ram Babu had been elected a member of the Bihar legislature and Mr. Yunus tried hard to win him over and offered him a place in his cabinet, so that he may get the support of the Harijan members. But Jagjivan Ram Babu unhesitatingly spurned his offer and Ministership that went along with it. Dr. Rajendra Prasad having come to know of it informed Mahatmaji. He was greatly pleased and made a mention of this fact in one of his articles. The other leaders could make out that Jagjivan Ram was not only a determined worker, but also he was second to none in sacrifice when occasion demanded it. Thereafter, he joined the Working Committee of the Bihar Provincial Congress Committee and when the Congress formed a ministry sometimes later, he was appointed as Parliamentary Secretary. Though he wished to be a minister, but did not press because of Mr. Jaglal Chaudhery's inclusion. In this post, he worked hard and fulfilled his responsibility very well, thereby received praise from all quarters. His relations with the congress workers became closer day by day and when the great movement launched by Mahatmaji started in 1940, he took due part in it.

When the congress decided to join Central Cabinet in 1946, Jagjivan Ram Babu naturally attracted the attention and was taken in the Congress cabinet. He was young. Perhaps, the youngest minister in the interim government. Still he managed the labour ministry well. He was in the minister of labour for about six years. The central Acts relating to labour passed during his regime as Labour minister indicate what he did a lot to improve workers' conditions. To have an adequate appreciation of his work, one must look at the change effected in the living condition of the workers.

Like Rajendra Babu and Mahatmaji, Jagjivan Ram not only believes in simplicity but also mlives simple. He had the zeal of a missionery. Hard work did not deter him and he had learnt to speak out his mind and act up to his beliefs. When he was confronted with a problem he formulated his opinion only after viewing it in all its aspects. But once his opinion is formed, nothing can make him waiver. His whole life is a story of dedication. [33]

As a fighter for freedom, Babu Jagjivan Ram is one of the pioneers of Trade Union Movement in India. There was a time when trade unions were looked upon as a threat to establish governments and threats they indeed were. One motivating force that guided trade union activity in the pre-independency India was the desire to wrest freedom from alien government, whether through the Non-cooperation days or the Quit India Movement. The trade unions in our country invariably responded to the call of the nation with all their organized force and ultimately paved the way for independence. It is due to selfless efforts and undefatigueable work of the men like Babu Jagjivan Ram that the energies of the farmers in the fields and workers in the factories were galvanized and trade unions in our country emerged as instruments of the nation in its historic struggle. [34]

While in Hazari Bagh Jail, the socialist prisoners organized classes on Marxim which was the raging fashion of the day. It attracted many young Congress workers who swallowed the teachings with avidity. Jagjivan Ram felt that the socialist teachers started with a bias in favour of Marxism and did not engourage independent thinking. The classes were an effort more at indoctrination than a quest for knowledge. Having read

Marxism independently, he himself started taking separate classes in Marxist's theory and practices. He would also lecture on Gandhian doctrines and their far-reaching implications and encouraged his liternes to learn, to evaluate critically, both Gandhism and Marxism. It would appear that Jagjivan Ram Babu had a deep interest in political thought and had an analytical mind to compare and crystalise his thinking vis-a-vis the political thought of Gandhiji and Marx. He would call out the political meaning which was directly in the interest of the masses of the people and shun all ideologies which run contra to their welfare and independent expression and existence.

Even though buried deep in his studies and taking his 'ASANS and PRANAYAM every day, Jagjivan Ram was no reclusile. He was full of human kindness. Just as injustice turned his heart into steel sufferings and distress made it equally soft. All this helped him to become extremely wise in political thinking and thus his political thought became an important instrument for liberating the masses of the millions of the depressed classes of India.

On coming out of jail, his first concern was to resume his ceaseless political and depressed classes league activities.

By June, 1942, India was anticipating the possible advent of the Japanese. The masses were so nurtured that they were prepared to think of them as liberators, But, Gandhiji was clear in his mind. The congress leaders also had no illusions. "I would rather shout than submit to the Japanese or any foreign power" wrote Gandhiji on July 26, 1942. the country was simmering, raged, frustration and discontent were struggling to find an outlet. Indian humanity was one vast bulk of highly inflammable material. The Govt. foolishly supplied the spark.

The All India Congress Committee met in Bombay on August 7, 1942 and adopted a resolution assuring the British that an Indian Government would resist aggression with all the armed as well as non-violent forces at its command and urged immediate declaration of independence. But if the appeal failed, the congress, resolution further said, would be compelled to start a civil disobedience movement. After the resolution was adopted, Gandhiji addressed the delegates after midnight on August 8. He wanted to have one more interview with the viceroy. But the British were in no mood for parleys. Gandhi, Nehru, Mrs. Naidu and scores of others were awakened sometime after they had gone to sleep and carried off to prison[36]

The whole of India was in revolt the next morning. Gandhiji had given only two slogans. He had declared to the British :-

"Quit India"

"He had told his countrymen"

"Do or die"[35]

The details of the movement were chalked out in the vaguest outline. Each man was to be his own leader after Gandhi and other leaders were arrested.

Jagjivan Ram and the late Prof. Abdul Bari and some others who were putting up in a hotel, were informed by a friendly source in the early hours of the morning about the arrest of national leaders. Gandhiji had expressed his desire to see both Jagjivan Ram and Abdul Bari on the 9th morning and they hoped to receive first hand guidance and instructions. Though there were whispers of Gandhiji's possible arrest, responsible congressment thought that the Govt. would not be foolish and will surely give Gandhiji a chance of meeting the Viceroy.

Jagjivan Ram left for Patna immediately. As secretary of the Bihar Congress, he would have much to do reaching there. He felt that organizational work had become more important than the agitational. If the congress was to lead the resistence movement, it must develop a resistence organization.

All important localities in Patna had been barricaded by British soldiers. The barricades could be crossed only on passes issued by the civil authorities. The passes were naturally not given to the leaders of the rebellions and they would not apply for it. The organization of a proper resistence movement, Jagjivan Ram felt, was not practicable. Congress volunteers had not the necessary training and the conditions were not propitious. The revolt could not be developed into an insurrection and the insurrection into a machinery for seizure of power. A country wide well coordinated resistence was not practicable and the only way out under the circumstances was to have widely scattered pockets of resistence unapproachable by armed units and where the spirit of the August Revolution would survive. The situation was handled in this manner by Jagjivan Ram. It was again an evidence of his political wisdom. [36]

When Khan Bahadur Omar, the Additional Magistrate went to arrest him, Jagjivan Ram had on his person several important papers and some money. But no search was made. Omar told him that he could take his own time in getting ready. But Jagjivan Ram was in no mood to incur obligation. He handed over the papers and the money to the congress workers gathered there and gave final instructions to Jamail Mazhari. Thus began Jagjivan Ram's second baptism of jail life.

What a galaxy of eminent men met him in the Bankipur Jail; Rajendra Prasad, Dr. S.K. Sinha, Dr. A.N. Sinha, Sarangdhar Singh, Satyanarayan, Maha Maya Prasad, Phulan Prasad Verma and many others were already there. They were lodged in the hospital jail in one room. Rajendra Babu was given the operation theatre. After a few days, came Dev Sharan Sinha who informed that the people were being terribly harassed and the soldiers were the masters of the situation. Yet, occasionally, the people held unpleasant surprises for them.

Jagjivan Ram was released after 14 months from the jail in indifferent health. The Bihar CID very diligently shadowed him wehreever he went and kept a close watch.

In September 1944, Jagjivan Ram undertook an extensive tour of Centra Povince and Bombay, both for Congress and the League work. At Nagpur, the working committee of the all India Depressed Classes League met under his president ship and prepared the memorandum which was presented on behalf of the all India Depressed Classes League to the Sapru Committee. Later , finding that effective and useful political work of the congress could not be carried on, he organized with the assistance of Prof. Abdul Bari, a constructive workers' organization at Patna which continued to do useful work till the end of 1945.

Jagjivan Ram was faced with a delicate situation. He could not, holding the views he did, assert that the untouchables were a separate nation. He could not at the same time, leave untouchables' interest completely unrepresented in any arrangement that took place or in any agreement that was to be made when Rajgopalacharya evolved a formula for congress leage understanding in June, 1944. the Harijans were certainly a part of the Indian nation, but, being the most persecuted minority, it was only fair that their interests should be safeguarded. [37]

Jagjivan Ram shows how the Mahatma applied his truth and non-violence to the question of untouchability and caste. The other link through which he wanted to forge a greater unity and integration was through abolition of untouchability and the revivl of *chaturvanic concept in all its purity*- month after mont, week after week, he returned to the theme in his *Young India* and later In the *Harijan* (page 242). Jagjivan Ram quotes Gandhi:

"If we do not efface untouchability we shall be effaced from the face of the earth – The four Varnas are fundamental, natural, esstential, while the innumerable castes and sub-castes aare excresence – Varnas fulfil nature's law of conservation of human energy and true economics. It is the classification of different systems of self-culture. It is the best possible adjustment of social stability and progress. It tries to include families of a particular way of purity of life, only it does not leave the decision whether a particular family belongs to a particular type, to the idiosyncracies or interested judgement of a few individuals. It trusts to the principle of heredity and being only a system of culture, does not hold that an injustice is done if an individual

or family has to remain in a group in spite of their decision to change their mode of life for the better. It is difficult to imagine a more harmonious adjustment. Caste does not connote superiority or inferiority. It simply recognizes different outlook and corresponding modes of life. Caste is the classification of different systems of selfculture. It is the extension of the principles of family. Both aare governed by blood and heredity. Its value from the economic point of view was very great. It ensured hereditary skill. It limited competition. It was a remedy against pauperism. It had the advantage of trade guilds. It was man's experiment in social adjustment in the laboratory of Indian society. If we fan prove it to be a success it can be offered to the world as a lesson and as the best remedy against heartless competition. Varana is inherent in human nature. Hinduisms has reduced it to a science. Caste, at present, is a distortion. But in our eagerness to abolish the distortion let lus not abolish the original. It is not human invention but an immutable law of nature, the statement of a tendency that is ever present and at work like Newton's Law of Gravitation."

After this revolting justification of Varna and caste, this grotesque glorification of a system which decrees inequility to be an eternal law of nature and which applies to heredity and blood for dtermining a man's status in society how can Jagjivan Ram say that Gandhi succeeded in shaking the foundations of the caste system? Shri Jagjivan Ram observes that ... "Mahatma Gandhi uses Varna and caste as intergangeable terms and believes that all types of men can be categorized under four broad occupations, viz., teaching, defending, wealth-producing and manual labour" and this is to be a hereditary system.

Hence, Jagjivan Ram became the victim of the caste Hindu leaders and accepted the thousand old system of varna based on birth.

Congress and Kamaraj

In the small town of Virudupatti, now known as Virudunagar, was born Kamaraj, on the 15 day of July, 1903, affectionately known as Kamatchi. Kamatchi Kamaraj, later known to the world as Kamaraswamy Kamaraj. Kamaraj belonged to Nadar community.[38] Nadars professionally were considered a community of toddy[39] tappers and were socially considered, in the rigid caste-ridden society of the early twenties, even beneath caste and would not be admitted to some of the Hindu temples. This social discrimination has been responsible for the spirit of protest and revolt, in Kamaraj's life and thought against social inequities and social injustice.

While still a growing child, Kamaraj had to face a series of calamities. Grand-father, Chinnappa passed away and a little later, father Kumarswami Nadar also died. Kamaraj was then in school and with these sudden deaths of the family bread-earners, family responsibilities fell on the two grief-stricken and elderly ladies. Grand-mother, Parvati Ammal and mother, Sivakami who themselves were naturally heart-broken and disheartened.[40] They were without the means to bring up child Kamaraj and his younger sister. Though they struggled to keep Kamaraj in school for some time, he had to leave school and part with his studies prematurely. This has had an imprint on Kamaraj's life and from this can be traced two other psychological influences in his life.

There is always an incident or two in the life of every great man that shapes his future; may it be frustration or a frustrated love, or, be it some humiliation that arouses the man in man, and each such incident becomes an emotional thrust in such lives.[41]

What was this Jallianwala incident that aroused the man Kamaraj into a national effort? Kamaraj, even as a youngman, was a very keen reader of the Tamil daily "*Swadeshimitran.*" Swadeshimitran can rightly and proudly claim to have informed and shaped young Kamaraj's mind, as in those hectic days of the national struggle, it was vividly reporting, within the limits of the forced censorship, the repressive acts of the British in the different parts of India, and therefore, to understand Kamaraj and his future, it is necessary to recreate "Jallianwala" which changed the course of his life and has continued to dominate his life and thought.[42]

This was the horror of Jallianwala Bagh which changed the life and course of young Kamaraj. The boy in him suddenly matured into a determined youth and the youth, in course of time, was to avenge the honour of his country by doing his all for the expulsion of the British from India, with all their O' Dwyers, Dyers, Johnsons, O' Briens, and Bosworth Smiths.[43]

The happenings of 1919 and the horror of Jallianwala made Kamaraj, though a young of bare 16, the determined man he is today or has been ever since. He had made up his mind, come what may. His relatives did not matter, nothing mattered; his country was a slave; he was a slave; Jallianwala had shown, with its brutal naked-ness, how a slave people could be trampled under, how a Bosworth Smith could tear the veil from over the face of helpless women and then trifle with the self-respect of self-respecting ladies.

1919 was a departure in more ways than one. He met with Dr. Varadarajulu Naidu in that year. Dr. Naidu was a political orator of his day and a nationalist of respect and repute. At Virudupatti, the home town of Kamaraj, Dr. Naidu and others addressed an influential public meeting which attracted an audience not only from the town but from rural parts, till then in age old slumber and political apathy. The meeting was organised by Kamaraj, a mere volunteer of small town Virudupatti. Dr. Naidu had seen even much smaller gatherings get disorganised but young Kamaraj had organised such a large gathering, so painstaking and so well to the last detail, that Dr. Naidu saw an altogether different touch in it. Dr. Naidu enquired about the excellence of the arrangements and young Kamaraj was presented to him. Varadarajulu Naidu, the great leader, was so impressed with the young man and his modest behaviour that to the audience itself, he was all praise for Kamaraj. Years later, this wayside association between a leader and a small town worker blossomed into friendship and admiration and a time came when in 1955, Dr. Naidu paid his tribute to Kamaraj saying:[44]

"I met him first in 1919 when I went to Virudunagar on Swarajist propaganda. I was surprised at the arrangements he had made at such a short notice for a very big meeting for me to address. He managed the situation very cleverly when there was some confusion as I was being taken in procession. Then he might have been twenty years of age. From that day to this he was serving the country in a manner which is well-known to Tamils. Only the unselfish can understand the incomparable service he has done to the Motherland. Those who expect him to confer favours on them will never understand his unspoilt life."

"If Kamaraj had not continued to be the undisputed leader of Tamilnad Congress, there is no doubt Tamilnad would have met the same fate as the Kerala and the Andhra Congress. So it is that the pride of place for safeguarding the Congress interests in Tamilnad goes to Kamaraj and good men will never forget it. He takes the first place among those who had served the country without the wherewithal of life, without any aspiration of building up fortune for himself or to enjoy life, and who had borne untold sufferings. A poor man to the poor, a servant to a servant, it is a virtue to praise Kamaraj."

"Many may recall that in 1946, Mahatma Gandhi issued a statement condemning Kamaraj. I wrote to the Mahatma then: Kamaraj is in the forefront of those in South India who have served Gandhism and the Congress with pure 'Bhakti'.[45] It is not proper that you should make a wrong statement on such a pure man as Kamaraj Nadar. I humbly inform you that it will be for the good of the country if you do not interfere."

"In a card, Gandhiji replied: "Alright, I will do so. I shall not hereafter interfere."

"Love of the country and service to the people are Kamaraj's religion. Equality and fraternity are his guides of conduct."[46]

"Kamaraj is a true Tamilian, a good man and an unselfish man. He possesses keen intelligence and discrimination in an abundant measure. He does not think on caste, communal or racial lines. Those who say he has them are themselves the self-seekers. One might say he has renounced everything. I am very glad that it has been left to him and his regime to shut the mouth of those who have been blabbering that only English educated lawyer pundits can rule the country and that others were unqualified for the task."

Reverting to the public meeting arranged for Dr. Naidu and the public praise showered on Kamaraj, we find that the relatives of Kamaraj got more perturbed; the young man must be sent out of Virudupatti for a brainwash. And so Kamaraj found himself brought to Tiruvantapuram, to be an apprentice at his maternal uncle's shop. To Kamaraj, the change was no brainwash; it was a brain stimulant. Kamaraj was looking for an opportunity to express himself and this he got soon enough.

Near Tiruvantapuram lay the small town of Vaikom. In Vaikom, bigotry reigned supreme. The diehards, the Sanatanists,[47] discriminated inhumanly against the Dalits and would not even let the poor Dalits use the public roads of the town. Religious fanaticism was so maddeningly perverse that a so called high caste would take an immediate purifying bath if perchance the shadow of a Dalits, walking on the good earth, happened to fall or was feared to have fallen on the sacrosanct high caste Hindu. The local Congress Party, therefore, decided to take up cudgels on behalf of the Harijans in pursuance of Mahatma Gandhi's Harijan uplift movement. Kamaraj enrolled himself as a Satyagrahi.[48]

Success at Vaikom spurred Kamaraj to further activity. In 1925, started the Flag Satyagraha in Nagpur, then the provincial capital of the Central Provinces and Berar. The British rulers had imposed a prohibition that no Indian could carry, on his person a dagger, spear, etc. This led to nation-wide protests in all parts of India. Kamaraj, then operating from Madurai, under the leadership of the local Congress leader Somyajulu, organised an impressive procession called "Pichchuvadu Oorvalam" i.e. procession of bearers of daggers and spears. The procession, in its bold defiance of British authority then in its imperial height, was a resounding success and this success established Kamaraj as a worker of more than Virudupatti standing it gave him the status of a district worker, and now deserving of more than local assignments.[49]

1927 was to see another success for Kamaraj which took him to the outer fringes of provincial party activity. Colonel Neill's statue, in a prominent thoroughfare of Madras, was a daily irritation to be self-respect of patriotic Indians. In the 1857 war of Indian Independence which the British, in their imperial haughtiness, seemed pleased to relegate as a native mutiny, Colonel Neill had blasted, rather mercilessly butchered, with his guns and cannon, hundreds of Indians; whose sin was their aspiration to independence. The Madras Congress Party joined issue with the British and demanded removal of Neill's statue. Bulusu Sambnurti was placed in charge of the agitation in Madras and Mahatma Gandhi blessed the people's movement. Batches of freedom fighters came from all over Tamilnad and on behalf of his native district of Ramanathapuram, Kamaraj led his devoted band of volunteers. Similar bands of workers came from other districts and in no time, the agitation was led loose in Madras with full force. The agitation finally succeeded and the despised and hated statue of Neill was ordered to be withdrawn. Kamaraj, amongst others, was the recipient of public recognition and this success of the cause in which Kamaraj had participated naturally enhanced his confidence in the righteousness of the path he had chosen as his life's ideal.

1927 was, in one sense, a cherished year for Kamaraj. That year, the Congress held its national session at Madras and resolved on independence as its goal. Jawahar Lal Nehru also attended the deliberations. Kamaraj convened the Indian Republican Congress under the leadership of Jawahar Lal Nehru and thus began virtually an era, first of acquaintance, then of friendship and later of comradeship between the man of the North and the man of the South; divergent in tastes but convergent in ideology. Nehru was an aristocrat and a western cosmopolitan while Kamaraj was a commoner and an Indian, with not a western air in him. The contrast between the two could not be greater but it is a remarkable get-together of history that the twin did meet.[50]

In 1933-34, Kamaraj got involved in the Virudunagar Bomb Case. The Madras Conspiracy Case had had inter-provincial repercussions and one of the approvers had implicated Kamaraj for his hand in armig the conspirators. Police investigation under a conscientious police Chief, reported a dead end and lack of clinching evidence against Kamaraj. The main case was, therefore, not pursued aginst Kamaraj. The subsidiary security proceedings asking Kamaraj to keep the king's peace were, however, initiated. His mentor, George Joseph, who along with Dr. Varadarajulu Naidu had come to entertain a very high opinion of Kamaraj, ably defended Kamaraj in court and it resulted in the discharge of Kamaraj from criminal proceedings. Thus ended too Kamaraj's way-side aberration into violence, His old friends recall that in 1939, Kamaraj used to stay at the Madras Mahajana Sabha Office, then functioning from Number 9, General Patters Road. Kamaraj's bed was in the Sabha library and was surrounded on all sides with the library almirahs and records; there was hardly any ventilation in the room and the old carpet on the floor was his bed. One of these days when he had hardly gone to bed and within minutes, the C.I.D. (Criminal Intelligence Department) followed him in pursuit but as the record room was surrounded by almirahs and files, Kamaraj was able to hide himself.[51] The C.I.D. searched the place but such has been the loyalty Kamaraj evokes in his colleagues that they denied having seen him anywhere there; knowing full well that if arrested, Kamaraj would get another jail term for a number of years. The situation was no doubt saved that day but to avoid future trouble and police risk, the inmates decided to ask one of the persons, running spray paint business, to sleep or stay in the record room, obstruct effectively the library passage and save Kamaraj in future at all costs.[52]

Kamaraj quietly borrowed a cart which took him to his modest house in town. Next morning, Kamaraj got up, quietly walked to the local Inspector who happened to be a friend of his, and asked him to arrest him. The Inspector-friend hesitated before doing an unpleasant and an anti-national job. Kamaraj, however, requested him to do his duty; telling him that by then, he had done his duty and, therefore, a police officer should do his duty. With the obstinate offering before him, the Inspector formally arrested Kamaraj and sent him to his earlier haunt, the Vellore Jail, and in the Vellore Jail and later in the Amravati Jail, Kamaraj was to spend nearly three years of his life, occupying his time reading books on history, classics. Thiru Kural and whatever else he could lay his hands on in Jail. In 1945, Kamaraj was released from Jail. [53]

Congress and G.D. Tapase

The political situation took a new turn in India when the Second World War broke out between Germany and her allies on the one side and England, America and their allies on the other. All the leaders of political parties in India were of the view that India had nothing to do with this War as it was confined to Europe and other remote places. But all of a sudden, one fine morning, the Viceroy of India proclaimed, on behalf of India, war against Germany and its allies. Thus, India was involved in the War without public opinion. Soldiers and arms, ammunition and other materials were rushed to the war-fields. On seeing these happenings, there was a country-wide discontent. Under the leadership of Gandhiji, the Congress decided to launch Non-Coooperation Movement. The Congress ministries in all the States, after ruling for a period of 27 months, resigned and the administration was taken over by the British bureaucrats.[54]

It was decided by me to offer the Satyagraha at 5.00 p.m. after attending a public meeting at Guruwar Paraj Maidan which was just in front of my office. My wife, with a small three-month old baby in her arms, had by then come back to Satara to attend the meeting. I spent the day meeting several friends. They all wished me well. Those who had offered the individual Satyagraha before me had been arrested and convicted. The maidan, where I was to address the meeting, calleing upon the people not to cooperate with the British War efforts, presented a good gathering. After seeing the crowd, the Sub-Inspector of Police, who was incharge of the meeting, decided to arrest me before I had addressed it. He did so and declared me arrested as a detenu. Sub-Inspector went in a tonga to the local sub-jail. It was very near our house. The news flashed rapidly. Police of the Government at that time was to arrest and convict the participants. For the Bombay Provincial Congress Committee, however, the policy of the Govt. was to detain such participants. According to the policy, Shri Shankar Rao Deo and Kaka Saheb Gadgil, leaders of M.P.C.C., were arrested and convicted after they had addressed the meetings. Even in Satara district, the President of the District Congress Committee, Shri Venkatrao pawar, who had offered the Satyagraha at Sirale, was arrested and convicted. My case was the first one in M.P.C.C. in which I had been detained.[55]

I was kept in the sub-jail for 14 days. During the night no light was provided in the cell. Though I was a detenu, yet my room used to be locked up during the day for some time and completely during the night. The District and Sessions Judge of Satara, Shri Salve, visited my cell. He inquired about me as I was known to him as a lawyer. I complained to him that though I was a political detenu, no light or reading facilities were provided to me whereas I was entitled to them. I heard that the authorities themselves were not aware of the facilities that should be given to such detenues. The only facility that I was getting was the home-cooked food. For 14 days or so, I was alone in the whole barrack. Still I passed my days happily, because I was voluntarily determined to face such an eventuality. Such a determination helped me a lot, not only on this occasion but also in several subsequent hours of trail.[56]

After the visit of the District and Sessions Judge, light was provided to me by fastening a lantern outside the door of my cell. Fortunately, the policeman on duty used to give me company for a while. On the 15th day, I was carried by bus to the railway station to make me catch a train for Poona. I was treated as a 'B' class detenu. As I reached Poona station, the son of Jedhe family, Shri Yeshwantrao Jedhe, a well known personality of M.P.CC., met me and inquired about me. He supplied me some reading material. The police insisted that I should travel by III class. I flatly refused to oblige them. Then by the morning train, which had a 'B' class compartment, I traveled to Nasik. Police took me to the Nasik Road where they asked me to take lunch at some hotel. They told me afterwards that henceforth I would be getting only the jail-food. I took my meals there. The hotel-owner refused to take any money from the police saying that he counted his gesture of providing food as humble service to the patriot. Then I was taken to the Cental Jail of Nasik.[57]

I was first taken by the warders to the camp number 3 where the Communist detenues were kept. There I saw some new faces – the workers and the leaders of the Communists Party of Bombay Province. Mr. Dange, the Communist Leader of international fame, was there. Mr. Chhannoo Singh of Sholapur, hero of the Marlial Law of Sholapur, welcomed me, while I thought that I had been wrongly put in the barrack of the Communists. I was theen taken to another barrack, where the leaders of the Bombay Provincial Congress Committee were kept.

During my stay in the jail, for about one year, only one interview took place. My elder brother and my wife came to see me. My daughter was also accompanying them. I tried to take my daughter in my arms but she was reluctant to come to me.

All of them were there for abut 10 minutes only. Then they left. I heard afterwards that my wife and brother, as they reached the Godavari Ramkund, wept bitterly because of the short duration of the meeting. After six months or so, the policy of the Government changed and the jail authorities started realizing the detenues one after another, according to their importance. As they started realeasing some of the senior and tried detenues started cutting jokes to me that I would have to stay for a longer period until my daughter was marriageable. I remained undaunted by such pranks and never worried as to when I would be set free. My turn came exactly after full one year of my detention. Coincidently, the same was the case with Mr. S.K. Patil. I returned home hale and hearty.[58]

I was relieved from Nasik Jail on Nov.30, 1941, alongwith Mr. S.K. Patil. At about 4.00 a.m. on 9th August, repeated knocks were heard by me. Then I woke up and made enquires as to who was knocking at the door. The Police (CID) Inspector told me that he had come to arrest me. He asked me to open the door. As a Gandhian, I immediately opened the door and asked for sometime to prepare myself for accompanying them. After about half an hour, I left my pregnant wife with a small baby on her side and accompanied the police. I took nothing with me and also there was no time left to think of such a thing.[59]

As I entered the jail-barrack, Bhausaheb Soman welcomed me by saying, "Ganpati, so you have come." Though there was no light provided in the barrack, yet we instantly recognized each othe by our intuition and voices.

After about 2 months, I got a fever that lasted some days. My friends were worried. Even Balasaheb Kher and morarjibhai used to visit me and make inquires about my health. My courage never failed me even when I was having a continuous fever. Fortunately for me, the fever came down soon. I was advised to take anea to clear my bowels. I had never administered such a thing before. A friend of mine did this for me. My redovery made everyone happy and cheerful because the feeling of brogherhood prevails in jail also in the meantime. After 15 months of my detention, one day, all of a sudden. I recived my orders for release.[60]

Congress and Peer Mohammed Munis (Dalit Muslim)

From the womb of renaissance, Peer Mohammed Munis was a committed Writer and journaliost who was in the darkness of history. He was related to the poor Dalit Muslim family.

He was born in 1882 in the Champaran, Betia Nagar, Bihar. He had not recived the school education, yet he started to write the stories related to the villages. His first article was published in 1907. In 1909, his second article was published in Karmyogi. Reacting the same, the famous writer, Balkrishna Bhatt, had to say... 'You write and always write. After some time, people would realize you and your article.'

When the movement was started by the farmers in the year of 1907-1908 and thousands were imprisoned by the British, he wrote the article- *"The 200 years rule of the British Empire"*.

He also toured Allahabad and met the famous writer and activist, Ganeash Shankar Vidyarthi. He joined the Congress and became one of its followers. He wanted to highlight the problems of thousands farmers of Champaran. From that point, Gandhiji had to start the Champaran Satyagrah. The year of 1937 was very important in the life of Munis because in that year, he was elected a member of the District Council of Champaran on the ticket of Congress. Munis was a social worker as well as a committed true patriot.

Many times, he was victimized by the Police and suffered a lot. His last days were full of miseries. He had to face financial problems as well.

On the 8th April, 1945, he had a setback, when his son, Mohammed Sulaiman died at the age of 26 after suffering from the deseas of Dibeties, 26 yaers old. He also died due to this desease.

References

1. Manoranjan Pandey, Congress Leadership in Workers and Peasant Movement, H.K. Publication, Shakti Nagar Extension Delhi. 52. 1992, p.1.
2. Sekhar Bandyopadhyay, From Plessey to Partition: A history of modern India, Orient Longman, New Delhi. p. 218.
3. Ibid, p. 219.
4. Bombay Gazette, (28 Dec. 1885).
5. Bombay Gazette, M. Pandey, p. 70.
6. Bombay Gazette, M. Pandey, p. 70.
7. Ibid, p. 222.
8. Ibid, p. 223.
9. Mlhrotra 1971: 412.
10. Shashi Joshi, Struggle for hegemony in India (1920-47), Sage Publications, New Delhi, 1992 p. 10.
11. S.A Gange, Gandhi versus Lenin, Bombey, 1921, photocopy, ACHI, JNU, New Delhi.
12. Antonio Gramsci, Selections from the Prison Notebooks, New York, 1971, p. 151.
13. Struggle for Hegemony, p. 11.
14. A.K. Gopalan, In the cause of the People, Bombay, 1973.
15. B.T.Ranadive, 'Caste, Class and Property Relations', in Economic and Political Weekly, Annual Number, 1969, Emphasis added.
16. Gramsci, Prison Notebooks, p. 167.
17. Roy, Present Events in India, Communist International, No. 3, 1921.
18. Abhikari, Documents. Vol. 1, p. 344.
19. Ibid, p. 350.
20. Dr. Naunihal Singh, Jagjivan Ram: Symbol of Social Change, Sandeep Prakashan, 1735 Tri Nagar, Delhi. 1977 p. 4.
21. Ibid, p. 5.
22. Devendra Prasad Sharma, Jagjivan Ram, The man and the times, Indian book company, 36C, connaught Place, New Delhi. 1974, p. 18.

23. Ibid, p. 19.
24. Ibid, p. 20.
25. Ibid, p. 21.
26. Ibid, p. 22.
27. Ibid, p. 23.
28. Ibid, p. 25.
29. Ibid, p. 26.
30. Ibid, p. 27.
31. Ibid, p. 28.
32. Jagjivan Ram : Symbol of Social Change, p. 22.
33. Ibid, p. 23.
34. Ibid, p. 39.
35. Ibid, p. 117.
36. Ibid, p. 118.
37. Ibid, p. 120.
38. R.P. Kapoor, Kamraj The Iron Man, Deepak Associates Private Limited c/circus, New Delhi, 1966, p. 29.
39. A mild alcoholic beverage.
40. Kamaraj The Iron Man, p. 41.
41. Ibid, p. 42.
42. Ibid, p. 59.
43. Ibid, p. 67.
44. Ibid, p. 68.
45. Devotion.
46. Kamaraj The Iron Man, p. 69.
47. The religious conservatives, with their emphasis reportedly more on ritual and symbolism, than on the essentials of ethics and spiritualism.
48. Kamaraj The Iron Man, p.70.
49. Ibid, p. 71.
50. Ibid, p. 72.
51. Ibid, p. 76.
52. Ibid, p. 77.
53. Ibid, p. 78.

54. G.D. Tapase, From Mudhouse to Rajbhavan, Sadhna Publication 29/16-A Chandigarh, 1983, p. 47.
55. Ibid., p. 48.
56. Ibid., p. 49.
57. Ibid., p. 50.
58. Ibid., p. 51.
59. Ibid., p. 52.
60. Ibid., p. 53.

7

Quit India Movement and the Mass[1]

Towards the close of the year, on August 9, 1942 and unparalleled congress rebellion of terrible magnitude reared its head and within a week crippled and paralysed the British Government. *Manager, Padri Circle, Raj Darbhanga, (n.d.)*

'The school students started the movement. They were joined by all sections of congress workers. The sober section of the Congress tried to keep the movement under control, but when they allowed the village mass to join, it became an serious question. *Beguserai Subdivisional Officer, 22 December 1942.*

In 1942, a massive movement swept across India. It began on 8th August when the All-India Congress Committee (A.I.C.C.) called for mass civil disobedience movement to force the British to 'Quit India'. The British reacted with speed and force: they declared the Indian National Congress an illegal organization, shut down its offices and printing presses, confiscated its records and funds and arrested its all prominent leaders. The attack on the Congress sparked off angry demonstrations, with which the police dealt harshly.[2]

Political pamphlets and journals were published almost everywhere in India during the Quit India Movement though the major centres were Bombay and Bengal.[3]

With the adoption of the famous 8th August Resolution, the entire country plunged into what was the last battle for freedom. Bengal was no exception. What separates Bengal from other provinces was the continuity of the movement when its pan-Indian counterpart was completely smashed. Of all the districts in Bengal, Midnapur added a new chapter in the nationalist movement by successfully challenging the British state during the 1942 August revolution. *Baplabi* is a document illustrating the growth and nature of the 1942 Quit India Movement in the district of Midnapur in Bengal. A weekly Bengali publication, *Biplabi* dealt with the day-to-day Congress-led anti British consult in the district and elsewhere in India. The journal was regularly published during the period between September 1942 and late August 1944 despite adverse circumstances. Like other propaganda materials for political purposes, *Biplabi* might have exaggerated Congress. Nonetheless it helped sustain 'the anti-British feelings' by constantly printing accounts of government brutality *vis-à-vis* the nationalists.[4]

The rebels were not scared of arrest; they were afraid of police raid on the suspect's house which, in most cases, led to indiscriminate beatings, destruction and loot of property as well. The congress counter offensive became effective gradually as people in large numbers participated in the movement. While narrating the inhuman conduct of security forces, the accounts of *Biplabi* run as follows,

.........the daroga (sub inspector of police) sprayed petrol and sprit over the roof with a syringe and set fire to the house of Dr. Janardan Hazra, a Congress volunteer of Sijberya. They allowed no one to come near the house to put out the fire. In cowshed cows started wailing pitifully. Five cows, five goats, two cocks and one cat were burnt alive in the fire.[5]

The bestial activities of the British and Indian police were constantly referred to in *Biplabi*. Police arson of villagers' hut was a terrible aspect of this movement. Nalini Raha, a police sub inspector of Mahisadal police station who seems to have enjoyed in arson, was identified as *ghar pora* (house burner). In its edition of 6 November 1942, *Biplabi* writes,[6]

On 15 October 1942, Nalini Raha accompanied by 25 armed sepoys and nearly 40 Muslims set fire to the house- under lock- of a distinguished Congressmen, Sri Nilmani Hazra of Rajarampur village. Soon afterwards, the police raided Matakari, an adjacent village, set fire to and looted fourteen houses.[7]

Volunteers arrested in Tamluk

On 20th September 1942, an armed group of soldiers raided Simulia village and arrested Sri Praphulla Chandra Bhuiya, the President of the Union Board, Sri Gopal Krishna Das, Sri Braja Gopal Das, Sri Gadadhar Chandra Kuinti and Sri Sashi Bhusan Mandal of Jaikrishanpur. They took Sri Asutosh Misra to the police *thana,* then later set him free. In order to protest their arrest, there was a *hartal* at Hijli *hat.*

On 9 September 1942 the *daroga,* with the help of 50 armed soldiers, searched the house of the wellknown Congress volunteer and president of Union 3, Sri Gundhar Bhowmik. Failing to find Guna-Babu, they took away a national flag.

On 3 September 1942 the President of Union 11, Shri Girish Chandra Das of Purbalakhya village, was arrested because he had led a procession in Mayna *thana.*[8]

Arrest in Mayna *thana*

On 21 September 1942 the police arrested Sri Satish Chandrs Bhowmik of Dakshin Harchuli village and took him to the police station. As soon as he was arrested, there was a procession which followed him [form Dakshin Harchuli] to Srirampur *ghat.* On the same day the students of Ijmalichak High School organized a procession to protest his arrest.

On 10 September 1942 the police arrested Sri Rajani Kanta Maiti and Sri Anadi Charan Das of Deuli village and sent them up to Tamluk police station.

On 20 September 1942, Sri Basudev Mandal of Dakshin Harjuli village was arrested and sent up to Tamluk police station.

On 29 September five processions approached Tamluk and Mahisadal police stations from different directions. Indian and foreign soldiers tried to block their advance. Once they reached the police stations, the police indiscriminately lathi charged and fired upon them. The young male volunteers asked their female counterparts to stay back because of the shooting. A 73 years old woman from Alilan village of Union No. 3 in Tamluk *thana,* Matangini Hazra, disregarded this advice and advanced with the national flag, chanting '*Bandemataram*!' She ran toward the enemy, asking to be shot. The second officer, Anil Bhattacharyya, personally ordered his men to shot her. She was shot twice in the arm, but continued to advance with the flag in her hands. When hit by a third bullet in the forehead, however , she fell but never let go for the flag. This heroic death inspires our movement to attain the goal of freedom. The people of Tamluk have lost their heroic mother ![9]

The late Matangini Hazra joined the [Tamluk] National Congress in 1932 and participated in the salt *satyagraha.* At that time she was beaten by the police for raising a national flag on top of the ciriminal court building. She was arrested and given six months of rigorous imprisonment for this offense. In Tamluk she also hoisted a black flag atop the Governor's House [*sic*]. Although she was old, she continued to serve the Congress sincerely from 1932 on. She had respect for Mahatmaji. Despite failing eyesight, she regularly spun [yarn] since the time of the [1932] *satyagraha.* She was religiously devoted to serving the people. The firing on that day caused five deaths- two in front of the police station and three on the Sankarara Bridge. Published by the Tamralipta Congress Committee on November 6, 1942 in its Issue Number Twelve, the following lines as ...

In the midst of the
fierce revolution

We hear the sound of your
conch-shell.

Arson at Congress Man's House

On October 15, 1942 the senior *daroga* of Mahisadal *thana,* accompanied by about 25 armed *sepoys* and nearly 40 Muslims, set fire to the house – under lock and key – of a distinguished Congress man, Sri Nilmani Hajra of Rajarampur village. Soon afterwards, the police party raided Mattatikari, an adjacent village, set fire to and looted the houses of the [14] persons whose names, along with estimated losses [*c.* Rs. 1600/-] are given below...... The police arrested Sri Kokil Jana and Sri Radhanath Saska and sent them to the *thana.* The women of this village showed great courage. The *sepoys* did not succeed in molesting them in any manner. On seeing the approaching policemen, the women armed themselves with *bati, katari,* etc. ... and remained together. Out of fear, the police did not dare at all to molest them. We request the women of all villages to emulate this policy during raids carried out by the police.[10]

On October 14, 1942, the senior *daroga,* alongwith 10 armed *sepoys,* raided the house of Sri Manindra Nath Samanta, a distinguished Congress worker of Chandipur under the pretext of carrying out a search : they destroyed numerous boxes and almirahs [tall wooden closets]. On October 23, 1942 the same police party searched the house of Sri Hangsadhwaj Maiti of Bhabanipur village, he is wellknown Congress worker and vice-chairman of the local board. They beat up Sri Tamradhwaj Maiti and his son, Sri Govinda Maiti, and kicked Bhaku Jana with their boots to extract information about the whereabouts of Hangsadhwaj Babu. During the search the police destroyed a lot of furniture and other articles. Next, the police party raided Bipin Bihari Mandal's house at Sitalpur, destroying a lot of property.[11]

On October 25, 1942 the junior *darogas* of Mahisadal and Tamluk *thanas,* accompanied by the ARP [Air Raid Precaution] commander of Tamluk and about 40 soldiers, raided the Chunakhali Congress office and arrested three volunteers : Sri Ekadasi Bhaumik, Sri Mukunda Mohan Jana, and Sri Rajkrishna Samanta. The police took all the furniture, etc. from the office and then burned it down. Afterwards, they searched the house of Sri Narayan Barman, Sri Surendra Nath Barman, Sri Tarendra Nath Barman and Sri Gorachand Barman. On October 20, 1942 a police party, while on its way to Sri Bipin Bihari Mandal's house at Sitalpur, asked two Muslims to accompany them to show the way. The two Muslims directed them in such a manner that many among the party fell into a tank [pond]. After rising from the tank, they severely beat the two muslims and let them off. On October 26, 1942 the seniour *daroga* of Mahisadal *thana* alongwith a party of soldiers raided Madargechhya and Rauturi villages and extorted money.

At 9 am on Saturday, October 24, 1942 the *daroga* of Mahisadal *thana* and the DSP [Deputy Superintendant of Police] suddenly arrived at the *hat* at Byabarta. They barred alal the entrances to the hat, which was filled to capacity with thousands of people engaged in buying and selling. Without letting anyone leave, they began searching for [congress] volunteers. They beat up all gentlemen wearing *jamas* [long shirts worn over lower garment], and especially those wearing clothes made of Khaddar. They made them wait in front of the president of the panchayet's shop. Many shopkeepers were beaten and asked to furnish information about the volunteers. Sri Praharilal Bhuia and Sri Rasiklal Bhuia were severely beaten for failing to name volunteers. The people were kept confined within the market till 2 pm and a huge quantity of vegetables was destroyed. The police arrested 25 innocent people on suspicion of being volunteers and took them to the thana. In the afternoon, they released everybody.

In parts of India repression contained protest, and after a few days the situation quietened. But in the middle Gangetic plain, a region comprising Bihar and the eastern United Provinces, the revolt intensified.[12]

The strength and fury of the revolt is epitomized in the following extract from an account by R. H. Niblett, an Anglo-Indian District Officer, of his tenacious defence of the Madhuban *thana* in the Misran area of Azamgarh district in the eastern United Provinces.[13]

1. *We reached Madhuban about noon. The police station stands on a plain, with a few trees and three or four houses only to east and north-east of it. A market is usually held here on Saturday afternoon, but not a soul was in sight. As we approached, the gaunt and lonely appearance of the thana, and the sentries on the roofs reminded me of tales of the Foreign Legion. The Station Officer and his staff had spent a sleepless night; but we found them ready and alert.*
2. *I then learnt of the incident at Rampur; and shortly after, of the one at Fatehpur as well. Other news of an alarming character also came in. Huge bodies of men were massing at Dubari and Fatehpur, with the intention of marching on the thana. Circle Inspector ... and I decided not to return to Mau; but to see things through at Madhuban .*
3. *Our garrison consisted, besides myself, of Circle Inspectors... Sub Inspectors.. and ... Head Constable ... an Under Officer, 18 Constables, 42 chaukidars (six of whom disappeared when trouble began), the Station Officer's son and nephew, and six servants (one being my driver...).*
4. *Our equipment consisted of 10 police muskets, 2 private guns, the revolvers with the three police officers, and four spears. The chaukidars, of course, had their lathis. (I may mention that police muskets are effective for only 100 to 120 yards).*
5. *We repeatedly warned our men of the gravity of the situation, of their duty and their dangers, and of the need for effective fire.*

About 15.00 hours, a crowd of about 1,000 people appeared from the west (that is on the roads from Ghosi and Dohrighat). Many were armed with lathis and spears. As we learnt later, some also carried plough-shares, hammers, saws and spades. They stood near the ruins of a house about three furlongs from the thana. When they saw us prepared for them, they picked up brick-bats, which they placed in the folds of their dhotis. With this contingent came two elephants with people on each. All waited and watched for forces from the east.

6. *Shortly after, two contingents approached from the east. One, which consisted of at least 3,000 men, came down the Dubari road. The other of about 1,000 came down the Bilauli road. The latter was the party which had operated at Rampur and Fatehpur with it were people from villages such as Maniar in the Ballia District, 24 miles away. Mostly were Dalits among them.*

7. *The Crowd now proceeded to burn the papers left in the Post Office, and to loot the residences of the Post Master, the Postman and also the neighbouring house of a Vaid. These places were in close proximity to the police station; but we could not allow ourselves to be diverted from our immediate defence.*

8. *The crowd now spread out, and attacked us from the north, east and west. Our sentries on the roofs shouted out that it was the order of the District Magistrate that no one should approach, and that anyone defying the order would do so at his peril. This was merely a formal warning; for we never expected the crowd to heed it. 'Inqalab Zindabad' and other slogans were heard all round.*

9. *The fight began with thousands of brick-bats being showered into the thana. Those from the north-west, especially appeared to be flung by people about 100 yards away. Obviously slings were being used. A brick-bat struck Circle Inspector ... on his turban. At least six fell on me;*

but, probably because of the distance from which they were thrown, I suffered a slight bruise only on my left arm. One large brick-bat did come with force; but it glanced off my helmet.

In the history of colonial India the striking parallel to the 1942 uprising is the Revolt of 1857. The Viceroy informed the British Government that, 'I am engaged here in meeting by far the most serious rebellion since that of 1857, the gravity and extent of which we have so far concealed from the world for reasons of military security.[14] Indeed, the challenge to imperial rule was even more serious than in '1857, in that the rebels of 1942 fought under the unifying banner of nationalism, and certainly would have achieved the success.

Harcourt has exposed the limitations the nationalist treatment of the 1942 rebellion, but unfortunately his exploration of the inner nature of the revolt develops into an unsuccessful attempt to prove Eric Wolf's thesis that **the 'middle peasants' characteristically provide the driving force of peasant insurrection**.[15] Accordingly Harcourt is unable to break the bonds of elite historiography: his vision is as monistic as that of conservative and nationalist historians, the differ-ence being merely that he offers a model of middle peasant mobiliza-tion in place of their model of elite-initiated revolt.

This essay seeks to provide a more adequate account of the context and development of the 1942 revolt in its storm-centre of Bihar and the eastern United Provinces.[8] It argues that **both the strength and nature of the revolt and its eventual defeat may only be understood through a consideration of the revolt's 'dual' quality, whereby it comprised not one but two interacting insurgencies. One insurgency was an elite nationalist uprising of the high caste rich peasants and small landlords who domi-nated the Congress. The other insurgency was a subaltern rebellion in which the initiative belonged to the poor, low caste people of the region.**[16]

In the middle Gangetic plain the response to the savage British blow against the leadership and organization of the Congress was swift and angry. In Bihar, for example, demonstrations and processions in the towns culminated on 11 August in a strongly supported march on the Patna Secretariat building. The police opened fire, killing seven people, all of them students, and wounding several others. The Governor, Sir Thomas Stewart, reported thus on what followed:

Though the firing checked the attack the crowd went back in an ugly mood in the evening and through the night engaged in widespread sabotage and road obstruction, the thoroughness of which had to be seen to be believed. Telegraph poles complete with their full equipment of wires were pulled over and branches of trees a foot and over in diameter were chopped down. This was not the work of five minutes or an hour but nevertheless no information came into headquarters that this wholesale destruction was going on. The ordinary police in the city as well as the civic sense of the citizen appears to have been paralysed by fright.[17]

The arrival of troops from Dinapur and Ranchi allowed the government to regain control of Patna but meanwhile unrest had developed in the countryside.

R.N. Lines, the Darbhanga District Officer, reported that 'all over the district, swarms of rioters and students took possession of the railways, and indulged in ticketless travel en masse, until the railways ceased to work'. Similarly, in the United Provinces 'rumours were afloat that students from Benares Hindu University had alighted in twos and threes at every station along the line to organize attacks on the railway'.[18] Clearly there is no validity to the claim of Francis G. Hutchins that the 1942 revolt occurred spontaneously without the lead being given by 'urban and intellectual elements'.[19]

However the contribution of students to the spreading of the call to insurrection should not be exaggerated. In Bihar and the eastern United Provinces even the largest towns lacked a distinct urban identity, and most of their inhabitants had strong and continually renewed links with the countryside. Even without the activity of the students, the usual to-and-froing between town and country certainly would have spread the news far and wide.

Whatever the precise means of transmission, the call to arms received an enthusiastic response. The Darbhanga District Officer reported as follows:

.. there were no disturbances on the 9th of August. But on the 10th of August demonstrations by students of all schools and colleges took place all over the district. These demonstrations continued at Laheriasarai each day until the 13th of August on which date 31 rioters and 28 Police men were injured in a clash, there were sporadic demonstrations on 14th, 15th and 16th August. but by that time the student leaders were scattered over the district creating havoc elsewhere.

In Darbhanga the rebels also attacked twenty of the district's police stations, capturing thirteen of them. They achieved similar victories elsewhere. At Rupauli in Purnea, in an echo of the Chauri Chaura killing of 1922, the crowd besieging a *thana* set it on fire, burning its defenders alive. In north Bhagalpur, all the *thanas* 'had been closed, locked and sealed by the Congress workers as early as the 13th August'. By 24 August in north Monghyr, all rural police stations had either been overrun or abandoned. By 19 August in Sitamarhi subdivision of Muzaffarpur, all the *thanas* except the one at the sub divisional headquarters had been overwhelmed. Seventeen of the district's twenty-three police stations came under attack and fourteen of them were taken. In Saran the authorities abandoned nine police stations.

The leading Left activist in the 1930s, Swami Sahajanand Saraswati, had gravitated towards the Communist Party of India. He supported Britain and U.S.S.R. in what he regarded as the 'People's. War' against international fascism, and hence he and his followers did not support the revolt.[20] Jaya Prakash

Narayan had already spent most of the time since March 1940 in jail, The other leading pro-revolt left-wingers were clapped into jail during the initial government clamp-down. At the height of the movement only those less influential left-wingers whom the British had regarded as too unimportant to arrest were still at large to engage in protest and propaganda.[21]

Ironically the authorities may themselves have been partly responsible for the tactics adopted by Congress supporters. To justify its draconic response to the passing of the Quit India resolution the government contended that the Congress had planned. wholesale sabotages and disruption. The wide publicity given this. claim apparently encouraged nationalist sympathizers to act bring it to fruition.[22]

But overall, neither the role of the Left nor that of authorities decisively determined the measures adopted by the supporters of the Quit India movement. Sabotage was an established weapon in the armoury of the Congress, and had been used extensively against toddy tappers and liquor merchants during the 1930-4 campaign. In the 1920s and 1930s there had been incidents in which Congress supporters sabotaged communications. Nor was strong antagonism to the police a new phenomenon. During previous mass campaigns there had been attacks both on policemen and on *thanas*. On a number of occasions and during the Non-cooperation Movement groups of demonstrators overran and occupied *thanas* and at Chauri Chaura in Gorakhpur in 1922 they had burnt down the *thana* with its occupants inside.[23] And several times during the Civil Disobedience Movement crowds of demonstrators attempted to raise the Congress flag over *thanas* but were repulsed with gunfire.[24]

The difference in 1942 was not that such events occurred, but that they occurred with a greater intensity and were concentrated within a shorter period of time than previously. The absence of the restraining influence of the senior Congress leaders because of their imprisonment allied with the angry reaction to their summary arrest did much to cause this frequency and intensity of protest. The depth and extent of hostility to the authorities, and particularly to the police, meant that government property and personnel provided a natural target. And when, throughout the countryside, the administration buckled under the strain, many people who were not regular Congress supporters felt further encouraged to participate in sabotage and disruption.[25]

The early triumphs of the insurgents were achieved in the absence of overall co-ordination. The arrest of the senior Congress leadership and of most of the leading local nationalist activists resulted in a situation broadly similar to that which prevailed at the high points of official repression during the civil disobedience campaigns of 1930-4. At the local level, less important activists and sympathizers took the lead.[26]

At Hajipur in Muzaffarpur Akshaya Kumar resigned from his high school post and assumed the leadership of the local students. In Purnea Jagannath Kundu, the son of Dr Kishori Lal Kundu, a prominent local Congressman, was among the leaders of an attack on the Katihar *thana*. At Madhipura in Bhagalpur, Birendra Prasad Singh, Bhupendra Narayan Mandal and Deota Prasad Singh were among the leading figures.[43] In the village of Garkha in Saran the lead was taken by Jaglal Choudhury, as famous dalit leader from Bihar assisted by two local men, Kumar Pashupati Singh and B. Firangi Singh. Choudhury, a Pasi by caste, had served as a minister in the Congress provincial government of 1937-9, but had been regarded as rather a nonentity who had been merely a token addition to the otherwise high-caste Congress ministry.[27]

At the names and the biographical fragments given above indicate, the local leaders did come mainly from the Hindus-caste backgrounds but also included lower caste men. Similarly their followers came from a broad spectrum of society. The social breadth of the insurrection gave it the appearance of a cohesive upheaval, and many historians have accepted this appearance as the reality. However a closer reading of the evidence reveals the essential duality of the revolt. In Bihar and the eastern United Provinces there erupted not one but two interacting insurgencies: an elite nationalist uprising and a subaltern rebellion.[28]

The subaltern rebellion got underway when the tumult of the elite nationalist uprising stimulated the poor to join in attacks on govern-ment buildings and property. These rebels were much the same people who had engaged in market looting earlier in the year and who had recently swelled the figures for petty crime.

Probably those who joined the revolt partly in the hope of acquiring provisions began taking part last and withdrew first when repression began, and accordingly are under-represented in the casualty and imprisonment figures. And possibly their numbers are understated because of the operation of a process of 'sanskritization' whereby Dalits attempted to increase their standing by, amongst other things, assuming characteristically Hindus caste names.[29]

The duality of the Quit India revolt is epitomized in the following extract from a report by the Madhubani Subdivisional Officer:

Most of the Hindus who took part the movement were from the higher castes ... There were agitators from other castes also. Generally people from lower castes or those belonging to the agricultural labourer class did not take part in the movement at first. They joined the movement in its later stage.

The element binding the two insurgencies together was the ideology of nationalism, and an awareness of the duality of the revolt permits us to appreciate more fully the inner diversity and complexity of nationalist consciousness,[48] Consider the use of the radical slogan 'Inqilab Zindabad' in the midst of the nominally Congress-controlled assault on the Madhuban *thana*. And what of Ram Nachchtar's claim during the assault that Gandhi had rendered the rebels invulnerable to gunfire?[49] Whether a cynical attempt to manipulate popular reli-gious feelings, or (more likely) an identification with the subaltern world vision in the heat of battle, this claim to invulnerability illustrates the permeation of popular nationalism with a characteristically subaltern religious consciousness.

M. V. Harcourt shows an awareness of the complexity of the revolt but does not perceive its dual quality. Instead he argues that the 'smallholder peasant' played a central role both in the peasant agitations of the late 1930s and in the revolt of 1942.[30]

The manager of the Raj Darbhanga circle of jhanjharpur in BhagaIpur wrote thus on 24 September:

Since the recent agitation I am daily receiving information from villages that people are not in perfect peace of mind as villages are daily being raided by the police both day and night and people being arrested. 'This has created another panic in the minds of the people because it is not known to them when their houses will either be burnt or looted by the police or who amongst them will be arrested.[31]

The capacity of the rebels to endure repression was restricted by their poor armament. Armed with spears, lathis and axes they first challenged policemen carrying muskets and then encountered soldiers armed with magazine rifles and machine guns and supported by air power, In one instance, students hurled brick-bats at British soldiers in a goods-train travelling from Samastipur to Muzaffarpur. The troops opened fire, killing twelve of them.[56] The rebels also displayed great tactical naivety. There were few attacks under cover of night and little attempt at concealment. An exception occurred at Marhowrah village in Saran district, where a crowd of villagers emerged from the cover of a tall standing maize crop and massacred five British soldiers and an Anglo-Indian civilian.[57] Only later, after the high point of the movement had passed, did greater tactical sophistication develop. Moreover, the widespread sabotage of com-munications combined with the flooding caused by the monsoon to limit the overall co-ordination of the revolt.[32]

Obviously, just as the initial successes of the revolt can be explained partly by the relative weakness of the coercive apparatus of the state, so its rapid suppression may be explained partly by reference to the deficiencies of the rebels' military efforts in the face of harsh repression by massive force. However, it is also clear that the limitations of the rebels' challenge to the colonial state were inseparable from the dual quality of the revolt.[33]

Many of those active in the Quit India revolt were driven by economic hardship, and for a period they operated in a context in which British rule had temporarily broken down. This might seem to have been an appropriate situation for the development of agrarian radicalism. The British administration had always supported the landlords, and during the 1930s officials and police had worked to contain extensive peasant protest. Hence their involvement in the Quit India revolt did not result from economic pressure. In contrast, their participation derived from loyalty to the Congress, sympathy with nationalism.[34]

References

1. I am obliged to Stephen Henningham to his essay "Quit India in Bihar and its Eastern united Provinces: The Dual Revol, published subalatern Studies II in preparation of this essay he has benefited greatly from the advice and criticism of Dipesh Chakrabarty, Ranjit Guha, Gail Pearson, Pauline Rule, Brian Stoodart and James wise. I am taking the abstract.
2. See M.H. Harcourt , The "Quit India" Movement, August 1942: A case study in Militant Indian Naitonalism' (University of Western Australia, M.A. thesis, 1967).
3. Bilabi, A journal of the 1942 open Rebellion, ed. Bidyut Chakrabarty, K.P. Bagchi & Company 286, BB Ganguli Street, Kolkata- 700012, 2002, p. 1.
4. Linlithgow to Churchill, Telegram : 31 Aug. 1942 in Nicholas Mansergh (ed), The Transfer of Power, Vol. II.: 'Quit India' (London, 1971), pp. 835-54.

5. India Office Records, London (IOR hereafter) R/3/2/36, a report by S.N. Mitra, Additional Superintendent of Police, Midnapur, 29 March 1943.
6. Biplabi, 11 October, 1942.
7. Biplabi, 6 November, 1942.
8. Biplabi, A Journal of the 1942 open Rebellion, p. 26.
9. Ibid, p. 33.
10. A common household knife. Sickle-shaped and attached at right angles to a peace of wood, used for cutting vegetables, etc. in a sitting position.
11. Biplabi, p. 53.
12. Ibid, p. 54.
13. EricStokes, The Peasant and the Raj. Studies in Agrarian Society and Peasant Rebellion in Colonial India (Cambridge, 1978), pp. 281, 284.
14. An earlier, less detailed version of this article is presented as Chapter 7 of my Peasant Movements in Colonial India: North Bihar, 1917-1942 (Australian National University South Asia Monograph Series; forthcoming).
15. Stewart to Linlithgow, 22 Aug. 1942, document 612 in Mansergh, op. cit.
16. Datta, op. cit., p. 45; R. N. Lines to Chief Secretary, 22 Dec. 1942, FMP f 84, 1920-42, BSA (hereafter Darbhanga Report); Niblett, op. cit., p. 7. See also Govind Sahai, '42 Rebellion: An Authentic Review of the Great Upheaval of 1942 (Delhi, 1947), p. 244.
17. Francis G. Hutchins, India's Revolution. Gandhi and the Quit India Movement (Cambridge, Massachusetts, 1973), p. 227.
18. Walter Hauser, 'The Bihar Provincial Kisan Sabha, 1929-1942. A Study of an Indian Peasant Movement' (University of Chicago Ph.D. thesis), pp. 148-51; Stewart to Linlithgow,24 March 1942, Mss Eur F 125/49, IOL; Surindra Gopal, 'Peasant Movement in Bihar During the Second World War', in A. N. Sinha Institute, Behavioural Scientist: Essays in Honour of Professor Sachchidananda (Patna, 1978).

19. Ajit Bhattacharjea, Jay Prakash. A Political Biography (Delhi, 1975), pp. 77-80; Datta, op. cit., Appendix H; P. N. Chopra (ed.), Quit India Movement- British Secret Report (Faridabad, 1976, a reprint of Wickenden's Report on the Disturbances of 1942-3, with appendices), pp. 262, 273-4; S. P. Sen (ed.), Dictionary of National Biography, Vol. IV (Calcutta, 1974), p. 113.
20. Bhuyan, op. cit., pp. 53, 90; Rajendra Prasad, Autobiography (Bombay, 1957), pp. 535-6,538,549-50; Sahai, op. cit., pp. 138,220,230.
21. Champaran Police Superintendent, Situation in Champaran up to 9 Nov. 1921, PS f 539,1921 BSA; United Provinces Government Press Communique, 6 Feb. 1922, HP f 563, 1922, NAI; GB FR(2) Dec. 1920; Memorandum from Saran Police Super-intendent to Inspector General Police, 6 Aug. 1930, BSA; HP f 5/80/1932, NAI.
22. Niblett, op. cit., pp. 13,15.
23. Judgement in High Court, Patna, on case of Jubba Mallah vs. King-Emperor, HP f 3/31/1944. NAI.
24. Datta, op. cit., pp. 60, 68, 161.
25. Confidential notes on the Ministers enclosed with Mainwaring to Puckle, 31 Aug. 1938, Mss Eur F 125/45, IOL; Judgement in Special Cases 4 and 5, 1942, King- Emperor vs. B. Jaglal Choudhary and others, 4 Nov. 1942, and Justice C. M. Agarwala. Criminal Review 2,1942,8 Dec. 1942, HP f 3/80/1942, NAI.
26. Bhawanipur AAR 1349 Fa (1941-2) f 16D2, C. Bhawanipur, 1942-3, RDA.
27. GB PS f 21, 1921.
28. See G. Pandey, 'Mobilization in a Mass Movement: Congress "Propaganda" in the United Provinces (India), 1930-34', Modem Asian Studies, 9:2 (1975), pp. 205-26.
29. See paragraphs 31 and 40 in the long quotation given above from Niblett, op. cit.
30. M. V. Harcourt, 'Kisan Populism and Revolution in Rural India: The 1942 Disturbances in Bihar and East United Provinces', in D. A. Low (ed.), Congress and the Raj: Facets of the Indian Struggle, 1919-1947 (London, New Delhi, 1977).

31. Beguserai Report.
32. Jhanjharpur Manager to Chief Manager, 24 Sept. 1942, f 16A2, C Head Office, G 1942-3, RDA. For further details of repression, see Datta, op. cit., and Niblett, op. cit.
33. Superintendent Police Laheria Sarai to Government of Bihar, 4 Feb. 1953, List of Killed, FMP f 69,1942.
34. H. P. Sinha, Saran District Officer, to Chief Secretary, 29 Jan. 1943, FMP f 84, 1942, BSA; GB FR(I) Dec. 1942.

8

Freedom Movement in Orissa, 1920-29 and Dalits

Orissa extends from 17°49' N to 22°34' N latitude and from 81 °29' E to 87°29' E longitude on the eastern coast of India. It has an area of around 155707 sq. km. Bounded by the states of West Bengal to the north-east, Jharkhand to the north, Chhatisgarh to the west, Andhra Pradesh to the south and the Bay of Bengal to the east, it was separated from Bihar and came into being on 1 April 1936. Today, the state is divided into 30 administrative districts and three revenue divisions. Since 1956, Bhubaneswar has been its capital. Until then, the capital was located in the historic city of Cuttack at the apex of the Mahanadi Delta.

Orissa was variously known as Kalinga, Utkal, Orissa, Odisa and Odra Desa in the past. However, in contemporary times, the term "Orissa", locally pronounced as "Odisha", has become more acceptable than all its other names. Both the people and the local language are known as "Oriya". Besides the Oriya-speaking people, who generally live in the plains and the foothills.

The large-scale deaths and scarcity due to drought and famine and the spread of epidemics like malaria and influenza created an atmosphere that became unfriendly, and at times quite hostile, towards the government. The nationalists not only articulated public resentment through the press and other forums like public meetings, but also organized relief for the victims. This led to their (nationalists) emergence as an alternative force to the government.[1] Further, the Montagu-Chelmsford Reforms Committee failed to satiate the local nationalist intelligentsia who had been moderately agitating for the amalgamation of all Oriya-speaking tracts under one political administration. The nationalists' hopes from the *mai-bap* nature of the British government were further belied when the "Punjab killings" took place in 1919. It nagged them into changing their understanding of the nature of the British rule in India. Many liberal thinkers were now convinced that the British decision to rule over India was against the interests of the local people. Besides, the discussion also focuses on the creation of a local ethos, use of local cultural symbols and mobilization of people through local issues by the leadership. Further, it discusses the response of different sections of people to the movement, the various forms of agitation, the reasons why some particular forms became popular, the different types of nationalist institutions created during the period, and their overall impact on the movement.

In 1803, the Marathas, who ruled Orissa since the decline of the Mughals, were defeated by the British and the state came under British sway. With this began a process of rapid colonization. At the same time, resistance movements against colonization and its various forms became quite conspicuous. Locally known as *melis* or *bidroha,* some of these movements were:

1. The Revolt of Jayi Rajguru, Khurda, 1804.
2. Paik Revolt, Khurda, 1817-24.
3. Kondh *Meli,* Ghumsar, 1835-37.
4. The Revolt of Surendra Sai, Sambalpur, 1829-48, 1857-62.

5. Banki *Meli,* 1840.
6. Angul Praja *Meli,* 1848.
7. Baud Praja *Meli,* 1862.
8. Mayurbhanj Santhal *Meli,* 1866.
9. Nilagiri Praja *Meli,* 1875.
10. Damapada *Meli,* 1876.
11. Narsinghpur *Meli,* 1876.
12. Nayagarh *Meli,* 1893-95.
13. Daspalla *Meli,* 1913-14.
14. Dhenkanal Praja *Meli,* 1922.
15. Kanika Praja *Meli,* 1921-22, etc.[2]

The emergence of a new educated class was a significant development of the late nineteenth century Oriyan history. Though a microscopic minority, this class showed interest in common societal issues concerning the general welfare of people, while the involvement of Dalits in the freedom movement was the important feature at that time.

The Congress could establish its provincial unit in Orissa only 35 years after its (Congress') formation. (The Congress was founded in December 1885 and the UPCC in December 1920.) However, this intervening period (1885-1920), despite the formal absence of the party, was not less tumultuous for Orissa. During the period (in fact, since the late 1860s) the ideas on Orissa-related issues crystallized into a definite movement striving for a linguistic and cultural identity of the people. The educated middle class, described as the intelligentsia, formed the core of this movement. As in politics, the intelligentsia's meaningful intervention in literature, as well as in other social and religious issues gave the movement a better grounding in the local society.[3]

The Non-Cooperation Movement (NCM) was the first major mass campaign against the British by the INC. Launched in August 1920, it continued unabated until its suspension following the "Chauri Chaura incident" in February 1922. The two immediate causes for the movement were the Punjab killings (1919) and the Treaty of Sevres (May 1920) described as "the Khilafat Wrong". Some of the main events included the surrender of official titles and honours, and boycott of foreign cloth, law courts and government-affiliated educational institutions. The main slogan, achievement of "*swaraj* within a year", greatly helped the movement to spread.

The cumulative effect of Gandhi's visit was reflected through a spontaneous *hartal* against "police *zulum*" in the Cuttack cantonment area in the last week of March. The local vendors refused to entertain the police constables' demand for certain food items at throwaway price.[4] When some 50 constables reacted by attacking the shops, a *hartal* was declared instantly. Shops were closed, public meetings were held and resolutions "expressing strong resentment and dissatisfaction at the act of the police" and on "losing faith" in the government were passed. Further, a union of sweepers, *khansamas*, washermen and vendors was formed to carry forward the struggle. Though there was no report about the "struggle" in the succeeding weeks, the *hartal* was believed to have "opened a new page in the history of Utkal".[5]

In Sambalpur, police actions and the non-cooperators' reactions became the focal point. The police warned people against attending Congress meetings. They assaulted Parameswar Behera, Dharanidhar[6] and fined Rs. 25 for publishing a nationalist song.[7] The song *Swaraj Bhaya Albat Hoga* by Nilakantha Das, given next, created a stir in all Congress meetings and processions there.

Oh great children of India!
Give up *golami,* march forward,
Don't frustrate your mother,
Don't live as *golam.*
Golami helps the *Raj* in its business.
Things go across the sea,
While you remain a beggar at home.
Remember, school, *kuchery* and council

Are chains of *golami.*
Forget not
Freedom, *golami* and *naukri* are only states of mind.
Liberate the mind
Let it decide on its own,
Break relations with the government,
Everything will be all right.[8]

The Congress reaction came in the form of a *hartal* on 19 April followed by a public meeting at Sambalpur on 25 April.[9] Besides, campaigns were intensified in the villages of Bargarh and Remenda by Anant Mishra from Puri and in Themra and adjoining villages by Chandra Sekhar Behera, Purna Chandra Das, Nilakantha Das and Ratan Singh Bhoi. They resulted in the enrolment of new members and the collection of swaraj fund.[10]

At Jaleswar and Bateswar in Balasore and Chachinda in Athgarh, Congressmen mobilized the *bauris,* an "untouchable" community, to hold meetings where oaths were taken under the guidance of their *pradhans* and *beheras* (community leaders) to wear *khadi.* Similar meetings of sweepers and *"chamars"* were held in Sambalpur during the *satyagraha* week in 1922. Dharanidhar Mishra, a DCC leader and a Brahmin by caste held *bhagabat path* in between the meetings which were generally organized in dalits localities.[11]

The emergence of dalit movements was a significant development of Orissa politics during the 1920s. On the one hand, it helped in the change of perception about caste and, on the other hand, it led to the radicalization of the national movement in the state.[12]

In Orissa, some of the caste names that are treated as socially "low" and "untouchable" are *Bauri, Pana, Doma, Kandara, Hadi, Ganda, Ghasi* and *Mochi.* Even suffixing them to a proper name would be considered "degrading" in the local society. Besides, there are castes like *Gauda* and *Teli* that are considered "low", but not as "untouchables" in the social hierarchy. Protest movements against caste repression as well as for social elevation by people belonging to these castes were not new in the local history.[13] However, during the period under study, two main changes were witnessed in the movement. One, most of these movements grew under the leadership of caste Hindu Congressmen. The leaders of "low" caste themselves, showed interest in the movement.

The second aspect of change, which became prominent from 1927 onwards, was in the sphere of leadership. Without any overt challenge to the Congress reformers for their caste Hindu identity, people from the dalit castes started to lead their movement. During the period, what was apparent was a kind of complementary relationship between the caste Hindu reformers and the "low" caste leadership, which consequently radicalized the Congress and the anti-untouchability and other movements in the subsequent period, that is, in the early 1930s upliftment of *Dandasi* in Ganjam. Traditionally, the *Dandasis* were considered a very "faithful" caste and were employed as guards for the purpose of safety and security. But the government had declared them as a denotified (criminal) tribe. This had lowered their status in the social sphere and motivated the Congressmen to take up the issue. The Congress leaders organized many *Dandasi Sabhas* where the government was asked to withdraw the said declaration and the *Dandasis* took a collective pledge to give up the habit of drinking liquor and eating carcasses of cows.[14] In another meeting held in early September 1925, some 200 *Dandasis* took a collective pledge and became members of the *sabha* by paying "four anna each" to be redeemed from the government Act.[15] In a similar tone, the *Asha* reported that some 500 *Dandasis* gathered in a meeting at Digapahandi on 15 June 1926. Presided over by Sashi Bhusan Rath, the *sabha* demanded the withdrawal of *Dandasis* from the Criminal Tribe List.[16]

The nationalists' assumption that the victims could be redeemed from untouchability "if they wished", motivated the *Asha* to demand higher social status for the *Bauris*. "They do not eat carcasses.... They are not untouchables by their actions. . .. They are called *Bhois* [and not Bauris] in Ganjam and are not treated as 'untouchables' in Parlakhemundi", it argued in June 1926.[17] In his reformatory zeal, Sarat Chandra Mahapatra organized a *Dandasi* meeting at Chandra Kaleswar Kota in Ganjam on 10 March 1925. Attended by some 500 *Dandasis.*

The movement from the side of dalits whether led by people belonging to the same caste, or by a few enthusiastic Congressmen, aimed at elevating their social status rather than at rooting out the British Empire. Definitely the caste organizations played a significant role in the freedom movement.

References

1. Pritish Acharya, National Movement and Politics in Orissa, 1920-29, Sage, New Delhi, 2008, p. xxii.
2. For details see Prasanna K. Mishm, *Political Unrest in Orissa in the Nineteenth Century,* Calcutta, 1983; K.M. Patra, *Orissa Under the East India Company,* New Delhi, 1971; Sadasib Pradhan, *Agrarian* and *Political Movement, States of Orissa,* New Delhi, 1986; Fakir Mohan Senapati, *Atmajibana Charita,* Cuttack, 1991 (reprint).
3. National Movement and Politics in Orissa, p. 48.
4. Gopabandhu Das in Samaj, 2 April 1921, in Das, G.B.R. Vol. VI, p. 68.
5. A.B. Patrika, 29 March, 1921.
6. *US*, 12 May 1921.
7. Samaj, 30 April 1921, in Das, *GBR,* Vol. VI, pp. 83-84.
8. See Das, *Atmajivam,* p. 188.
9. *US*, 12 May 1921; *Samaj,* 30 April 1921.
10. Seba, 18 and 28 May, 1921; Searchlight, 1 June 1921.
11. Samaj, 15 April 1922; Searchlight, 19 April 1922.
12. National movement and politics in Orissa, 1920-29, p. 240.
13. For details see Basant Kumar Mallik, *Paradigms of Dissent and Protest: Social Movements in Eastern India: 1400-1700*

A.D., New Delhi, 2004; A.C. Pradhan, *The Emergence of Depressed Classes*, Bhubaneswar, 1986.

14. The first meeting was held on 15 September 1923 where the pledge was taken. *Asha*. 4 February 1924.
15. *Asha*, 14 September 1925.
16. *Asha*, 21 June, 1926.
17. *Asha*, 28 June, 1926.

9

B.R. Ambedkar: A Social Revolutionary and a Great Patriot

Much has been and will yet be, written on Baba Saheb Dr. Ambedkar, when we study the remarkable personality like Ambedkar suddenly various images appear before us. Whether Ambedkar was the supporter of Britisher or true patriot or staunch fighter for social causes. These are undoubtedly aspects of his outstanding personality which demand both critical study and expert assessment at the hands of distinguished critics in those fields. At the time when India was submerged in the darkness of ignorance superstition and sorts of social prejudices, the birth of Ambedkar in a community considered untouchability really was historical event.

According B.G. Kunte Dr. Bhimrao Ambedkar, affectionately called Babasaheb, has always been held by me as among the greatest Indians of the first six decades of the twentieth century. Even before I had completed my seventeenth year I had fallen under his spell. He was then much hated by the Congress people, and even the radical circles, despite their commitment to the concept of equality as fundamental to a reordering of society, considered him to be a political reactionary and pro-imperialist.[1] According Madhu Limaye Dr. Ambedkar was not less of a patriot than the Congress leaders. Only his priorities were different. He wanted to "fight the two-thousand year old tyranny and oppression of the Caste Hindu and secure social equality" above everything else. He was not opposed to freedom; he ardently desired an immediate transfer of power – as much as the Congress people but he wanted for the Depressed Classes their rightful place under the Freedom's Sun – He could not fight on both the fronts. So he concentrated his fire on the issue of social oppression as against political freedom. He naturally sympathized with men like Mahatma Jyotiba Phule, M.G. Ranade and G.G. Agarkar.[2]

Dr. B.R. Ambedkar one of the top mostpoliticians state man of modern and who served the nation for about four decades. He was a social rebel and had revolutionized and influenced social thought in India. In 1919, when he was hardly 28 years of age on every sphere of social and political activity he left his imprint during this period.[3] Dr. Ambedkar as a true patriot and had cemented the broken India into strong and powerful nation. Dr Ambedkar is a great liberator and revolutionary, who waged a life long struggle in the emancipation of the suppressed and oppressed communities.[4]

The key to Ambedkar's thought and action is to be found in his contradictory motivations. He was on the one hand resolved to fight injustice and inequality; on the other he was an Indian in a profound sense. Despite the personal and collective humiliations which Hindu society had heaped on him and his community, at critical moments his patriotism would surface is an unexpected manner. There was in his perpetual yet creative tension between the keen desire for social justice and longing to see India rise to greatness.[5]

Whether in his evidence before the Simon Commission or his speeches at the Round Table Conference, except on the issue of special Schedule Caste representation, Ambedkar was no whit less nationalist than the most ardent patriot. He was opposed to the Federal Scheme and wanted both transfer of responsibility at the Centre and democratization of the administration of the Indian States.[6]

Speech delivered by Ambedkar at RTC-I[7]

For the first time in the history of India the untouchables were consulted in framing the constitution of the country. Dr. Ambedkar spoke in the conference and declared that he was placing the view point of one fifth of the total population of British India. A population as large as the population of England or France, which was reduced to a position worse than that of a serf or a slave. The untouchables in India were also for replacing the existing Govt. by a Govt. of the people, for the people and by the people.

British the British, we were in a loathsome condition due to untouchability. Has the British Government done anything to remove it? Before the British, we could not draw mater from the village well. Has the Govt. secured us the right to the well? Before the British we could not enter the temple. Can we enter now? Before the British we were denied entry into the police fore? Does the British Government admit us into the force? Before the British, we were not allowed to serve in the Military. Is that career now open to us? To none of these questions can we give an affirmative answer. Our wrongs have remained as open sore and they have not been righted, although 150 years of British rule have rolled away.

We do not accuse the British of indifference of want of sympathy. What we do find is that they are quite incompetent to tackle our problem. The Depressed Classes find that th British Government in India suffers from two very serious limitations. There is first lf all an internal limitation which arises from the character motives and interests of those who are in power, which prevents them appreciating the living forces operating in our society, makes them indifferent and inimical to its aspirations, and apathetic to our education. It is not because they cannot help us in these things but because it is against their character, motives and interests to do so. The second consideration that limits its authority is the moral fear it has of external resistance. The Government of India does realize the necessity of removing the social evils which are eating in to the vitals of Indian society and which have blighted the lives of the down trodden classes or so many years. The Government of India does realize that the landlords are squeezing the masses dry, and the capitalists are not giving the labourers a living wage and decent conditions of work. Yet it is most painful thing that it has not dared to touch any of these evils. Why? Is it because it has no legal powers to remove them? No. The reason why it dows not intervene is because it is afraid tha its intervention to amend the existing code of social and economic life, will give rise to resistance. Of what good is such a Government to any-body? Under a Government, paralyses between two such limitations, much that goes to make life good must remain held up. We must have a Government in which the men in power will give their individed allegiance to the best interest of the country. We must have a Government in which men in power, knowing where obedience will end and resistance will begin, will not be afraid to amend the social and economic code of life which the dictates of justice and expediency so urgently call for. This role the British Government will never be able to play.

We feel that nobody can remove our grievances as we can not remove them unless we get political power in our own hands. No share of this political power can evidently come to us so long as the British Government remains as it is. It is only in a Swaraj constitution that we stand any chance of getting the political power into our own hands, without which we cannot bring salvation to our people.

I am sorry Mr. President I had to speak in such plain words. But I saw no help. The Depressed Classes have had no friend. The Government has all along used them only as an excuse for its continued existence. The Hindus claim them only to deny them or, better still, to appropriate rights. The

Muhammedans refuse to recognize their separate existence, because they fear that their privilegers may be curtailed by the admission of a rival. Depressed by the Government, suppressed by the Hindu and disregarded by the Muslim, we are left in a most intolerable position of utter helplessness to which I am sure there is no paralled and to which I was bound to call attention.

I am afraid it is not sufficiently realized that in the present temper of the country, no constitution will be workable which is not acceptable to the majority of the people. The time when you were to choose and India was to accept is gone, never to return. Let the consent of the people and not the accident of logic be the touch stone of your new constitution, if you desire that it should be worked."

The powerful and fearless speech of Dr. Ambedkar brought the attention of the British politicians and newspapers towards the plight of the Depressed Classes in India. The Indian Daily Mail described this speech as one of the finest bits of oratory during the whole Conference. His Highness the Maharaja of Baroda was so pleased with this speech that with joyful tears in his eyes, he told his princely wife that their efforts and the money they had spent on the sparker of the day were all realized. He was full of admiration, satisfaction and high appreciation. He invited Dr. Ambedkar to a special dinner given by him in London to his choice friends.

Dr. Ambedkar was not content with the demand for Home Rule. He demanded full independence of the country with recognition of civil rights for Untouchables in free India. He also demanded equal citizenship, fundamental rights, adequate representation of Untouchables in legislature, adequate representation in Government services redress against prejudicial action or neglect of interests; special departmental care and the Depressed Classes to have representation in Cabinet.

Dr. Ambedkar created a tremendous impression on the foreign newspapers, delegates of the Conference and the British statesmen. The Sunday Chronicle, paying a glowing tribute to Dr. Ambedkar about his work, said, "At heart a true nationalist, he had to put up stern fight against the persuasive coquetry of the British diehard who are anxious to win him over to their side and at the same time his task as made more difficult by his anxiety to retain his brother delegate Rao Bahadur Srinivasan, within the nationalist fold. As the Chesterfield Gardens, time and again, he explainedthat Sir Tej Bahadur was giving more to the Princes in the process of give and take. But he admitted that Sir Tej Bahadur had to maneuver through a very difficult situation." The Indian Daily Mail wrote "Ambedkar pointed out that he had a mandate to see that no responsible Government was established, unless it was a the same time accompanied by a truly representative Government. He voiced a fear that the proposed form of Government would be one of the masses by the classes and his protest found much echoing sympathy in the Labour and Liberal Parties of Great Britain."

Dr Ambedkar arrived in Bombay on February 27, 1931. He was given an enthusiastic welcome at ballard Pier by his followed led by Shankarrao Wadvalkar.

Dr. Ambedkar paid a visit to Ahmedabad the headquater of Gandhi. He went there to look into the arrangements of the new Boarding which he had started for Dalit students.

He Kolaba Samachar, a hostile paper to Dr. Ambedkar in the matters of social reforms, expressed a debt of gratitude to Dr. Ambedkar for the patriotic service he had rendered to the country in the Chirner Trial. It recalled his services at the time of the visit of the Simon Commission and at the first session of the Round Table Conference; and it added that Dr. Ambedkar was a true patriot and whould fight to break the shackles of the country and help others do so at the second session of the Round Table Conference.

The Indian Daily Mail, congratulating Dr. Ambedkar upon his nomination to the Federal Structure Committee, paid a glowing tribute to him. It said, "Dr. Amhbedkar is a partriot and is vitally interested in securing self-government. In the future discussions which will centre on the frenchise of the Senate and Federal Assembly, this brilliant representative of the Depressed Classes is certain to play a most important part."

The Sunday Chronicle, The Kesari and several other newspapers expressed satisfaction at the nomination of Dr. Ambedkar. Congratulations Dr. Ambedkar and N.M. Joshi, the Journal of the Servants of India Society observed. "Being drawn from the humble ranks of the society, one representing the labour classes and the other the Depressed Classes, they are necessarily strangers to 'high politics' as they are understood in this country. They have the simple faith of the simple folk whose cause they have espoused and they will not be deterred by the superior smile of the eminent personages surrounding them, from insisting on the literal application of certain principles which they have been caught to hold as inviolable"

The London representative of the Free Press Journal, a leading nationalist in Bombay, in reply to Miss Mayo had eulogized the services which Dr. Ambedkar had rendered at the first session of the Round Table Conference, and said that Dr. Ambedkar was a fearless, independent and patriotic minded leader whose fearlessness was unbearable to both Hindus and Muslims, and that his opening speech at the first session of the round Table Conference was the best speech in the whole proceedings of the Conference. Congratulations were showed from all quarters of India and even from England.

Writing about the relationship between Gandhi and Ambedkar, Nagraj refers to the irony to the irony of ironies. This irony is that "to understand the nature of Babasaheb's political career one has to place it along with Gandhiji's for the divergence between the two will highlight the unique problems of the former". By the same token, it underlines how politics of passion puts itself forward against politics of Goodness, asserts its claim to be the only viable and legitimate basis for ordering public life, and makes the appearance of politics of Goodness in the phenomenal world well-nigh impossible.

The irony that Nagraj speaks of is not that of Ambedkar's political career alone. It is also the irony of Gandhi's political career. And, by extension, it is the irony of history-history understood in the sense of a moving field where the voice of reason does arise to curb the depredations of passion but gets muffled in the din of clashing interests. It is this that systematized in the relationship between Gandhi and Ambedkar although in a limited way and on a limited scale.

Gandhi wanted to discuss with Dr. Ambedkar the matter of special representation of Dalits. The two leaders met on August 14, 1931, for the first time. This meeting took place in the following way:-

Gandhi: Well, Doctor, what have you to say in the matter?

Ambedkar: You called me to hear your views, Please tell me what you have to say. Or you may please ask me some questions and I shall answer.

Gandhi: (with a staring look at Ambedkar): I understand that you have got some grievances against me and the Congress. I may tell you that I have been thinking over the problem of Untouchables ever since my school days-when you were not even born.

Ambedkar: It is true, Gandhiji, that you started to think about eh problem of Untouchables before I was born. All old and elderly persons always like to emphasize the point of age. It is also true that because of you, the Congress Party gave recognition to the problem. But let me tell you frankly that Congress did nothing beyond giving formal recognition to this problem.

I also say that the Hindus have not shown a change of heart in regard to our problem, and so long as they remain adamant we would believe neither the Congress nor the Hindus. We believe in self-help and self-respect. We are not prepared to have faith in great leaders and Mahatmas. Let me be brutally frank about it History tells that Mahatmas, like fleeting phantoms, raise dust, but raise no level. Why should the Congress-men oppose our movement and dub me a traitor?

Ambedkar now grew animated. His face flushed and eyes glowed. He paused for a moment and then continued in a bitter, indignant tone.

Ambedkar: Gandhiji, I have no homeland.

Gandhi: (taken aback and cutting him short): You have got a homeland, and from the reports that have reached me of your work at the Round Table Conference, I know you are a patriot of sterling worth.[8]

Speaking on the formation of a separate Karnataka Province on 4 April 1938, Ambedkar denounced parochialism and provincialism and declared his faith in the goal of building up a feeling that we are all Indians:[9]

I do not like what some people say, that we are Indians first and Hindu afterwards of Muslims afterwards. I am not satisfied with that, I frankly say that I am not satisfied with that. I do not want that our loyalty as Indians should be in the slightest way affected by any competitive loyalty, whether that loyalty arises out of religion, out of our culture, or out of our language. I want all people to be Indian first, Indian last and nothing else but Indians....

No nationalist could mach these words which came from the innermost recesses of Ambedkar's heart.[10]

But there was always a "but" to this. Ambedkar always entered a caveat. while speaking on the resolution introduced by the Premier of Bombay on dragging India into the War without consulting her wishes, there was a memorable passage-at-arms between Premier B.G. Kher and Ambedkar.

Ambedkar said that he had often been misunderstood in the country. His position was not properly understood. He loved the country, no doubt.

I will also leave no doubt in the minds of the people of this country that I have another loyalty to which I am bound.... That loyalty is to the community of untouchables, in which I am born.... And I say this to this House as strongly as I possibly can, that whenever there is any conflict of interest between the country and the untouchables, so far as I am concerned, the untouchables' interests will take precedence over the interests of the country. I am not going to support a tyrannizing majority simply because it happens to speak in the name of the county. I am not going to support a party because it happens to speak in the name of the country. I shall not do that. Let everybody here and everywhere understand that that is my position. As between the country and myself, the country will have precedence; as between the country and the Depressed Classes, the Depressed Classes will have precedence, the country will not have precedence.

Premier B.G. Kher in his reply referred to Ambedkar's statement: "As between me and the country, country has precedence." I support him in this, Kher declared, and I shall quote everyword of what he has said. I have known the honourable member's life and career intimately, and I can say that this is absolutely correct. He has always been willing to subordinate his personal advancement for the course of the country. He goes on to say, "as between the depressed classes and the country, the depressed classes have precedence with him."[11]

Dr. Ambedkar began by raising the old question of social reform vs. political advance that had divided the Indian National Congress into two camps. He referred to Tilak's opposition to the holding of Social Conference in the Congress Pandal, and the threat to burn the Pandal held out by the opponents of social reform. To Ambedkar the defeat of the social reform party was a tragedy. But this had not settled the question of the bearing of social reform on political reform in a conclusive manner. The victory of the political reform party as not a victory of the right nor was it a definitive victory. The question remained unresolved, and Dr. Ambedkar used the address to state forcefully the case not only of social reform, but of social revolution, of the need for a fundamental refashioning of the social structure.

Has there been any change in Hindu society's treatment of its most downtrodden sections in the last two centuries? Ambedkar first cited the condition of the Harijans under Peshwa rule in the eighteenth century and compared it with the contemporary treatment of the Scheduled Castes in the Indore State as I had been described in the Times of India of 4 January 1928. The Doctor said:

Under the rule of the Peshwas in the Maratha country the untouchable as not allowed to use the public streets if a Hindu was coming along lest he should pollute the Hindu by his shadow. The untouchable was required to have a black thread either on his wrist or in his neck as a sign or a mark of prevent the Hindus from getting themselves polluted by his touch through mistake. In Poona, the capital of the Peshwa, the untouchable was required to carry, strung from his waist, a broom to sweep away from behind the dust he treaded on least a Hindu talking on the same should be polluted. In Poona, the untouchable was required to carry an earthen pot, hung in his neck wherever he want, for holding his spit lest his spit falling on earth should pollute a Hindu who might unknowingly happen to tread on it.[12]

Now what was happening in contemporary Indore? There a Harijan caste called Balais was subjected to prohibitions and compulsory performance of certain duties by the Rajputs, Brahmins and Patels. They were not to do any of the following things as this constituted an affront to the upper castes' superiority and dignity: Balais must not wear gold laced pugrees, or coloured or fancy-bordered dhotis.[13] The Balais must convey intimation of death in any Caste Hindu families even to far away villages, and play music in the Caste Hindu marriages – of course without payment; Balai women must not wear ornaments and must attend on Caste Hindu women during their confinement. In the event of their failure to abide by these rules they were to leave the villages. Ambedkar gave many other more recent incidents of atrocities against the Scheduled Castes.

Ambedkar asked: Could any society which did these things to its followmen deserve to be called civilized and held worthy of wielding political power? If one country was not fit to rule another –as Congressmen never tire of telling the British – was one class fit to rule over another?

Ambedkar said that what was called for was not mild reform such as abolition of child marriage, permission for widow remarriage and so on. what was called for was a basic reform which would bring about the break up of the Caste System. Ambedkar drew the attention of his audience (or rather readers) to the Communal Award, and said that it was, in a way, "the nemesis following upon the indifference and neglect of social reform".

In 1934 a new party had arisen in the Indian National Congress wedded to the abolitions of economic exploitation and class rule, namely the Congress Social Party. Ambedkar addressed the major portion of his address to the Socialists. He asked them, could they neglect the social problem if they wanted to achieve economic reform?

Ambedkar said that the Socialist were trying to apply the economic interpretation of history to the realities of Indian society. The socialists propounded the doctrine that man was an "economic creature" that his activities and aspirations were bound by economic facts and that property was the only source of power. The Socialists, therefore, wanted economic change to have precedence over social change; in fact, it would not be wide off the mark if it was said that they claimed that social change was a function of economic change and would automatically follow the latter.

Ambedkar convincingly argued that Chaturvarnya and caste system have been responsible for crippling large numbers of the Indian people permanently. They could not bear arms and without arms they could not rebel. They were deprived of education, they were not allowed to partake of higher culture. They were denied a share in enlightenment and were condemned to servitude.

Because of the deadening and paralyzing effect of Caste India was subjected to "defeat and darkness" and damnation. There was only one period of freedom, greatness and glory. This was the period of the Maurya Empire, and this was the time when *Chaturvarnya* was in retreat.[14]

Much is made of Hindu society's capacity for survival. But mere survival had no value for Ambedkar. To him the mode of survival, the quality of life was important. Ambedkar thought the Hindus' existence has been a story of continuous defeat. "To beat a retreat, to surrender and to live the life of a captive is also a mode of survival." This he thought was scarcely comforting.

In another place and on another occasion Dr. Ambedkar raised this question again and answered it himself. "Why has our country lost its freedom again and again? Why have we been subjected to foreign domination so often"? The reason was that this country never stood as a *whole* against aggression. It was always a small section of society and whenever it was overpowered the country lay prostrate at the feet of the victor. "This was mainly due to the pernicious Caste System of the Hindus." Giving the example of Europe at war Ambedkar said that there soldiers who were killed in battle were immediately replaced by fresh recruits. A whole nation, fought not just one section. In India when the Kshatriyas were beaten in battle there could be no fresh recruitment or mass mobilization, since according to the abominable law of *Chaturvarnya* Kshatriyas alone were entitled to fight. "This is why the country has been enslaved many times. Had the right to bear arms not been denied to us, our country would never have lost her freedom and no invader could have succeeded in conquering her," Ambedkar declared.[15]

After the release of the Congress leaders in 1945, establishment of the interim government was son the agenda. The demand of the Muslim League and the adamant attitude of Jinnah were the hindrances. Some people tried to have rapprochement between the Congress and Ambedkar still persisted. He remarked: "Only a man who had no self-respect will cooperate with the Congress. I am al greater nationalist than any of the congressmen." According to him, the problem of independence was linked with the solution of the communal problem by the British government. He stressed the necessity of the political freedom of India and remarked that to make the independence dependent upon the agreement of the different communities was to postpone its solution indefinitely.

He emphasized that people should make the political democracy a social and economic democracy. The problem before the country was whether people would place the country above their creed or creed above country. "But is the parties place creed above country, our independence will be put in jeopardy... and probably be lost forever." Dr. Ambedkar warmed the people must determine "to defend the independence with the last drop of our blood".

The slogan of Ambedkar was: "Be a ruling race." He tried to transform the depressed classes into a political entity and pressed their political claims which were conceded in the Constitution of 1935 in the form of special representation of these classes. He considered that unless the Indian people secured political power and that power is also not shared by the socially suppressed section of the Indian society, it was not possible to completely wipe out all social, legal and cultural disabilities from which that section suffered.

Lalaji was caned by the police when he was leading the demonstration against the Simon Commission in Lahore on 30 October 1928, and he succumbed on 17 November 1928. When Ambedkar read this he burst into tears and in a public meeting condemned the police atrocities.[16] He wrote an article in Bahishkrit Bharat in which he said, "Lalaji was honest, selfless, ready to sacrifice for what he undertook. He did not separate politics and social reform." He praised all his precious qualities as a national leader, a social reformer, an educationist and a journalist (editor of the People). Thoush Lalaji's sympathetic attitude towards the upliftment of the untouchables was regarded as honest, still he regarded it as insufficient for the uplift of untouchables.[17]

Ambedkar considered that his life's mission was too not only the liberation of India from British rule. But, his mission was the liberation of the Depressed Classes from the strangle hold of Brahminism and the Caste System. Addressing the Railway Workers in 1938 Ambedkar said that the workers must fight two enemies: Brahminism and Capitalism. He did not mean the Brahmins as a group. By Brahminism he meant the negation of the spirit of equality, liberty and fraternity. This was not confined only to the Brahmins. It was rampant in all classes, although the Brahmins were its originators. This had to be fought.

At the Second Round Table Conference Gandhiji and Ambedkar clashed over the question of the representation of Depressed Classes. In the Minorities Committee Gandhiji said that it was a "travesty of the truth" to say that he was opposed to any representation of the Untouchables in the Legislatures. What he had said and what he felt impelled to repeat was that he was opposed to their special representation. He was convinced it would do them no good. The congress was wedded to adult franchise and he felt that with "untouchability fast disappearing" the nominees of the Depressed Classes would not be excluded or boycotted. He went to say that what these people needed more than election to the legislatures was protection from social and religious persecution. But thank God, Gandhiji said, untouchability would soon be a "relic of the past" now that the conscience of the Hindus had been stirred.[18]

In retrospect it seems clear that Gandhiji was overly optimistic about the speedy destruction of untouchability and all that it signified. It is also doubtful if in the absence of reservation the Depressed Classes would have secured any representation at all.

Dr. Ambedkar has been a symbol of that intense feeling which we must always remember – The intense feeling of the suppressed classes in India, who have suffered for ages past under Hindu Social Systems.

References

1. B.G. Kunte, Comp. Source Material on Dr. Baba Saheb Ambedkar and the Movement of Untouchables. Vol.1 (hereinafter cited as Source Materials) (Bombay 1882), p. 234.
2. Madhu Limaye, Prime Movers, Role of the Individual in History, Sangam Books Ltd., 57, London Fruit Exchange Brushfield Street, London, E.L.6.E.P M.K. 1889, p.181.
3. M.C. Chitkara, Dr. Dr. Ambedkar Towards Buddhism, APN Publishing Corporation, 5, Ansari Road New Delhi, 1997. p.6.
4. Ibid, p. 7.
5. Prime Movers, Rule of the Individual in History, p.190.
6. Ibid, p. 191.
7. Vasant Moon, Comp. and ed., Dr. Ambedkar, Writings and Speeches (Bombay, 1982).
8. L.R. Bali, Baba Saheb Dr. Ambedkar, Jallandhar.
9. Dr. Ambedkar, Writings and Speeches, Vol. II, p. 1982, p. 195.
10. Prime Movers, Rule of the Individual in History, p. 197.
11. Prime Movers, p. 192.
12. Dr. Babasaheb Ambedkar, Writings and speeches, Vol.II, p. 258.
13. Prime Movers, Rule of the Individual in History, p. 200.
14. Writings and Speeches, n. 6, Vol. 1, 39.
15. Bhagwan Das, ed.,Thus Spoke Ambedkar (Jalandhar,1977),n. 2, Vol. 11, 53-54.
16. Bindu Puri, Mahatma Gandhi and His Contemporaries, Indian Institute of Advanced Study, Rashtrapati Nivas, Shimla, 2001, p. 81.
17. Writings and Speeches, n. 14, Vol. 11, 660-1.
18. Prime Movers, p. 213.

10

Other Dalit Freedom Fighter

1. Sadhu Jitau

Sadhu Jitau was born on 2 January 1856 at village Sahijanpur[1], Lucknow district in Uttar Pradesh. He was Chamar by caste. His father Shri Kuberdasji was a railway employee. Jitau Jeetbahadur had no formal education; but he learnt Hindi, Urdu and English. When he was 25 years of age he became a disciple of Mahatma Mohandasji of Kamalpur who led him to convert to the Ravidas Panth. Since then he began to living in the company of Satsang sadhus and preached Ravidas Panth to his brethren.

He began taking part in national independence movement under the banner of Congress since 1926. He tried to muster the active support of the Depressed Classes in the independence struggle. He participated in the civil disobedience movement, for which he got jailed for a period of six months. During 1926 to 1933 he remained active in independence struggle. Thereafter he again turned towards religious work. He built the Ravidas temple at Belipur in Lucknow district. He had many disciples in the districts of Lucknow, Unnao, Kanpur, Faizabad and Hardoi.

His written works include *Rahasya Yuktalm, Shri Hare Ravi Bhajan Mala, Shri Sadguruji ki Amrit Vani* and *Shri Ravidas Satsang Sagar*.

His books are mainly based on the spiritual philosophy of Sant Ravidasji and reveal the rational thinking of the author.[2]

2. R. Srinivasan

R. Srinivasan (1859-1945) was born on 7 July 1859 at village Kozhialam in Madhauranthagam Taluka, Chengalpet district in Tamil Nadu. His father Rattamalal was a poor farmer. He belonged to Adi Dravida community. Srinivasan had keen interest in painting, as such he was sent to Government Arts College, Coimbatore for further education. There he acquired skill in arts and painting. He got a chance to serve on Hill Station of Nilgiri district. There he happened to meet Colonel Olcott and Madam Blatvastky. He came to Madras in 1890.[3]

He was, however, perturbed to see the abundant miseries of the Dalits in those days. He decided to fight against injustice on his brethren. In order to organize them, he formed *Adi-Dravida Mahajan Sabha* in the year 1891. He organized the first conference of the untouchables on 23 December 1893 and declared his "open war" on untouchability, caste system and religious myths. In order to bring a new awareness among the masses, he started one magazine named *Parayan* in 1893. He convened the next conference of the untouchables on 7 October 1895 at Victoria Hall in Madras.

In 1904 he joined the service of the South African Government as a translator in the courts. He remained in South Africa up to 1920. In South Africa he found that there were severe discriminations against the Blacks by Whites or British people merely on the ground of colour or race. An untouchable in India was treated as untouchable in South Africa also. During those days, he came to be acquainted with Mahatma Gandhi, who was an advocate for the Indian merchants in South Africa. R. Srinivasan taught Tamil to Mahatma Gandhi.

R. Srinivasan returned to India in 1920. He was nominated to the Madras Legislative Council as a representative of the Depressed Classes in 1923. He was also a member of the Legislature from 1923 to 1935. During his membership he could secure several amenities and educational facilities for the Depressed Classes. He had a unique opportunity of being nominated as a representative of the Depressed Classes in India to the Round Table Conference held during 1930-32 in London, alongside Dr. Babasaheb Ambedkar.

3. Kalicharan Nandagavali

Kalicharan Nandagavali (1860-1962) was born in 1862 at village Bothali, in Balaghat district in the then CP and Berar. He belonged to Mahar community. His father Ganuji Nandagavali was a prominent person in society.

Kalicharan got education upto the eighth class. He was deeply moved by pitiable and poor condition of his brethren and therefore he turned to Social Service. He was Mahanubav Panthi by birth and accordingly he was a vegetarian and a teetotaller and inclined towards spiritualism.[4]

He was of the opinion that education alone can bring the remarkable change in the lives of Dalits. To enable the girls to take education, he built a school for girls at his own expense at Gondia in the year 1910. In 1914 he became member of the Municipality of Gondia and in 1916 its Chairman. In the same year he established one Bharatiya Mahar Panchayat to took into the problems of the Mahars; and convened a conference on the issue of untouchability.

He gave evidence before the Southborough Franchise Committee and appealed to give representation to the Dalits in the legislature. He got nominated on CP and Berar Legislative Assembly in 1920 for a period of three years. He was Chairman of the reception committee of the First All India Depressed Classes Conference held in 1920 at Nagpur. Chhatrapati Shahu Maharaj of Kolhapur was presided over the Conference and Dr. Babasaheb Ambedkar came as chief guest.

Kalicharan Nandagavali through an important resolution in the Assembly on 16 March 1921, proposed that a committee should be set up to inquire into the condition of the Depressed Classes with regard to their employment in the government services; their education; their rights as *Kotwal;* boycotts in the villages and separate settlements for the Dalits. This resolution was passed by the Assembly. Accordingly the government of CP and Berar appointed a seven-member "Depressed Classes Inquiry Committee" in June 1921. The committee completed its task in 1922. Kalicharan Nandagavali along with Ganesh Akkaji Gawai was of as its member. He moved another resolution on 13 August 1923 regarding civil rights of the untouchables, such as right to access to public wells, bathing ghats and such other public places. Though, it was passed by the legislature; but it remained a mere resolution.

Kalicharan Nandagavali arranged a community dinner at the residence of Vishramji Savaitul in 1929 which was attended by many prominent persons including Pandit Jawaharlal Nehru, Subhash Chandra Bose, Sir Bhavani Shankar Niyogi. He wanted India to be free from British imperialism. Therefore he supported the Indian National Congress. He sent support to non-cooperation movement and participated in the *Salt Satyagraha* also. However, his activities were not acceptable to some other Dalit leaders. Therefore he was stopped from reading his welcome address at the All India Depressed Classes Conference, held at Nagpur in 1930.[5]

4. Mohini Mohan Das

Mohini Mohan Das (1886-1949) was born on 14 August 1886 at Chandsi district Barisal. This place is now in Bangladesh. He was a *Namashudra.* His father Padma Lochan Das was a medical practitioner. Mohini Mohan Das got education upto matric at Goila School, Barisal. He began his social activities in 1910. He mainly preached against beef-eating superstitions, idol worship, child marriage, untouchability and casteism. He led the Temple Entry Satyagraha at Kali temple in Dhaka in the year 1930. There he along with his wife and other colleagues was arrested and later on released.

Mohini Mohan loved classical music. For development of classical music in the society in general and among the Depressed Classes in particular started one school at Barisal. He joined the Congress under influence of Chittaranjan Das. Later he joined the *Swaraj* party founded by Chittaranjan Das in 1923. He was elected as a member of Bengal Legislative Assembly from 1922 to 1929. He was also a writer. He wrote a book in Bengali, named *Pashan Putra* and another book continuing poems titled *Pathayar.*

To bring a new socio-political awakening among the untouchables, he started a monthly *Sadhak* in 1923. It remained continuation till 1929. He wrote many articles in *Amrit Bazar Patrika* and *Bongwani.*

He stood for a separate electorate system which he thought would be beneficial to the untouchables.

First he married Sutrishna in 1909 and after her death in 1923 he married Sonomani. He had two sons and two daughters. He breathed his last on 27 October 1949 at the age of 63 at Calcutta.

M.B. Mullick

Mukunda Behari Mullick (1888-1974) was born on 27 December 1888 at village Kharasambal, Bagerhat Sub-Division, Khulna district (now in Bangladesh). He was a Namasudra. His father Prasanna Kumar Mullick was a rich landlord. Mukund Behari Mullick began his education at the age of six in his own house under a teacher Kuver Chandra Ghosh. In 1893, Mukunda Behari got admission into the Bagerhat High School. He completed his entrance in 1905; Intermediate in 1907 and his B.A. in 1909 from Presidency College, Calcutta.

He completed his M.A. in Pali in 1913 and his B.L. in 1914 from Calcutta University.

He got enrolled as lawyer in the High Court at Calcutta on 20 April 1914. From 1914 to 1974 he remained in legal profession including the period of his ministership during 1937-41. At the same time he was a lecturer in Pali in Calcutta University from 1914-1937. He served as a part time lecturer in Law in Calcutta University.

Mullick began his social service in 1912 when he apprised the Governor of the Miseries of his community. In order to unite his brethren he founded the Bengal Namasudra Association in the year 1912. Under the banner on this associate he organised many meetings and conferences at several places like Dhaka, Kulna, Jessore, Calcutta, Cuttack and Lucknow, which infused a new strength in the Dalit masses. He tried to boost up the morale of the people and tried to raise their confidence. Mukand Behari was an educationist. He was well educated, was a professor, fellow and senate member of Calcutta University during 1914-1937.[6]

He was active in politics also. He contested for Bengal Legislative Assembly in 1921 from Khulna constituency as an independent candidate, but lost. Again he contested from the same constituency in 1925, but failed. However, he was nominated by the government as a member of the Legislative Council. He continued to be so till 1936. In the elections held under the Act of 1935 in the year 1937, he contested from Khulna Assembly constituency (R) and won the election. He was again elected in 1946 as a member of Legislative Assembly of Bengal.

Mukand Behari represented the grievances of the untouchables a number of time to the authorities for getting redressal. He clearly mentioned to the governor in an appeal, submitted in December 1918 that "a vociferous and small band of organized castes could not pretend to represent the interests of the downtrodden." As President of All-Bengal Namasudra

Association, he submitted a memorandum to the Indian Statutory Commission headed by Sir John Simon, in 1929, in which he wrote, "Franchise should be based on population and not on any property or educational qualification". He gave support to the demand of separate electorate made by Babasaheb Ambedkar during the Round Table Conferences. M.B. Mullick took part in the Second All India Depressed Classes Congress at Kamptee, near Nagpur on 7-8 May 1932 and denounced the Rajah-Moonje Pact in a resolution. He appeared before the Lothian Committee and put forth the demand of increase in seats for the Depressed Classes.

M.B. Mullick was inducted as a minister in charge of co-operative credit and rural indebtedness in the first Fazlul Huq cabinet of Bengal from 1937 to 1941. During 1942-47 he served as Chairman of Coal Mines Stowing Board under the Government of Bengal.

He was elected as a member of the Constituent Assembly of India, when India was partitioned. After 1947 he resumed his legal practice in the Calcutta High Court and continued it till his last.

He worked towards the liberation of the untouchables all his life. He was, however, not attached to any political party. Being dedicated leaders, he had immense popularity among the Depressed Classes. They addressed him by the respectable appellation of *Jananayaka*. He was felicitated by the Bar Association of Calcutta High Court in April 1964 when he completed 50 years of legal practice in the High Court.

Shri M.B. Mullick expired on 4 August 1974 at the ripe age of 86 at Calcutta.

Bhola Paswan

Bhola Paswan (1914-1984) was born in 1914 at Bairgachhi, Purnea district in Bihar. He completed his 'Shastri' examination from Kashi Vidyapeth, Banaras. He belonged to Pasi community.

Bhola Paswan began his career as a member of the District Board of Purnea. He continued as its member from 1939 to 1941. He started took part in the independence struggle under the banner of Congress. He participated in the Quit India Movement in 1942, for which he got jailed for 21 months. He was the champion of the downtrodden communities in Bihar. He worked to improve their condition.[7]

Bhola Paswan got elected to Bihar Legislative Assembly in 1946. In 1952 he became Parliamentary Secretary to Minister for Local Self Government. During 1952-53 he was inducted as Cabinet Minister in Bihar Government. He got elected from Banmankhi (R) Assembly constituency in 1957 and 1962. In the general elections held in 1967 he again successfully contested from Korha (R) Assembly Constituency. However, in 1968, he left the Congress and formed his own party named Lok Tantric Congress. He became Chief Minister of Bihar in 1968 and continued in that position till June 1969. Again he became Chief Minister for a period of one year 1971-72. He again joined the Congress in 1972.

He was elected to the Rajya Sabha in 1972 and continued as member of Rajya Sabha till his death. He was Union Minister for Works and Housing during 1973-74 under the Prime Ministership of Indira Gandhi.

He became Chairman of the newly formed Scheduled Castes and Scheduled Tribes Commission, in August, 1978. The Commission prepared and submitted the first Report for 1978-79 on 8 February 1980 and its second report for 1979-80 on 25 May 1981 under his chairmanship.[8]

He started *Rashtra Sandesh* a weekly in Hindi. He was assistant editor of *Rastra Vani* published from Patna.

He expired on 10 September 1984 at the age of 70.

Jaglal Chaudhary

Jaglal Chaudhary born in 1895 at village Garkha, Saran district in Bihar, Jaglal Chaudhary belonged to the Pasi caste.

His father Mushan Choudhary was a toddy-seller. After passing the lower primary examination in 1903, he passed his matriculation in first division in 1912 from Chapra Zilla School. He passed his Intermediate (Science) examination in 1914 from Patna College. Thereafter, though he was admitted to Medical College, Calcutta, he left his education and joined the Non-cooperation Movement in 1921 answering the call of Mahatma Gandhi. Soon, he became a member of the District Congress Committee, Saran. During the Salt Satyagraha he courted arrest. He also had interest in the movement of Dalit liberation.

In 1937 he was elected on Congress ticket on the Bihar Legislative Assembly. Soon after he became the Minister for Public Health and Excise. Knowing fully well the adverse effects of liquor had in general and on the Depressed Classes in particular, he introduced prohibition in the districts of Saran, Ranchi, Muzaffarpur, Hazaribagh and Dhanbad. In November 1941, he was arrested and jailed for offering individual satyagraha. During the Quit India Movement 1942 he led a *satyagraha* and captured the post office and police station at Garkha. He was arrested on 23 August 1942 and sentenced to five years' imprisonment. During this movement one of his sons shot dead by the British force. On 30 March 1946 he was released from jail.[9]

Jaglal was elected to the Bihar Legislative Assembly in the elections held in 1946. Soon he became Minister for Public Health and Harijan Welfare in the second Congress Ministry formed in the Province in 1946.

In the first general elections held in 1952, he got elected the Bihar Legislative Assembly. He successfully contested election in 1957, 1962, 1967 and 1969 to the Bihar Legislative Assembly. In 1953, he wrote a book entitled *A Plan to Reconstruct Bharat*.

B.S. Murthy

Bayya Suryanarayan Murthy was born on 29 October 1906 at Nagarm, taluka Razole, East Godavari district in

Andhra Pradesh. His father was Bayya Nagayya. B.S. Murthy got his education at Rajahmundri and later at Madras. He was B.A., B.Ed.

Murthy became Secretary of the Andhra Pradesh Harijan Sevak Sangh in 1935. Later he became its President from 1940-49. He got elected as a member of the Madras Legislative Assembly in 1937. He was again elected in 1935. He became Minister for Industries and Labour in the then Madras Government from 1937-39 and from 1946-47. He contested in 1952 general elections for the Lok Sabha from Eluru (G and SC) constituency as a candidate of Kisan Mazdoor Praja Party and won. In 1957 he contested from Kakinada (G and SC) Lok Sabha constituency on Congress ticket and again won. He got elected in subsequent elections from Amalapuram (SC) constituency in 1962, 1967 and 1971 to the Lok Sabha. He was inducted as Deputy Minister for Health and Family Planning from 1962-67 in the Union Government.

B.S. Murthy led the temple entry *satyagraha* at Tirupati Hills demanding entry of the untouchables in the famous Venkateshwara temple in the year 1947, and was successful in his objective. He founded a hostel for the Scheduled Caste college students in Madras, named M.C. Rajah hostel.

He participated in national freedom movement. He offered individual satyagraha in 1940, for which he was given rigorous imprisonment (RI) of nine months and a fine of Rs. 300. He participated in Quit India Movement in 1942 and for this he was sentenced to one year RI and a fine of Rs. 100.

N.C. Laskar

Nibaran Chandra Laskar was born in February 1908 at village Nizphubari, Cachar district in Assam. His father Ratan Moni Laskar. Nibaran Chandra Laskar completed his matriculation from Haila-Kandi H.E. High School, B.A. from M.C. College, Sylhet, and M.A. in Sanskrit from Dacca University in 1931. He got appointed as Professor of Sanskrit and Bengali at G.C. College, Silchar in 1935 and remained in that position till 1945. After that he joined Congress and took part in national freedom movement and Dalit liberation movement.

Laskar began his political career as a member of Silchar Municipal Board in 1946 and continued to be so till 1949. He got elected to the Assam Legislative Assembly in 1947. Subsequently, he was elected to the Constituent Assembly in August 1947. He remained a member of the Constituent Assembly from 1947 to 1950. Later, he was joined the Ministry of Assam as Deputy Minister, Department of Relief and Rehabilitation in 1951.

In the first general elections held in 1952 he contested election from Cachar-Lushai Hills (G and SC) Lok Sabha Constituency and won. In the next general elections held in 1957, he had the unique honour of being elected unopposed from the same Lok Sabha Constituency.

He strived for the abolition of untouchability and for securing the legitimate rights for the welfare of the Scheduled Castes in Assam. He opined that the Scheduled Castes would have no future in Pakistan.

Ramchandra

Ramchandra was born in 1908 at Humanabad, Bidar District, in Karnataka. Veerappa was his father. Ramchandra could study only up to seventh class from Humanabad.

Ramchandra accepted Arya Samaj and he led his life strictly according to the tenets of this organization. He joined the Congress and participated in its various activities. He was opposed the Nizam's domination. He took part in the Hyderabad State independence movement under the banner of Congress. In those days the Razakar movement was doing harm to the interest to the society in general and the Scheduled Castes in particular. Under pressure of *Razakars* many untouchables were converting to Islam. Thus Scheduled Castes were being exploited on the one hand by the majority caste Hindus, and on the other by the Muslims. Therefore, the untouchables were caught in a very precarious and bewildered conditions. In such a situation Ramchandra came forward to their rescue. He could give them courage to face the situation and thus boasted their morale. He took part in the Quit India Movement in 1942 under the leadership of Pandit Shivacharanji. He also took part in the Hyderabad Independence Movement.[10]

He was active in the election of politics also. In the general elections held in 1957 he contested for Mysore (Karnataka) Legislative Assembly from Aland (G and SC) Constituency as a Congress candidate and won election.

P. Kakkan

P. Kakkan (1908-1981) was born on 18 June 1908 at village Thumpai Patti, in Melur Taluka, Madurai district, Tamil Nadu. His father was a worshipper of a community deity and was known as Poojari. Kakkan studied in Christian High School at Madurai. He left the school in 1922 after failing in the SSLC examination.

Thereafter, he served as a teacher for a period of four years and then turned to social work. He led the Satyagraha for Temple Entry at Meenakshi temple, Madurai in 1925. He had the honour of being the first untouchable *satyagrahi* to enter the temple.

Later he joined Congress and participated in the national freedom movement. He became Secretary of the Taluka congress committee and later the Treasurer of Madurai District Congress Committee.

P. Kakkan was a member of the Constituent Assembly during 1946 to 1950 and then a member of the Provisional Parliament. As a member of the Constituent Assembly, he served the cause of the people in general and the Scheduled Castes in particular. He strongly advocated reservation of appointments more so in police and military services.

He contested the first general elections held in 1952 as a Congress candidate from Madurai (G and SC) Lok Sabha constituency and won the seat. Thereafter he concentrated on State politics. He became President of the Madras Congress Committee in 1954. In the second general election held in 1957, he contested as Congress candidate from Melur (G and SC) Assembly Constituency and this time also he won. During his period he became Minister for PWD and SC Welfare, Madras Government. He was elected for the Madras Assembly from Samayanallur (R) Constituency in 1962. He again contested as Congress nominee in the year 1967 from Melur (SC) Assembly Constituency but this time he defeated by DMK candidate.

He lived a very simple life. He was known for his high moral and incorruptible character. He was honoured as freedom fighter for being actively associated with the freedom movement.

S. Nagappa

Sardar Nagappa was born on 6 October 1911 at Kurnool in Andhra Pradesh. He belonged to the Mala community. His father Sardar Buchayya worked in the home of a British Officer. Nagappa had passed his matric in 1932 from a local municipal high school, Kurnool. From 1933-36 he earned his livelihood by weaving and stitching khadi.

S. Nagappa joined the Congress in 1930. In order to create awareness and unity among the untouchables, he inspired the people to arrange Bhajan-Kirtan in every locality. His teacher Vaidyanath Aiyyer gave him a bicycle to move from place to place and teach the people in cleanliness and morality. Nagappa started a free hostel for the Scheduled Castes students at Kurnool in 1938. He and his wife used to prepare food for the students.

He won election to the erstwhile Madras State Legislative Assembly in 1937 from Kurnool constituency. He won again on Congress ticket from the same constituency in the year 1946.

He had the great honour of being elected to the Constituent Assembly from Madras Legislative Council in the year 1947. In the first general elections held in 1952 he contested as KMPP (Kisan Mazdoor Praja Party) candidate from Nandyal (G) Lok Sabha constituency, but faced defeat in the election. In 1967 he contested for Andhra Pradesh Legislative Assembly as a Congress nominee from Alur (SC) constituency, but here again he met with failure.

S. Nagappa participated actively in the national freedom struggle. He took part in the Quit India Movement in 1942 for which he was jailed for one year and six months. His wife Mrs. S. Amravati Devi also took part in the Quit India Movement for which she was detained in jail along with her infant son. Both of them offered satyagraha and courted arrest for several times. His contribution to the Constituent Assembly is of great value. He was convenor of the SC members. During that period he got to reside near the residence of Dr. Babasaheb Ambedkar. Babasaheb Ambedkar often used to invite him for informal discussions in the night. On being encouraged by Babasaheb Ambedkar, Sardar Nagappa moved an important resolution in the Constituent Assembly regarding "qualified joint electorate" for the Scheduled Castes. In resolution, he stated that the SC candidate, before being declared to have been elected to the seat reserved, shall have secured not less than 35 per cent of the votes polled by the Scheduled Castes in the election, and should have secured the highest votes polled by the general voters. However, the motion was not accepted by the members of the Constituent Assembly.

Both Shri and Smt. S. Nagappa received the honour as freedom fighters and got compensation of 30 acres of land for their livelihood. Nagappa was very proud to claim to be the 18th or 19th generation of his dynasty which heroically fought against the Raja of Kurnool under the command of Abdul Wahab who served under the Sultan of Bijapur and won the battle. Therefore, his ancestor got the title of 'Sardar' and also the house site near the Fort at Kurnool where Nagappa presently resides with his three sons. He claims with pleasure that D. Sanjivayya the first SC Chief Minister of Andhra Pradesh had received his early education under the former's parental care.

M. Jayaseelan

Jayaseelan was born on 20 December 1912 in Cantonment area, Bangalore. His father Shri Manickum was a businessman. He left the school and plunged into pclitics at a very young age in 1930.

Jayaseelan was a born Buddhist. His father had converted to Buddhism. His father-in-law Swami Pillai, who served in the Police Department of Burmese Government at Rangoon was also a Buddhist. Before conversion they were treated as untouchables.

He set up a hostel for the Scheduled Castes students, where students like L. Shivalingiah, who rose to the position of Chief Executive Engineer of Karnataka State, were boarders. He started one weekly in English named *Panch Sheela,* in the year 1956, which continued for a period of about three years. He also wrote a book titled *Poona Pact.*

He actively participated in the national independence movement as well as in the Mysore State independence movement. He was imprisoned four times in 1930 for 15 days, in 1937 for four and a half months, in 1942 for six months and in 1947 for one month. Thus altogether he spent one year in prison for the cause of independence. Hence, he got honoured as a freedom fighter by the Union and State Governments.

He began his political career by joining the Congress in the year 1930. He won nomination as a member to the Municipality of Bangalore cantonment during 1945-49. In the year 1951-52 he got elected as Deputy Mayor of Bangalore city and cantonment. He was also nominated as a member of All India Prohibition Council in the year 1971.

Pannalal Berupal

Pannalal Berupal was born on 6 April 1913 at Ramdeo Pathshala, Bikaner in Rajasthan. He was a Meghwal. Modaram Berupal was his father. Pannalal Berupal had no formal education. He was a cultivator and a petty businessmen.

He was President of *Meghwal Sudhar Sabha* and Rajasthan Provincial Depressed Classes League. He was a member of Harijan Welfare Board in 1944. He stood for the abolition of *Jagirdari* and *Begar* or bonded labour. He used to compose songs with messages aimed at creating social awareness among the Scheduled Castes. He joined the Congress in 1940. He contested in 1952 for the Lok Sabha as the Congress candidate from Ganganagar-Jhunjhunu (G and SC) and won the election. He contested regularly in 1957 (Bikaner), 1962 (Ganganagar), 1967 (Ganganagar) and 1971 (Ganganagar) and always won.[11]

He married Laxmi Devi. He is survived by an adopted son.

He wrote some books titled—*Hindu Samaj jin ko Achhoot Manta Hai, Kya Weh Achhoot Hain? Jati Pati aur Varna Vyavasta ka Rahasya; Harijan Pukar; Meghwal (Chamar) Jati ki Utpati aur Rasan Rivaj and Alakhiya Sampradaya.s*

Kanhaiya Lal Valmik

Sh. K. Valmiki was born on 14 March 1919 at village Khanai in Baluchistan, now in Pakistan. His family came to Bulandshahar in U.P. and settled there. Shri. Valmiki passed his matriculation from DAV High School, Bulandshar and Intermediate from Allahabad.

He joined the Congress in 1940. He activily participated in the Quit India Movement of 1942. When the police was in search of him, he went underground from August 1942 to May 1943. However, he was sentenced to imprisonment from 1943 to 1945. He became member of the DCC Bulandshar in 1950.

He was also active in Dalit Liberation movement. He was elected member of the provisional Parliament from 1950-52.

Karan Singh Kaen (1898-1990)

Sh. Karan Singh Kaen was born in Jatav community in 1898 at village Nagla Bhavani Singh, Agra. He passed his B.A. in 1926 from Agra College, Agra.

He joined the Congress and took active part in the freedom movement. He contested in 1937 to the UP State Assembly on Congress ticket from Agra City constituency and got elected. He came in contact with Dr. Babasaheb Ambedkar and accepted his leadership.

D. Sanjivayya (1921-1972)

He was born on 14 February, 1921 in village Peddayadoo, Kurnool district, Andhra Pradesh. His father Munia was a poor Dalit. He passed his B.A. from Madras Presidency College in 1942. As a student he supported the Quit India Movement started by Gandhiji.

After graduation he applied for a job and was appointed as Inspector in Food and Civil Supplies Department as the family was passing through financial crisis. In the meanwhile he passed his L.L.B. examination and took interest in the uplift and welfare of the poor downtrodden people.

From his childhood days Sanjivayya was very kind hearted, emotional and has a poetic heart.

These were the days when Periyar E. Ramaswami Naicker was challenging the Congress and party was loosing ground. The Congress party was looking for ground amongst the Dalits and the labouring classes. Congress leaders were influenced of Sanjivayya's oratory. He participated in the freedom movement.[12]

C. Rajagopalachari saw in him a promising Dalit leader who could save the Congress from defeat in elections, having mass popularity.

Both Rajagopalachari and B. Rama Krishna Rao impressed upon him to join the Congress.

In 1950 at the age of 29 years Sanjivayya was elected to the Provisional Parliament. After two years during first General Elections of 1952, he was elected to the Madras Assembly and appointed a Minister at the age on 31 only. For ten years continuously he was Minister in Madras and Andhra Pradesh (on these paration of new state.) In 1960 he was chosen as Chief Minister of Andhra Pradesh, being the first Dalit Chief Minister in the country and Nehru blessed him for his elevation. During this period he was a very popular C.M.

In 1962 he was appointed as Congress President, being the first Dalit in the Congress history of 77years. Again in 1971 he was made Congress President. As Congress President he was very popular and revitalised the party when Smt. Indira Gandhi faced many challenges.

During 1964 to 1971 Sanjivayya was continuously a Minister in the Union Cabinet. As Labour and Industry Minister he was a very successful minister and his work was appreciated throughout the country.

As Minister and Chief Minister of Madras and Andhra Pradesh, respectively as Congress President, as Union Minister he always thought and worked for the welfare and uplift of the masses specially the under-privileged classes.

Throughout the country he addressed several national level Dalit conferences. Every year during 1965 to 1970, Sanjivayya presided over the All India Dalit and Backward Classes Sessions organised by K.L. Chanchreek and Amin Chand Bhagat of the All India Harijan League in Delhi, and other places in which thousands of delegates participated.

He was a great Telugu poet and litterature and organised International Conference of Telugn Writers.

He also organised 'All India Scheduled Castes, Scheduled Tribes, Backward Classes and Minorities Employees Federation,' at New Delhi which is still functioning for the last

37 years or so from Sanjivayya Bhawan, Prasad Nagar, New Delhi under the supervision of K.R. Sunda and R. Sangeetha Rao.

A collection of his speeches on "Labour Problems in India" was published by Oxford/I.B.H., New Delhi. He was a great admirer of Dr. Ambedkar.

He died on 7 May, 1972 at the age of 51 only. In him the country lost a great and dynamic leader, to whom the cause of the poor and weaker sections was dear (Chanchreek: File).

References

1. Prof. Ramesh Chandra, Dr. Sangh Mittra, Dalit Leaders, Commonwealth Publishers, New Delhi, 2003, p. 73.
2. Ibid, p. 74.
3. Ibid, p. 75.
4. Gral interview with Mata Prasad, Lucknow, 10 March, 2007.
5. R.K. Kshirsagar, Dalit Movement in India and It's leaders, Prints India, New Delhi, 1994, p. 210.
6. Sekhar Bandyopadhyay, Caste, Protest and Identity in Colonial India, The Namasudras of Bengal, 1872-1947, p. 120.
7. Dalit Leaders, p. 144.
8. Ibid, p. 145.
9. Dalit Movement in India and Its Leaders, p. 215.
10. Dalit Leaders, p. 107.
11. Interview with Dr. Jetha Ram, Jodhpur, 20 April 2008.
12. Sh. K.R. Sunda ed. voice of the Weak, New Delhi.

Index

D

N

U

V

W

Y

Z